REFORMS

THE SPIRIT OF CHANGE:

Foundation of Social Evolution

LIFE, FREEDOM AND HAPPINESS

MIGUEL SOTO

Pi Manager,
Stanton, CA USA
First original release published by Pi Manager, dba in 2020

Photography in the book cover: sponsored by the book's designer.
Graphics, other images, and artwork are by the author.
ISBN book print version: 978-1-7347532-4-0
ISBN book electronic version: 978-1-7347532-5-7
Book printed in the United States of America.

Other works by Miguel Soto
Ciclos de Vida: El trabajo de los Espíritus
Life Cycles: The Work of the Spirits
Misterios: Amor, Luz y Vida
Project Information Manager, Vol. 1 Pre-construction phase
Angels in My Way

Disclaimer: This book content is a measured opinion of the author. The author declares that he is not a lawyer. He gives his opinion in exercise of his right to free speech. The author, a citizen of the United States, feels an obligation to present his interpretation of the history and events of recent decades. He holds these issues to deserve exposure to the public. His opinion does not accuse any private or public person. He suggests the United States of America government has faults, which prevent the fulfillment of the constitutional mandate to form a more perfect Union. No one can negate the rights of citizens to petition constitution reforms.

The author translated his book from Spanish, not literally but following the Spanish meaning to the English grammatical structure. Translations of the hyperlinks in Spanish may lead to different sites. The author invites you to conduct your own impartial analysis of current social, political, and economic situation, and ask reforms as desired. You have the right to do so.

CONTENTS

In colonial days, the people settled in rogue lands, outraged by the cruelties and inequalities of their government that controlled their lives and beliefs, in chorus said:

> *"We consider that these truths are evident, that all men are created equal, that they are endowed by their Creator with certain inalienable rights, which include Life, Freedom and the pursuit of Happiness..."*

And with this feeling of love for their communities and humanity, the people rose in arms; and without fear of the consequences, they fought against forces of that despotic monarchy until they achieved their independence and freedom. It wasn't easy; it cost many lives, and they wished to be free and overcame oppression. Life was like a fairy tale that ended with the Creator's gift, an award for their sorrows and sacrifices. They won a great nation along with their rights and freedom. By their noble sacrifice, one cannot admit or allow a person or group of selfish people to destroy this independence, the freedom. The popular sovereignty or the democratic republic, or the national sovereignty belong to the people. They must protect the popular sovereignty, or their democratic republic, or their national sovereignty.

Thematic discourse

The author admires the greatness of the United States from its forced birth by involuntary conditions imposed from Europe to the present time of real time information and illustration. He sets out the goal, or purpose of this book in this prologue, clarifying that is not about repeating historical records. The goals are to expose the principles of this great Union, collected in historical data.

The author defines a mirage of the constitution of the government, and the democracy of the United States, in this prologue. He gives details of this mirage, concluding that corruption is the product of political weakness, ambition and egotism. He talks of the constitution, reforms, the rule of law, and the government separation of powers.

In chapter 1, the author goes over historical events preceding the situation and the independence, in those days. And he goes after the intellectual framework and intention of the people in the English colonies of America. He looks for the reason or why the people left England. Present influences lay the foundations of the American colonies Union. The European people had the thoughts diversification for the fundamental greatness of this nation. They carried their longings and dreams derived from the enlightenment and rebirth period; man liberated his mind to manage his own life during this period. That dream had no racial traits; so, not a white supremacy. They escaped from an absolute and despotic monarchy, but Europeans escaped from many monarchies.

He explains the seven-year-war. This chapter sets out the weaknesses and vulnerabilities, according to the author's criteria, and the risks that precipitated from them. To these weaknesses, the author adds the fallibility of the Union, and presents the way of its formation, and the evidence. The author talks about the enlightenment that reaches the mind of man and separates himself from Theo centrism. People came out of the influence of Rome to the new concept of anthropocentrism. The author exposes the resentments settler had for building actions, for claiming their independence. And their actions gave certain warnings and consequences leading up to rethinking the situation. The author gives reasons in the last section of this chapter. About the justifications, the author explains the colonies' demographic composition, describing the character of the settlers.

The author speaks of the reasons certain Englishmen left the homeland—England—and venture into the discovered continent. He clarifies the cause or causes of the resentments of pilgrims in Britain, which compels them to emigrate. In this chapter, the author studies other forces that encouraged the urgent departure of Europeans to the new continent. The reasons included (1) escaping from the church of England coming out from under the Vatican influence and control; (2) escaping the consequences of the seven-year-war, (3) adopting the influence of the European age of illustration, (4) rebirth; and (5) seeking freedom to manage their own social, political, and economic destiny that they did not have. In reality, there was a lot in the minds and souls of desperate Europeans about to burst. Among the historical background we will see (1) the influence of the wars in Europe as the seven-year-war; and then (2) the despotism of the king of England, who provoked the great resentment of the English colonizers. This was the last drop that spilled the glass over.

The author discusses other concepts behind the colonies' drive for independence, such as the influence of the great European powers, Spain, France, and the Netherlands, and England. These influences were important factors in the mentality of settlers and leaders of the colonies that served as the basis for the independence argument. As an influence factor, the author mentions the social, political and economic phenomenon that brings the age of illustration and the rebirth of Europe. It was an illustration propagated to the world at the time, which the pilgrims and colonizers brought to the new continent. The author speaks of the character of the colonies, and presents certain concepts that influenced the independence declaration: factors such as demographic, diversification, civil rights, mercantilism, and autonomist.

In chapter Two, the author goes over the situation of the colonial days before the decision to declare themselves independent. He speaks about the nature of the constitution and exposes the place of failure, concluding that the Union is sick. People lived it with hatred, selfishness, racism, greed that takes it away from the principles of its constitution. The spirit, national and popular sovereignty, dies from this disease, corruption. The author predicts that republic and democracy are on the verge of a revolution for restoring the founders' dream. The author studies the disease of the Union and opens the constitution and its amendments, seeking the remedy for the spirit of the republic; he discusses other concepts behind the independence. He seeks the basis of deviation in areas of the constitution and amendments. He also studies concepts such as fallibility, the independence, the evidence of support and closes the chapter with warnings and consequences. In addition, in this chapter, the author sets out certain governments that let reforms in his judgment. The author expects that the antidote to Union disease is a general reform based on the causes found.

In chapter three, the author lists the Europeans as religious and political influences pushing their independence. The situation in Europe forced or influenced people to migrate to the new continent. Influences included concepts of physiocracy and subsidiarity. And the author studied the notion of separation of political powers, and the causes and consequences for seeking to be independent of Great Britain. He studied concepts of civil liberty and civil law in this chapter. He closes chapter three reviewing the definitions of the spirit of the law, Social Contract, and the natural rights.

In chapter four the author brings the text of independence declaration into this discourse as a theme of fundamental philosophical, social and political influences; thus, he opens the preamble to the constitution and the constitution. The author studies the character of settlers contributing to the text of the declaration of their independence, including concepts like:

(1) pluralism
(2) natural law
(3) popular sovereignty
(4) contract
(5) libertarianism
(6) civil liberties
(7) interventionism
(8) the concept of laissez-faire
(9) capitalism.

The author adds the ignored concept of *human capital*. He compares conditions to show that background situations do not change and stay the same through the time.

In chapter five, the author studies government forms in the colonies, which serve as the basis for the federation. He focuses on the profile of the founders and analyzes the sequence of events of the independence. He reviews the supporting causes, the legality of that action, and the outcome of the war. Here he discusses the legality of the independence, touching on the war, emphasizing distribution of power between state and federal government. He reviews the American dream definition, presenting social, political and economic injustice issues that today do not differ from the original dream; They have only changed their style. The background or its originality remains the same. The people established the legality of the movement. This legal basis remains in place and applies to current situations.

The Union is far from perfect. The author devotes chapter six to studying important aspects of the constitution, emphasizing government definition, division of powers, authority and size of government. Then he studies the state's authority and of the central government, in the constitution and in the amendments. In this chapter he studies the origin of political parties and the electoral process. Later he goes over the lessons learned during the history of the United States. He points out how constitutional reforms make a more perfect Union of the United States. In this chapter he discusses the concept of union. The author reviews the intellectual and moral principles of the people, underpinning the principle of unity. These principles include natural rights, human rights, civil rights, excluding geographical territories or the way they govern their territories.

Chapter seven delves into concepts, hypotheses and theories of progressive thoughts on freedom focused on forming a more perfect Union of the United States. He follows the idea—or dream—that the Union is of people under the same concept and not of governments or states. The book presents the constitution and amendments adopted, citing evidence supporting legislative changes to update the constitution. Updates include legal rules, and democracy to the social, economic, and political needs of today. Here the author compares the original intent of constitutional principles with the current social, economic, and political reality. He talks about human rights and natural rights as the main issues.

In chapter seven, the author presents lessons learned over two-and-a-half centuries, including racial status, political corruption, growing social rifts, etc. And he draws useful notions to change the interpretation and course of the American people's way of life, including freedoms and rights of the citizen. He correlates the lessons learned with historical records. The author categorizes the lessons learned from last year's events of American democracy, discussed in chapter five, in five aspects influencing the general welfare. These aspects are (1) economic, (2) educational, (3) social, (4) health, and (5) political. He also presents in this chapter the intention and basis of the need for general constitutional reform, as (1) Moral, (2) Ethics, (3) Transparency, (4) Honesty, and (5) Loyalty to the constitution of the Union.

In the epilogue, the author, concluding with closing comments, says, *"Maybe my ego falters within the mirage I mentioned; but the feeling that we are going astray does not betray my mind. The sufferings and pains of the people are evidence in my conscience."* The author's interest is not to create a separation or socio-political discord between citizens. He envisions a situation that claims a change in the people way of life. We need to return to a path within a legal, political, social conditions, leading to a more perfect government. He envisions a government framework closer to what founding fathers conceived. The author makes recommendations for effective change. He thinks every democracy depends on the will, or power, of the people, and when the government reduces their will or power, the people feel the pressure. And when this pressure reduces their rights and liberty, they react. Constant government abuses of power and authority push the people to the point of "zero tolerance"—the point of a big social explosion. We have no space between the point of "no more tolerance" and "the point of no return"; the time is short and we must find a solution right away. The pressure defines the social point of no return, including (1) History recorded the revolution of the English colonies of North America; (2) The people overthrew the French monarchy; and (3) people fought to gain independence from Spain in Latin America countries. We still have time, and the relief valve is a reform of the United States of America constitution.

Besides the above, the book includes a list of endnotes that give the reader the opportunity to delve into the different topics considered in this book. It also includes footnotes as references to information sources for expanding and supporting your reading.

image borrowed from the Internet

The mirage

The settlers' dream and the founders' vision is lost in the mirage of Justice, Equality and Freedom. Everything hides in the shadow of the effigy or is lost in the fog that covers the symbol, hope or longing of that dream—the mirage on the sand of an arid ethics, moral, and transparency of the representatives of the people in government. The goals of the constitution, the Republican government and democracy are falling behind its letter because its spirit is dying within this mirage. We only see the dream in the background as we see the symbol in this image. There are many personal interests, many agendas hidden in the minds and consciences of politicians managing their game behind the curtains that separate the public (the people). It's been over two hundred years and Benjamin Franklin's prediction has been fulfilled. Today it is up to us to raise the mirage.

People's dream is always their hope; but the reality may be different. There's always a goal, and most of the time that goal gets out of mind. That was why the founders wrote the need to "form a more perfect Union". In the dense haze of life, reality is unique and we cannot alter them. It doesn't matter the effort or commitment of those who want to change it. It may stay dormant, supplanted by virtual reality—it's the makeup with which the ambitious selfish people disguise the truth. Truth is the only reality kept in time, protected by the existence. What we see is not what is; we lose reality in the mirage that produces the desert of ignorance and human apathy. We form part of the mirage by following leaders, offering us the dream of our homeland knowing they cannot deliver. They seek to fulfill their personal and selfish purposes, aided by people with apathy.

Apathy reverts everything to the people when they ignore what politicians do with their heritage behind their backs, their elected representatives to public offices. Those are those who take and master people's dream and create and feed the mirage. That mirage is a grimace or grimaces from what the founding fathers of this American union conceived. It is the mirage of the form of government, and the democracy of America; it is the dream of the American people distorted by rigged policies or hidden agendas favoring the rich, famous, and powerful. And while people live in their daily chores—in their quest to survive—politicians take advantage of this situation to usurp the benefits of people's freedom. That mirage is the lie, the failure of the American dream that demagogues paint for the people perception; but it's a virtual reality. They make the people believe that they have a vocation to serve them. But they have the purpose of using the resources, the benefits of freedom of the people. That's the mirage.

In this mirage around us we see the desires for peace, freedom, prosperity, general welfare—like a dream, vanishing into a vacuum. This dream only exists in the mirage that vibrates in daily reality but not in the reality of our lives writhing on the hot surface of our environment. The politicians create with their actions mirages of what it can be. And after so many years of living in this involuntary unreality, a mirage becomes the current reality—virtual reality. Perhaps the day has come when a ruling clown with his customs tries to make us live in his circus—his virtual reality. And so, he disperses his magic, the anti-actual smoke, and imposed on us a monarchy, an autocratic government, or a life dictatorship. Patriotic fervor awakens and exalts the interest maintaining the form of republican government, democracy. The constitution and the spirit gives and maintains life and freedom in the United States of America.

The author is a citizen, as you are my reader, just like the others. He is not, nor does he pretend to be a lawyer; but as a citizen he feels a duty and commitment to contribute his simple ideas to improve the Union. He also submits this book and its content to the reader and public judgement. He thinks it is the time to study the effectiveness of the constitution and its regulations of laws applicable to the social, political state of the present time. Yes, because the constitution and its rule of laws age, growing weak with time; we must protect the developing society. The constitution is rigid while life is dynamic and changes with the time, its customs, its ideals, and its way of life.

The current situation is not commendable in all political, social and economic aspects of the country; there are big differences, social and economic gaps that affect the republic and democracy. Discrimination exists open and overlapping. You can see hate and vengeance; there are forces that deepen differences. And the exploitation of man by man is public. Free enterprise plays with human necessity, and the complicit government ignores these acts.

The United States government has failed, is failing, and will continue on that path while we, the people, do not wake up from our lethargy. The rulers changed the American dream declared in their independence, in the preamble to the constitution, in the constitution itself, and in the rules of law of the constitution. They have allowed, with ill intension and premeditation, the selfishness of private enterprise to take over the republic and democracy of America. A minority with its greed and selfishness destroyed the good principles and precepts of natural capitalism. Today what regulates the economy is mercantilism (anything for profit) and the concept of fair price rests in peace in history. The greed of capitalism took over the government and wants to end democracy. And we must change all that; that's the real kink that makes the American dream a mirage.

This concept is mercantilism; man rests his social, political and economic power on his accumulation (without limits) of wealth, at the expense of the middle and lower classes. That is the greed and selfishness the author mentioned. This concept is part of the mirage of man's life. It is an invalid, immoral economic theory that brings profound social, economic, political differences and consequences. History tells us of many men who had or have control of wealth and power, like monarchs, autocrats, and dictators in the world. That is the current mirage, the virtual reality, that selfish avarice has created for convenience. But that capitalism of the middle ages founded under the concept of fair price and based on the usefulness of products and services fell into selfish mercantilism. But, if capitalism adapted to the spirit and letter of the constitution of the United States, capitalism would foster the general welfare of the people. And it would contribute to form a more perfect Union, without altering national tranquility, and would promote the pursuit of happiness. Then leaving this economic system at large would be democratic capitalism; but never a socialism, because the constitution acknowledges the inalienable right of Life and this right entails the right to private property.

Abraham Lincoln envisioned *a government of the people, by the people and for the people*, but it is in coma. The misguided operation of capitalism distorts its sound intention. The ambition and greed of a few is ending with the life of the majority, general well-being and happiness. Those who have capital can buy justice. The national tranquility does not exist; the armies fight wars, defending the economic interests of the rich. The government does little or nothing to promote general welfare. The rich, and right-wing, call socialism to the general welfare. They think the benefits of freedom are only for the gigantic businesses and owners—they own the ninety-nine percent of total capital. The evidence is in the statistics, and in what those who own the capital-money do.

Yes, a few people have ninety-nine percent of the nation's wealth while ninety-nine percent of the people have only one percent of that wealth. The high cost of living is no problem for the rich, perhaps from the upper third of the middle-class up, but for two-thirds of that class down is limiting. The less affluent a people are the fewer chances they have for emerging and competing with others. They have no access to higher education, no possibility of saving an investment, or pay for its health, and cannot cover the cost of its education. And in this situation, it sinks day by day into poverty. But society asks, why so many homeless people live under a bridge, on the sidewalks of the streets. Where is the government responsible for ensuring general welfare? That's the question.

The mirage changes the image of the greatness of this nation to the world. It does not show that greatness of the few as a conspiracy aimed at keeping people marginalized, in poverty, occupied pursuing their survival. That's why they still don't recognize the actual value of human capital [knowledge, skills and experience]. The (free) labor market keeps the smallest wage at least value at the poverty level. The woman doesn't earn for the same job what the man earns. And the rich pays for the Justice to rule in their favor. The central government fails when it does not work on improving the social, political, and economic systems in its territory. The United States fails, not abiding by the spirit and letter of the constitution and the principles of the American Union. Nothing must stay or be above the law. This includes the capitalist system. So, the freedom of this economic system, the formation, and operation of the enterprise and the free market, must work complying with the constitution mandates.

COVID-19 (Coronavirus), the pandemic that appeared in 2020, shows the social, political and economic differences or social gaps. Those who cannot pay for their health die in solitude, because they have no insurance or they cannot pay their health bills. The constitution mandates to promote the general welfare, and within this welfare people have health and education. The governments are apathic, autocratic, supremacist; they are not interested in the people welfare. That's the reality. The mirage shows that everything is in conditions not seen. We remember that cruel and despotic conditions pushed the English colonies to seek independence in North America.

The concept of making "America Great Again" is part of this mirage. The conditions and circumstances of the time of independence are not the same as those the Union faces in recent years. Back then, the colony relationship was almost with the nations of Europe. And their social-political relationship was also with Britain. For that time, after the people created the Union, increasing corruption has invaded the fundamental principles of the nation; and with this the possibility of the republican government and democracy falling, as the Roman empire and the Soviet Socialist Union fell.

Several dozen years ago, it was time to update America's constitutional principles and adapt them to the current reality of American people's lives. We have the constitutional duty of studying the state of the Union and petition changes aimed to stabilizing the nation, focusing on the interests, freedoms, and rights of the people. Otherwise, the Union is just fifty two "Disunited States" of America and the people's dream is forever a mirage. Perhaps this is what Putin wants and Trump is delivering.

We, the people, must not allow the United States of America to become another corrupt nation; a nation that has no ethics, social, political, economic, and or moral. We must clarify the mirage of our political, social and economic reality. The social and economic balance is the correct and just approach for restoring people to equality; that is the dream people try to achieve or realize with their independence. This dream in which the people envision general welfare is top priority. It is their hope, the dream, to form a nation with sustained national tranquility, serving justice for all.

The land of free college education for junior people is where the government promotes and protects fair competition in the free market. And the nation is full of equal opportunities for people of all races and skin colors, and equal pay for equal work for woman and man. Is that just the dream, not the reality of life? No, it's not just a dream; incompatible purposes block the dream that stems from the constitution and the economic system chosen by the people. Capitalism is not a cause of the people's social and economic gaps; but people desires for unlimited profit is the cause. Corruption is not a chimera, and not the mirage the author explained. The cause of that mirage is the government failure to make that dream a reality.

Benjamin Franklin predicted the government would corrupt, and we would need to change it, as the republic ages. Those who step over the constitution and give away the nation to a form of corrupt capitalism are traitors. The politicians placing their interests above the duties of their offices are traitors. Franklin saw it in his visions and declare it.

> "We need a revolution every 200 years because all governments become obsolete and corrupt after that time."

Changes

The course of human events makes it necessary for us, the people, to seek alternative routes, procedures, policies, social, and economic ways to make a more perfect Union. It is our duty to improve our nation. We must ask government representatives to improve the Union; they must improve the general welfare, guard our national tranquility and justice under equal terms for all citizens. Then, we will break the mirage that the author mentioned earlier.

Over two hundred and forty-four years have passed since the thirteen colonies declared their independence. And the corruption and abuse of authority are obvious issues for the public. We are seeing Benjamin Franklin wisdom realized in these years, but we are overdue. Franklin meant an armed revolution, but now, the revolution is more intellectual than military. The printing invention gave people hopes. The industrial revolution that took us through the 18th and 19th centuries brought us prosperity. And we went through the Great Depression of 1929.

Four presidents have faced impeachment cases. These presidents are Johnson in 1868, Nixon in 1974, Clinton in 1999, and Trump (2020). And the last three went into a process of political dismissal. People changed their business procedures using electronic servers, databanks, and database applications. They changed business attitudes; and they changed business means and methods. We are now using inventions like computer servers, databases, and Internet. Technology and social networking brought us to new (instant) communication, not so long ago. We changed the way we think and communicate with each other using the Internet, which has unlimited information.

Donald Trump won the electoral votes and the presidency in the 2016 elections, aided by Russia's intervention, according to the intelligence community investigations. They found that Russia intervened in the 2016 elections. And because of Russia's intervention, new methodologies flourished, like cybersecurity. The Internet opened the door to a new phase of illustration that surpasses the Theo centrism and anthropocentrism of the 15th to 17th centuries. In these days people cannot hide the truth because electronic information brings the news on social media in actual time. Human thoughts have entered the instant recognition realm of mentality, abandoning the concept of a material being—that predominant material being was the notion of man. Man realizes that his mental values, knowledge and experience mixed with physical ability is true human capital—that is the source and strength of man's evolution.

In the political field diplomacy—the rules of social, domestic, local and international relationship—has fallen into the law of the strongest (the richest, most powerful). For example, president Trump's diplomacy is one of outrage, denigrating those who oppose him, dividing to defeat. It's an ancient philosophy by Nicola Machiavelli. Machiavelli suggested immoral theory: violence and deception in politics to divide the opponent and win. Dictators like Putin, Maduro, Ortega use this policy, and now president Trump is attempting to be like them. And after four cases of political impeachment, we see the constitutional crises that could destroy the republican government and democracy the founders had dreamed. All that has happened, and our constitution continues in its infancy. There are still obsolete vestiges in its spirit and letter; it is necessary to help it grow to its adult life, meeting our needs, the people in the present time.

The author notes that the constitution and its framework of laws have serious weaknesses that puts the national and popular sovereignty at risk. Since these two sovereignties are not equivalent, we need to make this distinction. In the hierarchy of power, popular sovereignty is over national sovereignty. The second derives power and authority from the first as the founders explained the declaration of independence and in the constitution. The power of the state derives from the power of the people. And national sovereignty only has the power stipulated in the constitution, and everything not sanctioned them belongs to the state or the people of this nation. The power and authority of the republic falls under the power of the states and or their people. We have seen, in recent decades, how autocratic presidents can destroy the balance of the powers of the Union, ignoring the constitution. They break the rule of law, dropping the democracy of the people, and overstepping the fifty-two states of the Union. The people must prevent, reduce and or end conditions, for a president to cut off the constitution of the United States. Otherwise, they cut democracy and implant an autocratic regime, monarchy or dictatorship.

Laws of combinations and permutations of the Existence show that if the legislative and judicial powers fall under the executive branch, the president can replace the government and its democracy. The president can install a dictatorial, despotic state, like the one in Russia, North Korea, or in Nicaragua, in Cuba, etc. An autocratic president can also install a monarchy like the one in Great Britain in 1776. We're seeing this possibility with president Trump and the republican party in control of the Senate. The three powers were in the republican's hands, but Trump did not have enough time to gain full control of the government. The danger exists and will stay possible, if the purpose and letter of the constitution does not prevent a situation like that. It is possible that one day that nation may fall under a permanent monarchy. The Union is not perfect, and the legislative branch has a responsibility to legislate to form a more perfect Union as the founding fathers dreamed of in 1776.

The constitution still bears traces of the situation of the year thousand seven hundred and seventy-six. For example, the need to have a militia is false when in the United States has the most powerful armed forces in the world. The constitutional organization of the national guard in each state is capable of resolving internal or external conflicts or situations. There is no need to, or legalize, a protective militia as when it was being stalked by the Army of Great Britain in the time of the colonies. The militia in the United States has already fulfilled its mission and now poses danger to common defense and national tranquility.

The approach of the vice-president taking over as president of the Senate contradicts the concept of separation of the powers of the state. In critical cases, he can cast his vote in favor of the party to which he belongs. The author raises this issue as themes for this book. Citizens, of the United States must awaken from their lethargy and see the dangers the Union and its democracy face in the nation's life. The founders saw these dangers and included the specific constitutional mandate to form a more perfect Union (every day). That mandate is a patriotic action not for a single moment but for the life of this nation.

For example, we destroy the popular sovereignty when the individual cannot choose its representatives, its presidents, and vice-presidents. The right of the people to vote is ineffective if we leave this right to the discretion of collegiate voters. The people have an undisputed right to pick the president and vice-president. The discretion of a few collegiate voters supplants the will of citizens (popular sovereignty) by choosing a candidate who does not win the popular vote. These college electors expose the people to internal and external influences of corruption, favoring a political party or candidate; the college voters may not follow the will of the majority. The Congress should design and sanction a more strengthened electoral method that ensures the freedom, security and accuracy of electoral suffrage.

Likewise, when the interests of a political party alter the role of the three powers, they violate the national sovereignty and betray the will of people; they depose the republic and democracy and install autocratic powers. This is the case when the chambers, supreme court magistrate, court judges, or the president do not work for the interests of the people. They work for hidden, personal, or third-party interests. They violate the oath of office with actions pointed out for this case. The president, vice-president or any representative commit treason to the nation's constitution; so, they attack the national and popular sovereignty. We should categorize such actions as treason, an attack on the constitution and the rule of law.

The constitution in its weakness allows political corruption to contaminate the principles supporting its integrity, the ethic and transparency of the three powers. For example, the president [of the executive branch] selects and nominates candidates to the judicial branch of the government. Current separation of powers is not effective, if the executive branch, the president, nominates candidates to hold the positions of the judiciary, magistrates and federal judges. The judiciary branch is so critical that the people must exercise the right to pick these officials by popular vote. If the people do not choose by vote, they have no separation of the powers. And we expose the government to political corruption—or favoritism toward a political party or an individual.

Likewise, the founders designed a nation with three separate powers for the central government. The power of the Union is what is in the constitution. Everything else not defined or detailed in it is the authority and power of the states, and or the people. A president's claim to have absolute power or rights over the sovereignty of states, or the people, and that is a misconception. For this reason, is necessary to amend article II of the constitution to clarify the power and authority of the president. There can, and should not be, a power higher than the popular sovereignty, from which the national sovereignty derives. That is the power and authority of representatives in the three powers of the state.

It is neither effective nor efficient to allow inept, inexperienced people to hold political offices. If we write and publish the requirements for a new position, open in private enterprises, we should specify requirements for the president and vice-president positions. Any candidate for these positions must submit their credentials compliant with the requirements. Political parties must submit candidates' credentials satisfying requirements for these positions. The best proposal wins the right to become a candidate to represent a political party in a campaign for the party nomination. People do not choose candidates for the positions of their government in this way. And that's why the people choose candidates who have no knowledge, skills or experience compatible with the position on the ballot. We know the constitution has three requirements, citizenship, domicile and age. So, we have been playing with the people, endangering their life, rights, freedom and democracy.

The authority given to a presidential candidate to choose his vice-president is a political risk. The president can pick an incompetent candidate for vice-presidency who can assume the presidency in the case the president leaves the post. We fail our nation by not pre qualifying the candidates to president and vice-president. Candidates for president must pre-qualify–knowledge, skills and experience before entering their presidential campaigns. A party nominated presidential candidate must seek prequalification of the vice-president candidate.

The changes are nothing new. Changes occurred even before the states ratified the original constitution, exposing the will, the sovereignty of the people of the peoples of the colonies. Four states did not ratify the constitution at once after its enactment because its peoples insisted that it did not meet the requirements that could satisfy their popular sovereignty. The people considered adding twelve amendments to the constitution, they approved although only ten Two of these twelve amendments are still pending.

image borrowed from the Internet

CHAPTER 1

Historical background

No event happens if supporting conditions or circumstances, or other events, are not given. And each set of conditions and circumstances allows events that satisfy them at the moment. The actions of living entities conform to the conditions and circumstances of each moment. But, according to the law of cause and effect, the results are effects or consequences. But actions always give results, positive and negative, according to this law. And casual events occurring at random, do not alter the end or purpose of causal events. Life will always have its events based on conditions and circumstances making the event.

The independence of the English colonies in North America depended on obvious causes. And the need to write the constitution of the United States had its causes. Settlers had causes in their minds along with their idiosyncrasies and common understanding of their conditions. The resulting event was inevitable by conditions and circumstances, forcing the outcome—their independence. Europeans thinking changed concepts by the end of the middle ages, the end of feudalism, the end of Rome's control over the minds of people. But control over the poor and innocent continues. Man discovers that he can live without religions, but religions cannot live without men. Nature teaches us that species inferior to man exist without having a library of laws regulating their interrelationships. But man needs laws to regulate his actions. Man needs three principles to keep his relations with other men at peace. These principles are (1) to love your fellow man as yourself; (2) to share with others what we exploit from the universe; and (3) to respect the right of others.

The author finds an article on the Internet that narrates important historical notes. Interest in science disputes the belief that God was the center of everything. The controversial point of this about thought began in the 15th to 17th centuries. The new mentality focused and developed an interest in new values, new knowledge and implanted confidence in the sciences, such as medicine, biology and botany, astronomy, physics, mathematics, among others. This movement injected an optimistic push towards scientific advancement, seeking alternative possibilities to improve man's lives. Social value changes help common welfare at different rates and different times. We saw that change brought different ways of thinking that included the study of nature and reason of beauty in the time of illustration. That alternative way of thinking supported secular (non-religious) life and had an optimistic feeling–the *enjoyment and living life in the present.* Settlers had a new mentality they brought to the new continent. And they saw the alternative (the choice) of freedom opposed to the repression imposed by the absolute monarchies of those times—*their luck was cast.*

Modern thought aroused scientific research, philosophy and dependence on reason, rather than resting in faith. Man leaned over the anthropocentrism opposed to the Theo centrism. Intellectual freedom of medieval and religious obscurantism created a fresh man. Man discovers that he can be free from the iron control that the church held over the mind of man. History recorded the holy inquisition and persecution of witches in Spain, in 1610, besides suppression of heresy by the catholic church, from 1478 to 1834. We find historical records of the Portuguese inquisition in the same years. We find the Roman inquisition that began in 1542 and lasted until 1965, extending to the conquered (expropriated) territories in America. Despotic kings had tight grip on people's lives. People had no freedom of worship; they did not control their lives, and they did not even have right to sexual tendencies (homosexuality). But Nature keeps its equilibrium or balance, its status quo, as long as the balance maintains the conformity (quiet) of the system—a sustained state.

These are suffocating conditions and circumstances creating hostile environments. But, sometimes, changes come by will of Nature like the COVID-19 pandemic. And when these suffocating conditions and circumstances occur, conditions and circumstances open steps to changes, justifying people's decisions and actions. And the settlers say it in their declarations of protest against England.

> *"When in the course of human events, it becomes necessary for a people to dissolve the political bands that have connected them with another, and to assume among the powers of the earth, the separate and egalitarian estation to which the Laws of Nature and the God of Nature gives them the right, a decent respect for the opinions of humanity requires them to declare the causes that drive them to separation."*

The Creator of Nature and the laws of Nature regulate the behavior of the universe, giving man the sacred attributes of life, freedom, and free choice. And in this life man receives together with the inalienable rights to enjoy life, all that the universe has in a state of tranquility, equality, and well-being. No man has the power to alter, reduce, or deny such attributes and rights to any other man. We have seen one man in this nation, over and over, altering, reducing and trying to cut the inalienable rights of man.

Let us note that the intellectual change of that time led to the growth of a middle-class, the bourgeoisie, that uses education to reach comfortable positions in societies—the new bourgeois class.

And the bourgeoisie is an agent of change. Let us note the rise of a nation comes from the working-class and middle-class; but wealth accumulated in the hands of few does not reach the poor sitting at the bottom in any society. Perhaps from this understanding comes the phrase *"only the people save the people"*. This is a correct phrase because we have seen it that the selfishness of the rich and powerful first thinks about the multiplication of their own wealth. The social and anthropological phenomenon shows that the general well-being of every society is born and grows with the growth of the middle-class; and it raises the level of the marginalized poor class. While wealth in the hands of a monarchy or a few individuals creates gaps and separation of classes, rich and poor, gaps increase. Those who block general welfare and promote injustice instigate rebellions and wars in societies of the world, as we read in the records of history. The release of free education to the middle class and down promotes the general welfare, liberty, and facilitate the pursue of happiness. Education and implementation will make the social changes needed to promote overall and equality for all.

In reality, there will always be social, political and economic changes in nations—no one can avoid them; man develops because of changes in life. The founders of the United States knew that the Union—states and citizens—was not perfect and must follow many changes for the Union to achieve perfection. We can achieve this perfection increasing our knowledge and applying it; because the more knowledge we gain the better life condition we have, and the more frequent we need a change. So, education must be free and uniform, establishing a uniform advancement and a stable distribution of the benefits of freedom. The founding fathers, bright and wise, saw and embodied this notion in their statement of independence, and they define the justification and necessity of the change. This Nirvana state does not yet exist; and the governments are responsible of perfecting our Union to achieve that state. The mental framework of Europeans had changed, because of the intellectual impact of the 15th-century renaissance period. Already the people of the old continent had awakened to the modern age—the wish for freedom and the sacred right of free choice.

People say the renaissance kicks off in the fall's wake of Constantinople in 1453, when the Byzantine empire—the eastern part of the Roman empire fell. [1] It happened a few years before the discovery of America. And the change shows abandonment of feudalism and the agricultural economy, opening the door to the concept and practice of the commercial economy.

---

[1] https://es.wikipedia.org/wiki/Imperio_bizantino

> The commercial economy is a system of centralized and despotic control imposed on trade and export during the 16th to 18th centuries. This system regulates the economy under the premise that a nation's boom depends on the accumulated capital represented by the accumulation of gold and silver, mostly.

That's the saying, *how much you have is how much you're worth.* Mercantilist thinking still exists as an intrinsic part of the current capitalist system, [2] is unlimited enrichment, the want for profit, if restrictive regulations—speculation. The term nation does not welcome the people but only the ruler on the dome of governments— in this case the monarchies. Today we still experience influences of backing the currency used in daily transactions in the world with precious metals.

Feudalism organizes society around land tenure for services or jobs. Peasants get possession of a piece of land, paying the price with work, service and loyalty to the landowner, the Lord. The Creator does not create the land and its content for the few. God did not sell or grant exclusive rights to certain individuals such as lords, feudal, monarchs, or powerful rich people of today. The earth and its contents are of all and for all, but certain individuals or groups of individuals, usurped it by force. There is no man who can present an original title of ownership that the Creator has given to anyone. For this reason, the resources of the universe belong to all living creatures, men, and animals, alike.

Mercantilism, feudalism, the absolute power of monarchies, and the religious control of Rome made or created hostile environments— unbearable—in Europe. We understand the change in people's mindset (according to historical data collection), by analysis and or synthesis, and with what we know of events of that time. At the end of middle age, humans took the spotlight and diluted the theocentric belief. And when Constantinople fell in the hands of the Turkish

---

[2]   https://es.wikipedia.org/wiki/Mercantilismo

empire, the Byzantine empire also fell and with it, the Vatican iron control in Rome. [3]

Why did the English leave England?

Fame, wealth, and power cannot be more explicit than what encloses the Anglican reform and the *act of supremacy—a document*. The parliament of England approved this document to confirm the monarch, Henry VIII, absolute power. The act formalizes the English Reformation, 1534. It was a political game in the upper echelons of the power of Spain, England and the Vatican. This game involved Pope Clement VII, the catholic kings of Spain, Henry VIII and the English parliament. Catherine of Aragon, daughter of Elizabeth and Ferdinand, the kings of Spain—Wife of Henry VIII, had married to Arturo Tudor, elder brother of Henry VIII. The English people or the Spanish people do not take part in these games, but people pay for the broken dishes of their controversies. In this entanglement, Henry VIII furious because Catherine did not give him a son as first descendant, he annuls the marriage. The Pope opposes it; the catholic Ferdinand consented. And the parliament of England agreed that king Henry VIII is the highest authority and made him supreme head of the church of England. This game favored Henry VIII's mistress Anne Boleyn, Mother of Queen Elizabeth I. The crown charged, convicted and executed Ana for crimes of adultery, incest, and treason to the king. Ana's execution was more fuel igniting political and religious upheavals and boosting English reform. In this period the sequence of events led the British empire to separate the church of England from the Vatican. [4]

People did not escape England by their will; they escape the selfish whim of the king. England was going through tough times, in the early years of the 1600 century; it was a serious political and economic socio-political situation.

---

[3] https://www.aboutespanol.com/que-es-el-renacimiento-2206950
[4] https://es.wikipedia.org/wiki/Catalina_de_Aragorn.

Henry VIII, who sought to void his marriage, created cracks in his (already troubled) relationship with the Vatican in Rome. And the king's whim caused a political, if not theological, dispute. Then, by the *royal act of supremacy,* the king became the supreme head of the church, independent of Rome. And by *the law of betrayal,* accompanying that supremacy act, he classified as a traitor whoever denied the king's supremacy. The king's attitude created irreconcilable conflicts. A separatist group broke with the church of England; they felt that the church of England did not represent, rather, Christian, biblical values. The English kingdom had already unleashed a religious persecution against all those who opposed or broke with the church of England—the king considered traitors. The separatists, the so-called pilgrims, fled England, by the mid-1600, never to return to England, escaping the threats of the Anglican Reformation. So, the pilgrims came to America by the year in 1620 and founded the Plymouth colony—in what is now the state of Massachusetts. They arrived poor, frightened, and without expecting help from the English crown. According to history records, half starved to death in the first few months on American soil. And if it hadn't been for the natives of America, the rest would have died too. Native Americans taught pilgrims how to live in these lands and in this climate. But even though they had fled England, and came to the Americas, the pilgrims were still subjecting of the English crown. [56] They were like property of the king, and so they were under the king's wishes. That's how the colonies started. The Creator and the laws of Nature consider man, (or anything in the universe) is not property of any man. Corrupt man contaminated their societies, their governments, their economic and their political systems, falling with their corruption. We have seen this corruption undressed in the United States. It's galloping and it's on the rise. If this government does not stop it, this democracy and this nation will not live many more years. Perhaps history repeats itself, and we learn of people uprising to gain freedom as settlers did two hundred and forty-four

[5] https://www.allabouthistory.org/spanish/peregrinos.htm
[6] https://Es.wikipedia.org/wiki/reforma_anglicana

years ago. The Senate, and republicans covered-up Trump's behavior in the impeachment process. Police assassinated George's in public. These events signal the need for constitutional reforms to find and plug the holes through which rats ran into our political system. [7]

The system of Spanish colonization style is not the same as the system of English colonization. These are two different systems. The Spanish system comprised conquests– armed rather military invasions executed with expeditions allowed by catholic kings to certain territories. The Spaniards imposed evangelization and European culture. It was not a process of conquest to unite natives out of their own free will by the charms of European culture. It was a system of exploitation with the wish to extract the richest, precious metals, from the new continent and bring them to catholic kings (that is mercantilism). This system worked with two components, the hiring house and the Indian Council. The first part controlled commercial activity, and the other represented the form of government. [8]

The conquests had only one purpose; that is the economic end: They had the purpose of exploiting America's richness, including extraction of minerals like gold and silver. They conquest America and took advantage of the natives, forcing into slavery. Their purpose was obvious, to enrich themselves by exploiting the new continent. Settlers in the colonies had to pay taxes for living, producing and marketing what they could since they arrived. Natives had no help from this operation—except submission to catholic kings—and had no freedom to market on their own; they only received European enculturation in return.

The situation of the American colonies was different. European emigrants came with the wish to produce on their own, independent of the English crown; they sought to be free to choose their religion, way of life, production, and commerce—that was their dream—and they did not plan to return to England. European had advanced industrial thinking, and migrants brought their knowledge, skills,

---

[7]   https://historiaybiografias.com/trece_colonias/
[8]   https://iesalagon.educarex.es/web/departamentos/sociales/
      documentos/trabajo moderno.

and experiences to America. They were eager to produce independent of the English crown. In deference of how the Spanish and English saw the new continent is negligible. They both saw the opportunity to usurp land—even by exterminating the Americans. Their goal was exploiting them for their own interests and benefits. And about the English crown, and even though the colonizers had certain rights, or freedom to act, the English crown did not allow them to process raw materials. They dragged the chains that tied them to the English empire for life. The crown reserved the right to process the raw material on its own. Likewise, the English crown did not allow the colonizers to trade internationally and reserved that role for the crown. We know England handled the colonies under a mercantilist system, through which the central government administration controlled its possessions, trade, and exports for its help. One cannot say that Britain practiced a targeted economy; what the settlers produced was not as important as it was to control what they produced for the economic help of the crown. The crown attitude violated the inalienable rights that the Creator gives on men. [9, 10]

The story is simple. The Huns came down from Mongolia and swept through much of Europe. They expropriating the lands of their residents, killed children, adults and, stealing what they had of value. In Europe, monarchies, and people did the same. Also, the Vatican with the crusades that in the cross's name caused disasters, ruins, and massacres. It's always been the same. And the settlers expropriated and almost exterminated the native Americans. History does not hide details and shows man's behavior as he is. Men drag their dishonesty, greed, and selfishness around the world.

In North America, the thirteen colonies had about one and a half million inhabitants by 1750 and operated with success. England managed the colonies through a British Chamber of *Commerce,* and a Royal Council and parliament—it was a system-like control system used by Spain. But despite this control, the colonies implemented

---

[9] https:// theelbirthofclio.wordpress.com/2013/04/27/sociedad-y-economia-en-the-13.

[10] https://es.wikipedia.org/wiki/Trece_Colonias

their independent way of acting outside British control. This prevailing economic regime in Europe—mercantilism—during that time of the 18th century, had a significant influence on the colonies of America. Mercantilism is an unscrupulous want aimed to control, produce and trade any form or method to make unreasonable gains—under the end justifies the means. [11] Mercantilism embraces a management system that regulates international production and trade to promote the development and infrastructure of Britain and not the colonies. [12] The mercantilism of that time followed regulatory rules in three fundamental components, control of the currency, control of relations between political power and economic activities contingent on government intervention. The State controlled all production, the market, natural resources, domestic, and external markets—export and import—and even population growth. But there was subsidiary favoritism for private enterprise, making it easy to create privileged monopolies—clear state corruption. The king-imposed tariffs on foreign products regulating export—the aim was to mint the currency in gold and silver. The government intervened in the economy, according to the absolute power of the English reign for its benefits. Abuse, exploitation, and restriction of the freedoms that the colonizers rejected. The scenario, conditions, and circumstances, almost ended the period of social, political and economic gestation, laying the foundations for radical change. Besides all the above, they say mercantilism was a mechanism of social, political, economic control for the help of European monarchies—an obvious exploitation of man by man. They drafted the constitution to change, reduce, and cut that form of government in stages.

People were hardworking, entrepreneurial, and the wealth of the great American continent led to production—almost limitless. But the colonies had no firm control over their primary operational work—international production and trade. Having religious, political and economic freedom was a dream that looked workable in the new continent (as they called it), and English and European emigrants

---

[11] https://economipedia.com/definiciones/comercialismo.html
[12] Mercantilismo: https://es.wikipedia.org/wiki/Mercantilismo

continued to arrive in America. The flow of immigrants did not stop, in particular people skilled in industrial production from England and Europe. They came eager to work, stay here, and make a new life. This land was for the free and the warriors. The people is willing to work hard to gain freedom, of religion, and personal and economic freedoms. This land was, in the words of Thomas Paine, *"the asylum for persecuted lovers of civil and religious liberties from all over Europe"*.

The Europeans brought with them philosophical foundations to make a great nation. They do not limit the development of this philosophy of civil and religious freedoms to the people of the colonies. The settlers did not object to subordinating themselves to Britain and were happy to be part of that empire. It resulted from the war in Britain and France, in which France loses. History points out that the loser in this conflict was Britain. The purpose of this book is not to repeat the narrative of the history, this war episode between these two nations. But the causes and consequences of this war are of basic importance to the American colonies. And it was those consequences that caused the settlers' change in attitudes.

The European situation in 1490

So many things happened in that time, so many things. Only by living the moments, we know the actions, second by second; but when time compacts the facts. And the density of the past is so high that the human mind, or its understanding, only sees the surface of what happened. The nature of our reality is what we see on its surface.

Existence has two realities, obvious reality, and latent reality. The obvious reality is what perception captures and processes, while latent reality is the knowledge obtained through reasoning, deductive and inductive. So, we need to expand our wise vision, before we do a deep analysis and synthesis, perhaps so, we can untangle the skein of history. Fortunately, knowledge is progressive, from lowest to highest, and only in that direction; so, we acquire the total image of truth discovered as new knowledge.

The situation at the end of the middle ages, in the fifteenth, sixteenth and eighteenth centuries in Europe, was like a game of commercial, economic, and political chess. This was a game for monarchies and the Vatican in Rome. Incessant intrigues, hidden interest strategies fueled wars for power and territorial dominance, rather than social dominance. Perhaps it didn't matter and peoples were nothing but system pawns. But, the social, or rather mental, part reached a new stage, a level of knowledge, which dragged the world into discoveries. Today's consumer societies are like cattle, pig, poultry farms—a comparison with the human situation not so eloquent—but it explains the situation. The farmer feeds these species with a single purpose feed the food chain. In consumer societies, they induce him to spend everything he earns from his job and leave him no choice but to keep working. The module of the general economic model for the working-class has been constant since man entered societies.

The man works, earns his wage or salary and spends it. But this model is not natural and is not a problem; problems are born when those who control capital-money manipulate the income of the working-class on a balance with their basic consumption. In this module the capitalist model controls the value of human capital—the sum of knowledge, skills and individual experience. What the worker earns is equal to or less than what he consumes. The consumer lives daily, from pay-to-pay, and has no chance of saving to make their own investments (savings = income - expenses = 0). The problem is greater when those who control the means of production and services take advantage of workers. They give credit to people living on future earnings, knowing their financial condition. So, they become pawns enslaves by debts, short or long term. The difficult payment of the debt make workers slaves of the (pattern) job.

European expansion was eminent; Europe does no longer fit on its territory under the political pressure of the moment. The fall of Constantinople by the Turks reduced the power of the roman empire and brought the end of the middle ages to Europe. And the geographical position of the Turkish empire blocked trade with the East, Chinese, and Indian. There was one way out for Europeans; it was the Atlantic Ocean, and they began looking for alternative routes to reach those distant places. There was no alternative, the west or the despotic, decadent European situation. They marked fate, America, and the wealth of the new continent was the salvation, the effective change, of Europe—and so the history records.

The Portuguese were the skilled navigators of that time. And for this and with the new idea that the world was round they thought to sail west to reach the east. And in that effort of exploration and recognition Christopher Colon touches the shores of a new continent. But long before Colon came other humans came to what is now Alaska in the Americas crossing the Bering Strait about twenty thousand years ago. This is according to the historical compilation,. The lives of Europeans on American lands are only 400 years old, at 2020. So, if anyone had the right to claim land in America they were (and is) the people who [13] crossed that strait. These people populated North America and are the true (native) [i]Americans, these people populated the entire American continent, from the seven caves to Patagonia Argentina. They came because their traces and presence are clear. About a thousand years ago the Vikings came to the east coast through Greenland. But we have no evidence of permanent settlements on this continent. In the early 1600 (Christian era) the Dutch arrived in the northeastern region of what are now the United states. And a little later (about 1620) came the first pilgrims from England—but they were not late.

The seven-year war

This war is an important issue, Europe was bleeding to death with the war of years resulting from the Austrian war of succession. It was a war between several European nations that serves as a prologue to the seven-year war. Russians sent military support to the UK in fight against France; French sent military aid to Prussia, and the diplomatic revolution begins—named for reversing certain alliances between European nations, according to the article in footnote 14

---

[13] https://www.libertyellisfoundation.org/immigration-timeline

on page 43. United Kingdom formed an alliance with Prussia and does not help the Austrians because they did not serve the British cause. UK decides not to help Prussia recover Silesia. Austria and France signed an aid pact for Austria to take back control of Silesia. The UK's policy was that what happened in America outside the responsibility of the settlers, but hostile relations between France and the United Kingdom were not. France increased its aggression after several defeats of colonial forces. This causes the English to increase their involvement in colony operations. The UK was fighting with France for north American rule. France claimed Canada and the great lakes as its own territory. Spain fought Against Britain over territories and colonies in various parts of the globe including its possessions in the Americas. And it came with the treaty of Paris. It was an agreement to distribute colonial possessions around the world among the great powers of Western Europe. It was something like handing out the loot after the assault. The people don't count, they don't have a voice or a vote.

We can consider the seven-year war as a world war. The great powers of the old continent took part in that war. In fact, it was a war between these powers for the domination and control of territorial possessions around the world, including American territory. For readers passionate of knowledge, the author points out certain articles published on the Internet. The author explains in this book factors that clarify the philosophy and basic thoughts of how to form the United States of America. For example, the "treaty of Paris" with which the seven-year war ends on 10 February 1763.[14]

The people in the colonies declared their independence on July 1776. Thirteen years after, Europe went through the seven-year war. According to historical recounts, we know the outcome of that seven-year war. In particular, the result affects the colonies in North America. For example, "The United Kingdom receives all French

---

[14] Links on the Seven Years' War:
    (1) https://www.lifeder.com/guerra-siete-anos/;
    (2) https://es.wikipedia.org/wiki/Guerra_de_los_Siete_Años

territories in Canada, the territories east of the Mississippi River, and west of the Appalachian Mountains (except New Orleans), in America. He also receives Florida from Spain, in exchange for removing English troops stationed in Manila City (Philippines) and in the port of Havana, Cuba. They also obtained the right of free navigation along the Mississippi River. The kingdom of Spain: by the treaty of Fontainebleau of 1762, France gives Louisiana to the west of the Mississippi, including its capital, New Orleans."

During the time of colonization, the English crown increases its possessions in America apart from the thirteen colonies, which by that time had grown economically. There are other factors that help shape the mental framework of settlers for independence. The colonies received many influences from various nations, such as Spain, France and the Netherlands. But in reality, the diversity of cultures, beliefs, education, and knowledge came from all over Europe.

The situation in Europe opened a new scenario on the new continent where they continue their political and military play. They aim at increasing their power and wealth. All monarchies in Europe take part in the game. But, the monarchs and emperors, including the Vatican are the players—the people do not play in this game, not in the same way. This game that was then feudal, then mercantilist, and is now capitalism, following the same purpose with different rules of the game, the prize is wealth and power. The fight for land, gold, silver as of other natural treasures opened a new tournament on the new continent. The rich and powerful played by increasing their winnings, and the workers play their game for surviving.

Dutch influence

Netherlands' influence on the people of the colonies of North America is a historical evidence, since the 16th century. It was long a county of the Holy Roman [15] empire—a political grouping. A long list of counts ruled Holland; the last count was Philip II of Spain. The Netherlands, during the reign of Louis I Bonaparte, of

---

[15] https://es.wikipedia.org/wiki/Holanda

French origin, related to France. In the Dutch rebellion against the Habsburgs during the Eighty Years' war, the rebels' naval forces—the "sea beggars"—established their first permanent base in Brie in 1572. Thus, the Netherlands, now with sovereign status in a larger Dutch confederation, became the center of the rebellion. In the 17th century, the Netherlands became the cultural, political and economic center of the United Provinces. They became one of the largest European powers in a process known as the Dutch golden age. After the king of Spain ended as Earl of Holland, the executive, and legislative power fell to the states making up the United Provinces. John de Witt (the Grand Pensioner) led negotiations—as a Prime Minister—.[16]

Dutch merchants entered established colonies, or founded new colonies at the beginning. New Amsterdam was the first Dutch colony in 1625—around the same time as the Mayflower ship reached the northeast coast of America, in 1620. The Dutch thought about the help of regionalism that attracted them to a specific area. Powerful influence of the Dutch explorer played a prominent role in the colonization of the United States, the introduction of fundamental principles.

Influence of Spain

Spain began the exploration of North America shortly after Christopher Colon discovered this continent, in the crown's service of Castile, on October 12, 1492. The Spanish explored American territory—about 128 years—before the first English arrived in 1620. Thus, they had time to instill, and perhaps impose on the natives of America, the European culture of that time. Spain covered almost the entire continent with its tireless conquests during the 14th to 17th centuries. These conquests spread from North America, throughout the Caribbean, Central and South America, including Alaska and Florida. And I add Louisiana to this list of territory when the treaty of Paris signed on September 3, 1783.

---

[16] https://es.wikipedia.org/wiki/Gran_Pensionario

image borrowed from the Internet

Influence of France

France collaborated with funds, giving the colonies weapons and soldiers in their efforts to achieve their independence, believing that the United Kingdom would weaken. France contributed its thoughts and modern philosophy—from that time—.

English colonies, a thought [17, 18]

Even today we see evidence of Dutch influence. The island of Staten and Harlem prove the first Dutch settlements in the territory's northeast of the United States of America. Then the war between French and English ended the commercial empire of the Dutch with the English capturing the colony New Holland. And they changed the name to New York. But many Dutch stayed in that colony with the English.

---

[17] https://www.ecured.cu/Trece_colonias
[18] https://concepto.de/las-trece-colonias/

image borrowed from the Internet

On another migratory front, since the first group of Englishmen arrived in 1620, they began, with great difficulty, to set up settlements along the east coast of the continent. Their difficulties were with native Americans and with the French—their longtime rivals. They did all colonization in the name of the English reign. For example, the area of Virginia, an area named after the virginity condition of Queen Elizabeth I. They established Jamestown in the year thousand six hundred and ten. English immigrants obeyed or were submissive to the orders of the British crown; despite the religious persecution of the colony against the opposed to the new church in England. The colonization sequence did not have chronological planning but was a casual emigration depending on the need to escape to the new continent. All were agricultural settlements controlled by the English monarchy imposing their mercantilist system. Under this system, the crown controlled the settler's assets for the people living in England [Europe]. But why did the settlers have to work for the people of England? Was that the land tenure payment? Perhaps it extended the feudal system moved to America, although it had already disappeared in Europe.

Under this regime, they found the colonies one by one, always agriculturally. And within a century, immigrants established the thirteen colonies. They found the colony of Virginia on May 13, 1607, thirteen years before pilgrims on the mayflower ship in 1620, when they founded the Massachusetts colony. Three years after founding this colony, new settlers founded the colony of New Hampshire in 1623. Thirteen years later, other immigrants established the Rhode Island colonies in 1636. During this time the English disputes against the Dutch continued and about 28 years. Later the English stayed with the Dutch colony of New Holland, which they at once called New York.

The settler's resentment [19]

The resentment of the settlers counts a lot in the causes to gain the independence. The king's repression against those who rejected the church of England is one of the causes. But it was not just for social rights, at first. At the start, the means of production in the settlements was a cause due to the economic restrictions imposed by the king. Everything changed from religious persecution to matters of justice and freedom, economic, and commercial rights. The dawn of an independence movement came because of these economic, trade, and fiscal matters. In reality, the movement was not of the people as a people, but the bourgeoisie instigated the middle-class, agitating the people to protect their interests. The affairs were economic to Britain, and survival for the colonies. It was a matter of freedom. In our time we have seen revolts in protests over the death of Rodney King; later, we saw demonstrations for the murder of George Floyd. These events created resentment of the people in a package of violations of the inalienable rights of the people. This package includes racism, injustice, abuse of authority by law enforcement and the president.

---

[19] https://enciclopediadehistoria.com/independencia-de-estados-unidos/

The protesters call for reforms to police procedures with the people of the village.

By the end of the seven-year war against France, on American territory, England had been bankrupt. That is why Britain and to balance its finances orders to create tax laws on trades. Such impositions affected the economy of the colonies in America. The people reacted with demonstrations, protests, riots and social uprisings. English action terrified created deep resentments that settlers could not could not ignore. The abuse was obvious. For example, the tea *act* of 1773 creates a monopoly on the exchange of tea favoring the East Indian Company; and the colonizers regarded such act as a tax tyranny, instigating the famous tea party in Boston. In retaliation, the British parliament passed the *Coerciti act* in 1774, closing the port of Boston for merchants' shipments.

The king ordered new impositions besides restrictions on international free marketing—such as the industry and timber products—on the colonies. And the people showed popular discontent with demonstrations and popular protest. These resentments were for commercial and business affairs. People marched demonstrating their discontent and protested issues dealing with discrimination, abuse of power and authority such as social and political injustice, as history records the events. The marches and demonstrations of that time are no different from the protest marches of today. For example, we see the demonstrations for the murders of Rodney King in 1992 and George Floyd in May and June 2020. In both cases, marches led to vandalism and mass destruction of private property by infiltrators who acted to change the course of peaceful demonstrations.

The origin of the war that Britain declares to the colonies of America was economic. But the purpose was taxation, so much as of a religious, social, or political motives. The war begins with the "Boston massacre" in 1770. And the merchants agitate the working-class, the people, to show themselves. The colonies react and set up their own sovereign government, creating in 1787 their own constitution and forming a state with 3 independent powers (legislative, judicial and executive). [20] What was the help of the working-class in this matter? This is the crucial point, the ownership of power and popular sovereignty. Trader claims are not enough cause to claim independence; it was necessary for the people to claim, as popular sovereignty, their right to be independent. And the debate, philosophical and or political, moves to the list of topics. The separation movement was no longer a matter of religious repression, now it was a matter of middle-class trade and economics.

One good news was the war of independence ended with six main battles. Britain emerges victorious in only two of them—the game ends 4 to 2 in favor of the colonies. The important thing about this story is the origin of the war of independence; it was for commercial matters. In fact, it was a war between the producers, traders of the colonies and the English crown. The colonies then faced the glorious task of giving character and direction to the nascent nation. And for this, the leaders of the revolution should have solid philosophical, religious, social, political and economic concepts and plan a structure that would protect new American citizens. Luck was on their side, because within their leaders there were true patriots who had everything they needed, in terms of experience and knowledge. Idiosyncrasies of leaders in the colonies showed that an independence movement must succeed from all points of view, not only political, but legal, economic and social. Settlers needed solid foundations, form, background and legal arguments. The evidence of in the written result (of the thought of the founders) embodied in their independence declaration. We should mention that the colonies received help from the European countries such as France, Spain, and the Netherlands; the latter provided financial support and official recognition from the United States. Without the help of these countries, which also sought to take advantage of England, the independence of the thirteen colonies would have had a different course.

The author believes that the founders studied the basis of such action. They confirm this notion with the obvious spirit drafted in documents supporting independence. And to confirm this study the

---

[20] https://es.wikipedia.org/wiki/Separaciorón_de_poderes.

author reviews the nature and characteristics of the mental framework of the colonizers. The ideological effervescence of Europe started and only needed a spark to ignite the bonfire of popular discontent; And so, it was. What was going on in Europe? In Europe, what was happening in the English colonies on this new continent, America. In reality, oppressed people only resist for a definite time, but the conditions, circumstances and oppressive level blows up people's patience come. This is when life no longer matters if death really hovers around at all hours. The author has seen this phenomenon in living action for the dictatorships of Anastasio Somoza and Daniel Ortega. He followed the news of dictatorships of Fidel Castro and others in South America. They say there's light at the end of the tunnel, but we don't know what light lights up and we only know it when we get out of the tunnel. Today the people are getting to that point, they are walking to the edge of risk and as Benjamin Franklin said we need a revolution.

The Austrian war of succession

This war was complex and caused by Spain actions related to English smuggling ships in America. [21] It was almost a general war involving several European nations. They all had their reasons. We see Prussia's objectives, rivalries between England and France over the colonies in North America, problems of Italy, and the grudges between Britain and Spain in 1739. These were the causes that undermined European stability. Upon the death of Charles VI and the political crisis created by the succession to the throne, Germany became the diplomatic pivot of that time. This conflict is complicated. We can say that it was all because of the ambition of power and expansionist character among the monarchs of those nations. We see among them Charles VI (Emperor of Austria); Frederick II of Prussia; Augustus III king of Poland; Maria Theresa, Empress of Austria; Philip V king of the Bourbon House' and Louis XV king of France. In this entanglement came the war of succession of Austria in 1740 that

---

[21] https://www.artehistoria.com/es/contexto/la-sucesión-Austrian

ended in 1748. It was all because of the succession of Maria Theresa in the Habsburg monarchy. North America was not exempt and was involved in King George's War in British America for matters of territorial possessions. It should be mentioned that this war is not one of the peoples of the countries involved but of the vagaries and ambitions of the monarchies of that time. But it's always the people who pay for the broken plates. But the republican government's vulnerability and weakness, is in its three powers. We saw this in 2020 thanks to president Trump's attitude. Trump has lack of knowledge, disrespect to the constitution's rules and a framework of laws. And he has declared admiration for several world dictators, such as Putin of Russia, Kim Un Jung of North Korea. Trump has created [22]great divisions in the American people that may take many years to close.

Demographic diversification

Despite the pilgrims populated the colonies first, puritans, dissidents, came to the shores of North America escaping religious persecution in England. The demographic profile soon mingled in a remarkable diversification. Here came Dutch, French, English, Spanish, Italian, and also Scottish and Irish, and from other countries in Europe. Different cultures, thoughts, philosophies, and morals merged into a single social composition. It is not the color of the skin or the bodily appearance of the people that makes America great. The greatness of the homogeneous *citizens* thoughts truly is—*E Pluribus Unum.* They all had the same thought, the same dream and common purpose of pursuing a perfect social union. And that's how it was in the colonies. Everyone wanted social, political, economic and religious freedom, equality and general welfare, for all. This welfare is a state of personal tranquility, satisfaction and gratitude, working to achieve an equal but higher state—without greed, selfishness or envy. That's the American dream. President D. Trump set himself against illegal migrants and promised on his 2016 campaign to build an impenetrable wall to stop the entry of illegal immigrants. The

---

[22] https://es.wikipedia.org/wiki/Guerra_de_sucesiorn_austriaca

truth of the settlers' story is that they were illegal immigrants coming from all over Europe to the shores of North America. But he ignores the advantages of a diversified population.

The good news is that the era of rebirth and illustration was all over Europe, and the settlers were exposed to these concepts. So, starting a new collective life in freedom and with autonomy was interesting point. Demographic composition involves important information on the cultural and intellectual profile of settlers. It is an indicator pointing to potential form of actions in specific situations. They had the desire of declaring the independence of the thirteen colonies of North America. In fact, the constitution of the Connecticut colony was a declaration of independence and at the same time a constitution—fundamental orders of Connecticut in 1639.

Colony demographics

The colonies were unable to keep English characteristics. The open shores received those who arrived and the people crossed the Atlantic voluntarily, escaping the absolutism of European monarchies. The population of the colonies felt an accelerated population explosion in the 17th century. By 1717 the colonial population was mostly of English origin, but the Dutch influence was in America before the English arrived. By the year thousand seven hundred and fifty the population was one and a half million inhabitants. And by one thousand and sixty the population of the colonies reached more than two million inhabitants. And a few years before the war for independence, the aggregate population of the colonies passed the two million and a half inhabitants. By this time this population censused about one hundred thousand inhabitants of Spanish origin. [23]

According to history, each wave of immigrants arriving brought new news, new thoughts and quickly the character and ethnic

---

[23] https://www.laguia2000.com/inglaterra/poblacion-e-inmigracion-en-las-colonias-norteamericanas

makeup of the population of the colonies changed. So, by the end of the seven-year war, the population of the colonies had consolidated their own identity. Apparently, the migration flow of Europeans had reasons, for instance, the overpopulation of Europe, in particular England. But the main reason was their freedom of worshiping, the opportunity to own land in America, and de desire of achieving economic independence.

With this and the abundance of resources of these lands and trade with European markets, the colonies achieved a highly productive economy. The formula was simple, population, with work plus resources represented the rise of the colonies. Meanwhile the population continued to increase, with the arrival of more and more immigrants, of all kinds, and even undesirable people. The British parliament punished tens of thousands of criminals with the banishment of the new continent, its colonies. Most of them arrived in Virginia and Maryland. At about the half-century people from all over Europe came to the colonies. The demographic profile of English origin remained in New England because they refused to receive immigrants. They wanted to keep homogeneous ethnicity living up to the name of the colony. This concept of segregation was not kept in the other colonies satisfying their characteristics, including the concept of regionalism. Demographics were not homogeneous, because people from different backgrounds formed groups from their home nation. For example, Germans, Irish, Jews, French, Scots, Sephardic, Welsh, and so formed their own communities. It was interesting that they lived peacefully in mutual support, and they all supported the formation of the Union—the United States of America.

It has been seen that the uniqueness of humanity appears when we are in times of crisis; and evidence that humans have in their soul and mind the ultimate notion of taking care of each other and sharing with other humans to survive. These attitudes prove that nature, in its natural course, is made with love, for love and *to love* mankind. For this powerful reason the native Americans reached out to the pilgrims and the settlers. They shared with the colonizers their way of living under the North American climate, and taught them to cultivate the land. How about that? the savages, as they called them, gave the pilgrims classes of love and humanism; Europeans who were going through the age of enlightenment and rebirth? It was clear that the way people live in the colonies was different from life in Europe, although their bases were based on European ideologies.

Character of the colonies

All these influences contributed to the formation of the socio-political and economic character of the colonies, although in reality it was the common denominating character of Europe. In the years between 1756 and—1763—almost a century and a half after the arrival of the mayflower ship to American shores, Europe was living a virtually world war. The result of this great strife brought many changes.

The character of the colony union reflects the composite character of settlers—religious formation for the most part. In fact, this compound character reflects the joint and integrated thinking, the mental framework, under which the settlers acted at the time. Despite being subordinate to the king of England, the colonies had their own character. A character that was born of its colonizers. It was their way of thinking, their beliefs, and their interpretation of the concept of community, freedoms, and sovereignty. The result was a reflection of his longings, a want for freedom within his popular sovereignty. At the same time, this mental framework obviously met their needs and priorities at the time. We understand that citizens' needs and priorities change with the evolution of the mental framework, from generation to generation, and all this changes over time. The priorities and needs of that time do not show or meet the priorities and needs of today. But we cannot crystallize into the situation of almost four hundred years ago. Generally, as history tells, settlers were religious, educated, industrial workers, eager to get broad individual and collective freedom. Great thinkers were among them, and from colony to colony, the intention of mutual aid was genuine.

Colony of Massachusetts

On 21 December 1620, the pilgrim fathers, a dissident group that had separated from the Anglican church arrived on the north coasts of the new continent. Later a group of puritans also religious dissidents, dissatisfied with the religious situation in England also arrived. And with the 'great migration', a thousand other puritans landed off the coast of Massachusetts. At the time, most of Massachusetts colonizers were of Puritan origin; and there were also Presbyterians. The belief and faith of puritans was (or is) that secular governors are accountable to God for protecting and rewarding virtue, including 'true religion', and for punishing evildoers. They thought there were honest people who could represent the people and manage their affairs with ethics and transparency for the well-being of all. Their desires were to achieve a good education and illustration (so they could read the Bible). Puritans see the seventh day for rest, although they are very dedicated to work and moderate manners (without promiscuity). In other words, the character of Massachusetts colonizers was religious, considering God to be the supreme authority. The story holds a long list of prominent puritans detailed in that 27th quote. This religious thinking is important in later events in search of independence. [24, 25]

Colony of Nueva Hampshire

It is important to note that the car license plates in New Hampshire carry the sign "live free or die". A concept that reflects the primary goal right to Life with freedom of movement, choice, expression, and belief granted by the Creator and the laws of Nature. The mentality of the colonizers was highly productive, especially in the cotton textile industry. New Hampshire was the first colony to set up a government independent of the authority of the Great Britain kingdom on Jan. 5, 1776. Six months later it was one of the

---

[24] https://www.voyagesphotosmanu.com/historia_massachusetts.html
[25] https://es.wikipedia.org/wiki/Puritanismo

first colonies to sign the declaration of independence. [26] The New Hampshire constitution is a civilian government serving the public good that frees the people from this colony from England oppression, and so declares.

> ... because of many laws of the British Parliament, which have deprived us of our natural and constitutional rights and privileges; [that] to make us obey such laws, the ministry of Britain has commanded a powerful navy and an army against this country, and in a cruel and immoral exercise of abuse of power, In many places it has destroyed the lives and property of the settlers to iron and fire, have taken away the ships and charters of many of the laborious and honest inhabitants of this colony who are engaged in trade , complying with the laws and customs applied here for a long time.

Obviously, the complaint is the common denominator of all the colonies. At this stage they understood the extent of the concept of civil liberty, and civil and natural right—a product of the era of European illustration.

New Hampshire appears as the second colony of French descent. But his political mindset transcends libertarian ideas— Libertarian Party [that promotes civil liberties, non-interventionism, laissez-faire, capitalism, and the scope and size of government]. [27] The original thought of independence included these conceptions; but we study and compare the truth and consequences of the result of its application. And we review constitutional mandates, as we go ahead with this study.

---

[26] https://en.wikipedia.org/wiki/New_Hampshire
[27] https://en.wikipedia.org/wiki/Libertarian_Party_(United_States)

The Colony of Rhode Island

The beginning of this colony was not easy; Roger Williams arrived in this territory after being expelled from the colony of Massachusetts for his controversial religious beliefs. Colonization, although it began with a friendly relationship with native American communities residing in this region, soon deteriorated. But what matters is not the friendly association that existed between the tribes of native Americans and the colonizers. The importance was the change in relationship when colonizers began to attacking the natives, capturing and use them as slaves in forced labor, or to sell them into slavery. Yes, that existed, no denying. Such attitudes break with the human principles that their religion preached. The important thing is to study the mental framework, the economic, political and social form of people before the independence revolution. The mindset was open to the idea of slavery and there was really trafficking Africans and native Americans. But also dedicated to industrial production. That is, religious concepts did not include complete morality—humanism was lacking—making possible the exploitation of man by man and the inclement use of slavery. One of the commercial activities of this colony was the slave trade. Notes of history show that Rhode Island ships brought more than 100,000 Africans to America to sell them as slaves. These ships also transported captive Africans to the southern states or Caribbean where they were exchanged for molasses or rum. A census of that time showed that about fourteen percent of households had slaves, so Rhode Island residents had more slaves per capita than any other state. It was a situation that one could, nor can now, reconcile the concept of a magnanimous Creator and an ignorance of the human life of slaves.

The Colony of Connecticut

Connecticut's first colonizers were Dutch. A Dutchman, Adriaen Block was the first explorer in the Connecticut area, in 1614, including the Long Island Sound coast; Block went up to the place that is now Hartford. The Dutch company of the West Indies traded furs with this settlement—called House of Hope (or Fort Hoop, Good Hope). But English settlers arrived and forced the Dutch to withdraw from the siege in 1650 with the Hartford treaty. According to this article, the first European[28] settlers were Dutch and settled in a small colony called Fort Hoop in Hartford. Half of Connecticut was part of the New Dutch colony. But the English, followers of Thomas Hooker left the colony of Massachusetts and established firm settlements to the south by 1630. Hooker was a Puritan leader at odds with the leaders of the Massachusetts colony. Hooker was the second Puritan leader expelled from the Massachusetts colony after Roger Williams. It is important to note that the Connecticut and New Haven colonies established the documents of the fundamental orders, which they say. *"The government is based on individual's rights, and the orders detail the rights, as well as how they are guaranteed by the government. It provides that all free men share the choice of their magistrates and use secret ballots. It sets the powers of government and the limits within which that power is exercised."*

The document "Connecticut Fundamental Orders" was published on January 14, 1639—that—is, nineteen years after the Mayflower ship docked off the coast of North America. [29]Literally *"secret ballots"* means the exercise of electoral suffrage and popular sovereignty to elect their representatives in government. The elector had the condition the elected ensure (the people) the fulfillment of detailed orders (of course) in a document (which can be called a constitution).

The Colony of New York

The Florentine navigator, Giovanni Verrazano, arrived in New York Bay and named it New Angler. Later the English Henry Hudson entered New York Bay, on behalf of the Dutch East Indies company. Henry climbed the river that today bears his name, Hudson. So,

---

[28] https://en.wikipedia.org/wiki/Historia_de_Connecticut

[29] https://constitucionweb.blogspot.com/2012/03/ordenes-fundamentales-de-conneticut.html

the Dutch occupied the territory of New York on the banks of the Hudson River. In 1614 the colony of New Amsterdam was officially founded. Later in 1626 Pierre Minuit bought the island of Manhattan from the Indians and thus became the official founder of the city. Here is another Dutch influence helped forming the United States of America. This trade led by Puritans settled there on, producing flour. They also traded African slaves as their main business. This is the strange controversy of beliefs most people were puritans, but they did not consider "that all men are equal." [30]

The Colony of Pennsylvania

William Penn acquired a letter of law from Charles II of these lands, in 1681. That letter was the commitment to repaid a debt of approximately $30 million owed to Admiral Penn, William's father. The lands were named Pennsylvania (or Pennsylvania) after William. An important point was that Penn established an innovative government that later served as a reference, observing the maintenance of the law and freedom of worship. Pennsylvania created its own currency without gold backing, issuing credit notes as valid as gold coins. Benjamin Franklin participated in the creation of this money. John Dickinson wrote the Bill of Rights and Complaints, which claimed that American settlers were equal to other British citizens. They protested against the application of taxes without corresponding colonial representation. It establishes (partial) citizen equality and the concept of taxes with representation. The political philosophy followed the model of West New Jersey. The government of this colony had a governor, and a parliament with two houses, the council or the upper house, empowered to create legislation, and the whole, the lower house [31], consisted of small owners—, (the private company of that time) without legislative power, although it had the right to accept or reject legislative proposals from the council. Note, however, that citizens apparently had no representation in government.

---

[30] https://www.nuevayork.org/historia/
[31] https://es.wikipedia.org/wiki/Pensilvania

The Colony of Nueva Jersey

It was Sir Henry Hudson who discovered cape May in 1609; but it was the Swedes and Dutch who colonized the entire territory. The area was then apprehended by the English and kept under control until the time of the American Revolution. Here we see again the influence of the Dutch. It should be mentioned that before the arrival of Hudson and the Dutch, the area was populated by the Lenape tribe, usually dedicated to agriculture. Peter Minuit bought the land from the Lenape and established the colony of New Sweden. In 1664 an English fleet under Colonel Richard Nicholls took control of Fort Amsterdam, annexing that entire province. New Jersey characterized by its ethnic and religious diversification. Congregationalists lived next door to Scottish Presbyterians and Dutch reformed migrants. A second wave of immigrants came from other colonies, including Quakers. New Jersey was a colony dedicated to rural agriculture, sporadic commercial agriculture, and port services for New York and Philadelphia. Here we are seeing that what binds the settlers is the need to cultivate, produce, and perform in capital, the product and or services resulting from their efforts; while it's beliefs and philosophies that separate people. It is obvious then that the repression of the English reign against religious beliefs or choices was not enough causes for independence. But when the king's absolutism, autocracy, or absolute power touches freedom of enterprise is when man says "free life or dying." [32]

The Colony of Delaware

Delaware was initially colonized by Dutch and Swedes, who were the first to attempt to populate that area, discovered by Henry Hudson. [33] Originally populated by the Amerindian tribe of Algonquins. After fighting with the Swedes, the English expel the Dutch from the region. Possession of Delaware was granted to

---

[32] https://es.wikipedia.org/wiki/Nueva_Jersey
[33] https://es.wikipedia.org/wiki/Delaware

Pennsylvania in 1682 and William Penn divided Delaware into three counties and the rest of Pennsylvania into three different counties, so Delaware and Pennsylvania had the same number of representatives in the Pennsylvania government.

The Colony of Maryland

The history of this colony is interesting from the point of cultural diversification. The ruler of the Spanish colony, Pedro Menéndez de Avilés arrived in the Bay of Chesapeake in 1572. It was a Briton, William Claiborne, who founded the first trading post. But the British Crown accepted George Calvert's request and granted him the right of ownership and government of the Bay Area, in 1632 (the territory now occupied by the state of Maryland and Delaware).

Europe was a mixture of ideas by then, diverse customs and thoughts. And you couldn't expect anything less than that diversification here in the colonies. There was never a simple line, so America's greatness is not entirely English. For example, Henry Mary of France, married to Charles I of England, was the daughter of King Henry IV of France and Mary of Medici; she was born in Florence Italy, a member of the powerful and rich house of Medici. The Médicis owned banks, dominated finance in Italy and much of Europe. Coincidentally it was for this that Henry IV, whose reign having economic and dynastic problems and debts with the bank of the Medici, chose to marry Mary; she would receive a dowry of 600,000 gold shields from the Medici family. Obviously, Mary was of Catholic origin, and perhaps not by coincidence, George Calvert got permission and King Charles I to colonize and rule the Maryland colony. Calvert wanted a colony where Catholics could practice their religion in freedom. The government of this colony passed to the son of Caecilius, on the death of George, with the consent of King Charles I. Then the Maryland colony was founded under Catholic influence. The history of this colony is complicated by political controversies between William Claiborne and George Calvert, Lord Baltimore. But it was finally that Oliver Cromwell, Lord Protector of England, recognized the title of the colony for Lord Baltimore, Charles Calvert, son of George Calvert. [34] [35] [36]

The Colony of Virginia

The case of the Virginia colony is evidence that the American continent was not wasteful, uninhabited, or empty. Native Americans lived here for about 10,000 (or more) years, before the arrival of Europeans. When immigrants from Europe, on an expedition of about 100 people from the Virginia Company arrived in 1607, about 30 tribes of natives were organized into a large federation —which some historians call the *Powhatan Confederation;* they worked agriculture and practiced hunting, occupying that region of the Atlantic coast. It is interesting this point of organization (defense and commerce obviously), as a wild people (as they were called) had intellectual scope to form a strong defense and administration organization. That expedition founded the first English colony, Jamestown, permanently. The colonizers faced serious problems of famine and conflicts with the natives of that region until more English arrived in 1610. The conflicts of colonizers with the natives are resolved with the marriage of John Rolfe and Pocahontas, the daughter of Chief Algonquian of the Powhatan Federation. By 1620, when pilgrims arrived on the Mayflower ship, the Jamestown colonizers had expanded throughout the area east of this village. The people of Jamestown devoted the work to the cultivation and process of tobacco. The Virginia company's original intention was to search for gold and silver deposits and find a river or route that would take them to the Pacific to establish trade with the East. Jamestown's problem is a complete story on its own. There you will find, ambition, political intrigue, conflicts of interest, disloyalty and betrayal. Maybe that's the true nature of the human being. This caused rebellions, armed conflicts against government authorities, even massacres of Native Americans. All this happened

---

[34] https://es.wikipedia.org/wiki/Maria_de_Médici
[35] https://en.wikipedia.org/wiki/Casa_de_Médici
[36] https://www.voyagesphotosmanu.com/historia_maryland.html

until, in 1624, four years after the arrival of the pilgrims, King James dissolved the Virginia Company and made Virginia an official colony of the crown. [37] [38]

The Colony of Carolina del Norte

Like the colony of Virginia, the territory of North Carolina was populated—by fourteen or more tribes—of— Native Americans from many centuries before the arrival of European colonizers. Charles I of Spain authorized Lucas Vasquez of Ayllón in 1523 to explore the North Carolina region, with the idea of finding a way to reach the Islands of the Species. It is unclear whether Lucas found such a step, but he explored and made a map of Chesapeake Bay, and established a village he called San Miguel de Guadalupe. Then another Spaniard, Juan Pardo, arrived and explored the interior of that region with the intention of claiming it for the Spanish colony of Florida, and establishing an exit route (safe) for the silver mines in Mexico. The Spanish interference and influence in that region was evident, until, in 1584, Queen Elizabeth I of England in a letter to Sir Walter Raleigh naming the capital of the North Carolina colony, as Raleigh. The first English settlers came down to Southern Virginia. It is interesting to note the demographics of North Carolina-settled colonizers strongly enough to split the colony in two [39]—east and northern part. Immigrants from England populated the eastern part, while the Scots, Irish and Protestants of Germany populated the western part. This division influences the political, social and economic life of the colony. In 1710 the colony was divided into two by matters of governorship, North Carolina and South Carolina. There is an important point in the political development of North Carolina. Delegates in this colony (now a state) did not want to ratify the constitution because the central government gained, or received too much power. Apparently, this state was inclined towards a reduced

---

[37] https://www.history.com/topics/colonial-america/jamestown
[38] https://es.wikipedia.org/wiki/Historia_de_Virginia
[39] https://www.ecured.cu/Estado_de_Carolina_del_Norte_(Estados_Unidos)

central government with less power. This way of thinking reflected concepts of subsidiarity —philosophy that has been explained above.

The Colony of Carolina del Sur

History records that about 30 or more Native American tribes lived in those lands when the first explorers arrived, Lucas Vasquez of Ayllón, mentioned above. In 1527, a year after the Spanish settlers left San Miguel de Guadalupe, the Spanish and now the French claimed the region, who failed to colonize the area because of the strong conflict with the Native Americans. In 1629 King Charles I of England ceded that entire region to Robert Heath, a territory comprising North Carolina, South Carolina, Georgia and Tennessee. But Charles II of England confiscates those lands and gave them to eight lords for political reasons. The interest of the owners was only economic and political and helped very little to the settlers in defending against the Spaniards, the French and native Americans. The political and economic differences of the people of Craven and Alertmarle counties caused the separation of the region in North Carolina and South Carolina in 1712. The territory was part of North Carolina, but split in two in 1712 under the reign of Charles II of England. [40]

The Colony of Georgia

We notice two points again, one, that it was the Spaniards, with Lucas Vásquez de Ayllón, who came to this territory and, two, that the territory was populated by Native Americans from thousands of years before European explorers. Hernando de Soto, another Spaniard, explored part of the Georgia area towards the Mississippi River. The French Protestants, Huguenots, incurred the area and founded a French colony called Fort Caroline in 1564. They left the territory because of the attitude of the King of France, Philip II, who consented to heretics in their territories. Here we see the

---

[40] https://es.wikipedia.org/wiki/Carolina_del_Sur

segregation, that is, the separation factor, of men. Pedro Menéndez de Avilés took care of this problem on the orders of his monarch. The French were expelled; and founded a chain of forts on the Atlantic coast. Spanish Jesuits arrived from Florida, settling in 1570 on a mission called Ajacan in present-day Virginia. That Society of Jesus was withdrawn and replaced by the Order of San Francisco. After the Spaniards withdrew, the English arrived and claimed that territory. In the same year, King Charles I of England created a colony that I call [41]*Carolinas.* Later, a group of Englishmen created a colony they named Georgia on behalf of George II.

We have read the founding of the English colonies. And they're English because they were all finally vindicated by England. However, we see that the colonies had influences in part by Spaniards, French, Dutch, Scottish, Irish, Italian and people from other nations. It is obvious that demographic diversification marked the character of settlers, hauling a bit of thought from all parts of Europe. No one can say that America only has English roots when the influence of other nations are obviously intense and evident.

> America's greatness is coincidentally diversification and the desire to create general welfare under a regime of tranquility and freedom.

The idea of making America great again is to deny that this nation started with its diversification and social, cultural, intellectual diversification that makes the Union great.

Society and economy

History notes that before the independence movement, the colonies had reached a stable economic level, although it was only based on agriculture. The United Kingdom blocked the industrial

---

[41] https://en.wikipedia.org/wiki/Georgia_(Estados_Unidos)

development of the colonies by denying them the manufacturing license and only allowed the production of matter and reserved the right of manufacture for the Kingdom. Traders and the new bourgeoisie claimed the right to make their own manufacturing. It is obvious that the resentment of the settlers grew to the point of "no more tolerance" and they were looking for a way to free themselves from that tyranny. Note that the resentment is of the production companies, not the workers, because they work in the production of products and services regardless of who, the reign or a rich settler, who offers the work. England's refusal to give manufacturing licenses was one of the factors that pushed the colonies into independence.

There are certain anthropological and or social factors that influence the character of a society. And the author considers it important to give them some study and attention.

Regionalism

The author finds certain articles that define this topic. Regionalism is a way of thinking that supports political action that, despite accepting that there is superior political power, such as a nation, seeks the defense of one of its parts, an area that is identified with the purpose by its ethnic, ideological and cultural homogeneity. It is a conservative thinking tending to maintain the status quo of the people. The author is not thinking about the commercial and industrial characteristics that the territory's resources give to its inhabitants, for example, tobacco in Virginia. In a way it implies the tendency that the will is in the hands of the people, and in turn, regional autonomy entails "obtaining and maintaining political autonomy in a region, which is an implicit form of a sovereign position. [42]

The intention to create an area with customs, way of life, religious beliefs, ethnic, and philosophical thoughts clearly identifies an area or region. This is what the Dutch tried to do with their settlements. Currently the people of each state are distinguished

---

[42] https://es.wikipedia.org/wiki/Autonomismo_regional

by the characteristics of the environment of their territory, their social habits, and exploitation and production of the resources of their area. There are distinction areas; for example, the differences between California and New York, or California and Texas, etc. It may also be the nationalist idea of a nation. It is also an example what George Calvert wanted to do with the Maryland settlement; wanted to make a fully Catholic colony so that people could practice this religion in freedom. But not only the Dutch promoted regionalism, some colonies tried to create homogeneous colonies (of a homogeneous culture).

Massachusetts – The people of Massachusetts had their religious thinking that distinguished them from other migrants who arrived in North America. Puritans believed that governors are accountable to God for protecting and rewarding virtue and punishing wrongdoers. But after 'the great migration', the population was more puritans than pilgrims. And if they founded their form of government and fought to maintain it. Today it is one of the most liberal states in the United States. [43]

New Hampshire. Car license plates carry an inscription that says "live free or die." This is a way of thinking, its spirit of struggle, supported by all the citizens of this colony. It is a thought that distinguishes the social attitude of the people of this colony. Rhode Island. It was the point of human trafficking, of slaves brought from Africa. It is difficult to reconcile the Theo centrist idea separated from the humanist idea, that is. *all men are created equal to certain inalienable rights. such as Life, Freedom and the Pursuit of Happiness, while* mistreating other human beings, created in the same way, with slavery.

Likewise, each state had its idiosyncrasies or innate characteristics. And the land of the free and hardened man opened its doors with a history and character that endures through time. Then people learned to live in the cultural and intellectual diversification of those times. Under this way of thinking the declaration of independence is born, establishing the principle of equality *"that the laws of Nature*

---

[43] https://www.laguia2000.com/inglaterra/la-fundacion-de-massachusetts

and the God of Nature gives to man". A truth that then emphasized by saying, *"that all men are created equal... inalienable rights.".* To make this nation, America, great again, is to create reforms to the constitution and its derived laws to form a more perfect Union under those principles.

These statements identify the nature and character of the United States and define the regionalism of the land of the free and brave man.

"... a nation under God, indivisible, with freedom and justice for all.

It is "... a land with equality and opportunity."

"God bless America, land I love. Stand next to her and guide her. Through the night with the light above. From the mountains to the meadows, to the oceans of white foams. God bless America, my home sweet home. God bless America, land I love."

image borrowed from the Internet

CHAPTER 2

The situation

Considering: 1 —that the Creator gives life, 2—that the Creator put in the universe, in fact, on earth, all resources for the sole purpose of promoting, generating, protecting, and maintaining life, 3—and that He also opened omniscience and put all knowledge for the life of man, 4—that God creates beauty and art to express its greatness. So, it is natural for life to include the infallible and inalienable right to (live) life as everyone chooses. And when men come together in groups or societies, the composition of their lives becomes one. This is why everything that promotes, improves the way of life, protects and maintains life is an infallible part of life and the right to it. Life is the highest mood—life is the living sovereignty of existence; and there's nothing higher about it. Likewise, the association of lives, mainly of men, constitutes popular sovereignty. So, governments created, organized, and administered by men are nothing more than agreements (procedures or laws) accepted to manage the relationship of men's lives in society. And that is implied by the declaration of independence of the thirteen English colonies in North America, in 1776.

"That whenever any form of government becomes destructive to these purposes, it is the right of the people to alter or abolish it, and to institute a new government, laying its

foundations on principles and the organization of their powers in such a way, as far as they will seem more likely than indeed their Security and Happiness.

This statement is not explicitly written in the constitution, in fact it should be included, because it is a fundamental instrument for sealing the political tunnels through which the corrupt infiltrate. The people need their sovereignty to be explicitly defined in the constitution and in its derived laws with a reform that includes the conditions for ousted an official in public office, including the president. In the system of government that the founders conceived obviously had that intention and it is clear that this was because they clearly say *"form a more perfect union",* which is only achieved with reforms over time.

It is clear that no government is above popular sovereignty or the rules of laws that control the government, nor does it have more power, authority, or value than what men of society or people give it. And though *"... humanity is more willing to suffer, while evils are suffering", "... to straighten themselves out"* needs a *"... abolition of the ways to which they're used to it.".*

"But when a long train of abuse and usurpation, invariably pursuing the same Object, evidences a design for reducing them under absolute despotism, it is their right, it is their duty to discard that government, and provide new guards for their future security. "Such has been the patient suffering of these colonies; and such is now the need for them to alter their former Government Systems..."

This declaration is nothing more than a declaration of popular sovereignty; the will of the people is above any form of government.

That's right, and it's true what Benjamin Franklin said, a revolution is needed every 200 years.

Our Union is sick, it has sacked a part of its soul; it is infested with selfishness, racist hatred, greed. A cancer, racism, took hold of his ego that makes him delirious with a supremacy that does not exist in the spirit of The United States. The principle of this nation is that *all men are created equally with inalienable rights endowed by their Creator*. And under this concept, we, the people, of the United States of America remember that national sovereignty is the will of each individual integrated into one voice and volition; and there is no higher sovereignty than the will of the people. This popular sovereignty and by agreement of the citizens of the people are formed the government to manage their social, political and economic interests. And this popular sovereignty defines national sovereignty in a single document, a magna letter or the constitution of the Union, defining a government that represents the people, with limited [but never general] powers and authorities sanctioned in that contract or political agreement. And there is and will not be higher power than the power of the people.

The social, political and economic interests of the people are implicitly included in the objectives of the constitution listed in its preamble: *Perfecting the Union, establishing justice, ensuring national tranquility and promoting general well-being.* This is the mandate, the responsibility, that an administrator of the interests of the people, the president, has. The Union is not yet the optimal version, far from that point, although the basic principles are cemented in truth and supreme justice. The constitutional commitment to perfect the Union is not only government; it is also of the people; this duty is the right of all, we the people, through the government that represents us.

It is a citizens' duty to preserve and foster the dream of our founding fathers—a dream designed for us, our posterity. We cannot ignore what our republic has been through in recent decades and is still happening today. The people must restore their government and democracy over the course that the founding fathers set out in 1776. The time has come [actually behind] the revolution that Benjamin

Franklin anticipated, in his vision, more than two hundred and forty years ago. This revolution is in front of us and with it comes a historical critique; but the way has only two choices, (1) letting certain political forces along with the company and private market destroy this Republican government and its democracy; or (2) reform the constitution and its sanctioned laws to perfect the Union of our states, complying with its preamble; to ensure that the fundamental principles that created this Union are fulfilled.

Sanity and wisdom, however, advises us to study the weaknesses of the state of the Union in order to provide the supporting reasons for the social, political and economic change that is needed. Our republic and its democracy are sick and if we do not cure it may die without seeing your dream realized. There are certain situations that we must consider about the state of our Union. Perhaps if we list the weaknesses and vulnerabilities, they will serve as the basis for the changes needed to improve the Union.

The constitution is pure, the government fails.

1.—The vulnerabilities and weaknesses of the country's system, political, social and economic, are clear and obvious. Weak or vulnerable areas are in the dark definitions of the powers, authorities, and functions of the three state powers that do not meet the six objectives of the preamble to the constitution. The government has failed; has not fulfilled the intention of the constitution, during the two hundred and forty-four years of independence. It is failing in the mandates.

> *... to form a more perfect Union, to establish justice, to ensure national peace of mind, to tend to the common defense, to promote general well-being and to ensure the benefits of freedom for us and for our subsequent...*

2.—Form a more perfect Union: The government shows no interest in establishing rules to perfect the Union, periodically reviewing the rules of law and its implementation in a way that meets the Union's objectives, Periodic Constitutional Reforms—there must be a constitutional mechanism or rules (amendments) to identify the flaws and achievements of the republican government and popular democracy, by means of a legislative committee, establishing legislatures to correct the course of the Union.

3.—Establishing Justice: The government has long failed to establish Justice under the basics of declaration of independence as is the consideration of the obvious truth,

> ... that all men are created equal, that they are endowed by their Creator with certain inalienable rights, which include life, freedom and the pursuit of Happiness.

It is clear and obvious that this nation is divided and one-half cling to the concept of a racist supremacy that does not fit in the form of government and democracy of the Union. The justice that the founders conceived is based on these inalienable rights. The people find situations where the application of the Justice betrays the original constitutional intention. It is obvious that the application does not apply equally to the citizens of the people, but is done according to the influence of fame, political power, economic status, and racial status of the citizen. Cases of civil and criminal injustice are many to list in this book, but they are available as public resources if this point needs to be sustained. The people have witnessed cases of racial crimes, sexual abuse of minors and adult women. The rich, powerful and famous go unpunished. Is this justice? Aiding, abating, and covering up, helping with and reducing a crime or crimes is a crime. The author lets the reader's mind extract from public institutions and the news media library evidence and proof of these assertions.

Social, political, and economic differences expose that men are not treated equally in the United States. We have seen that there is still a minority white supremacy in the Union which expresses repressed social resentments. The old KKK still takes to the streets to express its racial hatred—it is the great desire to establish the slavery that the colonies had before and after independence. These supremacists do not accept that men are created equally with rights endowed by their Creator. They want to have slaves again to make "America Great Again." They haven't made the result of the civil war they lost. They forgot that they themselves created slavery—as in Virginia where they set up black breeding centers to sell them as slaves. And it is possible that members of this clan have infiltrated the structure of the United States government. The attitudes of certain civil servants demonstrate this possibility. Possibilities that the people must (is in their constitutional right) to sue an investigation of such suspicions. The murder of the Reverend Martin Luther King, Jr., by a frank marksman, manifests racial resentment and hatred against innocent black-skinned people (1968). Within the equality of men, and the application of Justice, we see that women do not enjoy the same opportunities, nor equal pay for equal work, women remain a second-class citizen. How long? Inequality is obvious, in education, in health, in access to opportunities. Inequality is seen in small businesses competing with economic monsters that monopolize economic means. We see the inequality in the ability to acquire knowledge, the rich acquire education in the best institutions while the poor barely reach a scholarship. These differences are neither fair nor a result of social equality (to opportunities). Wealth, fame, and power creates social gaps.

4.—National tranquility: As long as there is no equality or equal justice, social, political, and economic differences will continue to unsettle the citizens of this nation; and there will be no national tranquility when the principle of all in one, "*e pluribus unum*" is not a reality. And as long as these differences last, there's no peace of mind (national tranquility).

As long as social, political and economic discrimination persists there will be no national reassurance. There can be no peace of mind as long as there are citizen differences; as long as women earn three-quarters of what men earn by doing the same job. As long as a citizen goes out on the street in fear of being arrested, beaten, beaten by a policeman and killed and then accused of resisting arrest, there will be no national tranquility.

George Floyd – killed by police brutality on May 25, 2020.

image borrowed from the Internet

We, the people, lived demonstrations for several consecutive months that began with civility and respect, and in some days ended in violence, raiding private ownership of small and medium-sized businesses, implanting chaos—plus generally peaceful marches in recent days. There will be no national peace of mind until there is a common defense and the president does not order the armed forces to crack down on protesters, abusing power and constitutional authority. And as long as resentment continues and there are socio-economic gaps, there can be no national peace of mind, no general welfare, and the inalienable rights of man are trashed, not respected.

5.—To tender for common defense: security and defense for all states of the Union against domestic enemies as foreign, visible and invisible; this is the national security that ensures the safety of the people. You cannot pretend to have and or maintain common defense when there is latent and obvious hatred and resentment among members of society. The origin of the Latin the word defense, comes from Latin *defending,* and we understand its meaning as the action of the verb defend —to care, safeguard or preserve a principle, a position, physical or mental, with the intention of giving protection in any way (defend). The common defense is to care for, safeguard or preserve the safety and welfare of all (the people). The government has failed and continues to fail to establish and tend to common defense as long as there are inequalities and injustices that favor only a part of the people.

6.—General Welfare: Without equal Justice, without the Equality of man, without a firm and permanent national tranquility, without a common defense of local security, we do not encourage general welfare. What is welfare? It is a way of life, a physical and psychological or mental state that provides a quality of life full of joy, satisfaction and gratitude–continuous tranquility. And it is in general a quality of life for all of us, the people, citizens of every state, and of the United States.

The cost of living creates great inequalities to the point that the middle class down is marginalized and does not receive the constitutionally promised benefits of Freedom; the upper-middle class and the powerful rich hoard these benefits, and the government allows it. The problem of citizens living on the streets, in bell tent camps on sidewalks, is the product of social conditions, difficult living conditions. As long as justice is not equal and or is applied with preferential treatment, as long as inequality continues in society, political participation in the economy, we, the people, will not attain the general welfare that the constitution sanctions; the government has failed, and continues to fail to promote and maintain that welfare as a primary goal of the constitution. There can be no general welfare when the differences between the minority that makes up ninety-nine percent of the nation's wealth and ninety-nine percent of the people (mostly) have only one percent of that wealth, there can be no general welfare. And as long as the strength of capital, private enterprise manipulates or controls the scale of wages and salaries, and the minimum wage at pauper levels, there will be no general welfare. As long as the government allows the mercantilism and speculation of private enterprise, of the big businesses and producers that set prices for products and services in the market without control, there will be neither general welfare nor will Happiness come.

Even when every day, the number of homeless people increases, there can be no general welfare. And when the ticket to watch a basketball game, football, hockey, or concert, or a musical presentation, Disneyland, etc., only for the rich, there can be no general welfare. There will only be poverty and the resentment that this situation brings to society. The government has failed for two hundred and forty-four years and continues to fail. The evidence is obvious with the actions of the Donald Trump administration that we, the people, do not count; and it is proven that society is divided into two classes, those that have and can influence its benefits and those that it does not have and cannot aspire to influence to survive. This is the state of the imperfect Union in the present time—the rich and famous becomes richer and more powerful, and the people, the poor class becomes poorer, at the mercy of the rich. The representatives of the people with their apathy, negligence or complicity have allowed the private company to control the government's efforts over the years to reduce or eliminate the dream of the founders. As long as this situation endures, there will be no possibility of equal opportunities and general welfare mentioned in the constitution.

7.—The benefits of freedom: The people cannot enjoy these benefits, nor enjoy egalitarian life, quiet, sure, sustained or permanent general welfare, to seek and achieve individual Happiness, of the people and their posterity This is the dream of America that for four hundred years is nothing more than a mirage in the wilderness of the unscrupulous selfishness of the few who hoard political power, the wealth, social and economic of the Union. The government has failed and continues to fail (1) to establish the equality that the Creator has endowed to man and the people and before the law of the Union, (2) in fostering the pursuit of the Happiness of all. Without justice, without equality, without national tranquility, without security, without general welfare there are and will be no benefits of Freedom for the people and their posterity—without all that, there is no Happiness.

That dream was a dream or a mirage of a dream because from the beginning man's equality did not exist. Independence was only of Europeans, that equality did not include the slave-man, treated as animals of cargo and labor, forced. The cruelty of slavery was so profound that in Virginia places were established for the reproduction of blacks in order to sell them as slaves. Great thinkers or philosophers such as Henry D. Thoreau and Ralph Waldo Emerson "questioned the government as representatives of individuals." Eighty-seven years passed and a bloody civil war after Independence Day to "form a more perfect Union," without slavery, but it left hatred, resentment, and vengeance against those who achieved emancipation; although the abolition of slavery became constitutionally legal through the thirteenth amendment. The American dream was only the mirage of a dream and still is; there will be no peace of mind as long as the KKK can march through the streets and the lynching is feasible.[44]

According to the NAACP, "there were 4,472 lynching between 1882 and 1968, most of them with black people killed at the hands of white mobs." [45] There will be no peace of mind or general welfare as long as hate is publicly expressed with murders like George Floyd's. We are far from forming a more perfect Union as the founders of the homeland dreamed in 1776. We are far from establishing Justice, obtaining national tranquility, or General Welfare. Today the benefits of freedom are only for a few who hold wealth and power. We are far from making a union more perfect. And this situation is the mirage of the intention of the preamble to the constitution.

There can be none of the six objectives of the constitution if a president, autocrat, dictatorial, abusing of his power is allowed to take full powers, abuse his authority, ignore the rules of law, and threaten to destroy the separation of powers from the government

---

[44] https://historiaybiografias.com/esclavitud-estados-unidos-origen-y-abolicion/
[45] Karine Jean-Pierre @K_Jean-Pierre [Tweeter]

to enact his own personal interests. These are the cases of Presidents Richard Nixon and Donald Trump.

The Union is ill

It is the author's view that "there is no intention or expression more sincere and beautiful than the constitution of the United States of America. The introduction to his articulation speaks of *"We"* without leaving behind any of his citizens, without discrimination of race, skin color, religious beliefs, philosophical inclination. We, the people, declare a dream to form a more perfect Union, and in five other explicit goals express the details of a dream, including *"ensuring for us and our prosperity the benefits of freedom."* All of this is an intrinsic part of the dream of the people of the United States in the spirit of their letter. But in the action of the ego, will it be just the mirage of a beautiful intention?

While some had their minds and pure conscience others saw an opportunity to use the American dream for their personal benefits. The Union was born with a part of his body sick with selfishness, greed, and hatred. The symptoms are still noticeable in the performance of modern society in 2020. There is a lot of work to be done to form a more perfect Union; to achieve true Justice, and general welfare, which guarantees the inner tranquility of the soul of every citizen. When that day comes, we, the people and our posterity, will enjoy the benefits of the freedom that our ancestors bought with their blood.

The intention of independence is embodied in the letter and spirit in its declaration and in the constitution. That is the reason of the Union. But their integrity and permanence were exposed to the corruption of dishonest officials who can abandon the people's objectives and use the Union for personal gain. Benjamin Franklin prevented this situation, anticipating that a revolution is needed every two hundred years due to corruption. The constitution has certain voids, that is, "darkness in its meaning" that lend themselves to misinterpretations. These misinterpretations can cause irreparable harm to the republic and its democracy.

For example, President Donald Trump thinks that he has absolute powers and that he can do whatever he wants under Article II of the constitution. And apparently, he thinks the other two powers of the state are under his executive powers. He may be right, perhaps not, but the separation of the three powers, the constitution must clearly define the separation of powers from the state, the functions of each and the scope of these powers. The precept that no one is above the law is something that must be sanctioned with an amendment to the constitution with a precise definition. This amendment should detail the extent of the powers and authorities that the constitution sanctions for each of the three powers. Article I and II should be clarified in detail. At the same time, the constitution must sanction the consequences resulting from violations of such mandates.

Articles I and II of the constitution deals with the power of the president and of congress—the two chambers—and the responsibility to prosecute political positions in the house of representatives and open political trials in the Senate. The deficiency of these articles is the lack of clarity of the powers of the congress and the president of the republic. The president's power and authority must be explicitly clear to avoid misinterpretations by the president. No president has the right or authority to deny, reject, ignore, the responsibilities, rights and authorities of the other two constitutionally established powers. To do the opposite is an attack on the constitution and such an act is a high political crime—subverting the constitution.

Amendments to the Constitution

Amendments: In addition, the same amendments to the constitution are causally sanctioned to perfect the original Union when its constitution requires reform. Let us remember that of the first twelve amendments only ten were ratified in a short time after the constitution was proposed. But some are still pending. [46]

---

[46] https://es.wikipedia.org/wiki/Anexo:Enmiendas_a_la_Constitución_de_los_Estados_Unidos.

The right of the American people to possess and bear arms is not written in the articulation of the constitution. It is an added right by the second amendment. It's a controversial issue in terms of objectives, and efficiency is concerned. The militia is neither organized nor has a hierarchy of military authority; therefore, it is not an organized military corp. The purpose of the civilian militia is a subject for discussion. There were many settlers who argued against the need to form militias. The original purpose of the militia was to articulate an armed body of effective defense against despot and autocratic governments, but it must be organized, properly armed and trained. The danger of a civilian militia is at risk of being politicized for corrupt and parties' purposes, covered under the (artificial) right to possess and carry weapons; in this case the militia becomes an army of a political party. And this brings the formation of another militia from other political parties under the same rights to possess and carry weapons–common security, national tranquility and general welfare is lost, *de facto*. Moreover, the disorganization of the militia puts in the hands of skilled politicians a possibility of manipulating it for lucrative personal purposes.

The government has failed and will continue to fail to shape and make the militia apolitical; fails to organize it and give it military character, as it should be. An organized and trained militia has no end and must be integrated into the military reserve as a permanent. The argument that the militia is necessary for the security of a state is weak and ineffective. However, it is a citizen's right to carry weapons for hunting purposes.

Article 1, Section 8 establishes the authority to organize and discipline the Military Reserve shared between the central government and the states for specific state and federal defense purposes. Why is a civilian militia necessary? It is time to make the militia, if necessary, efficient and effective for domestic defense, integrating it into the national reserve, which has similar objectives. But such a reform of the amendment that made possible the militia can make or transfigure the militia for the benefit of general welfare and national tranquility, not only for the common defense, but also to ensure the benefits of Freedom equally for all of us, the people. This is the real goal of the militia, not to go hunting a duck with a high caliber machine gun with automatic repetition that leaves no trace of the duck.

Amendment V does not penalize a person having the right not to be investigated for crimes committed, civil or criminal. And although the amendment states that will not be compelled to testify against itself, the law does not provide that evidence attesting to his innocence cannot be requested. Legislative power has failed and continues to fail not to clarify this matter, especially when it relates to the investigation of crimes and crimes in political cases. Amendment V does not immunize anyone. That is, the impeachment does not have or seek to prove that the indicted is or not guilty of the crimes committed, that is the matter of the courts, but is, and should be sufficient necessary to establish suspicions with reliable evidence that the suspect can be prosecuted in the normal courts, consequently the ratification of the evidence by a grand Jury could, or should, be part of the evidence in the formal charges in cases of political dismissal. And so, the guilty individual must be removed from the office held.

Amendment X separates central and state government rights. But it does not establish the authority of the executive branch over the states, being that national sovereignty is granted by popular sovereignty (the people of each state or all together). It is understood that what is not explicitly sanctioned in the constitution, power or authority, is property and right of the states or the people of those states. In the case of the president's threats to command, as in fact he did and is doing, federal troops to appease, frighten, restrict, reduce, dominate, or eliminate popular protests in a state is an act that is not clear. And the president **assumes** that he has the power to execute such an action.

Amendment XIV in reference to citizenship specifies only persons born or naturalized in the United States. It does not specify or mention legal persons as corporations as American citizens. The controversy comes out of the definition of citizenship. The problem with idea of forming corporations that are simple properties or associated with, is that the owners- citizens acquire by this means rights and powers, perhaps duplicated, that other citizens do not have. This situation violates the equality of men, equal according to that inalienable right.

Amendment XV, the right to electoral suffrage is sacrosanct, and we cannot ignore it. No one shall undermine that right to citizens of the United States on the basis of race or color, prior social status. However, we have witnessed how political division is used by both major parties trying to gain an unfair political advantage that manipulates district boundaries. Similarly, we have seen a variety of methods of suppressing or restricting voting, including intervention in electoral processes by foreign governments in open violation of U.S. national sovereignty. Any intentional attempt or manipulation to alter the natural order of electoral suffrage in order to gain advantages for a political party violates popular sovereignty. It is an attack on democracy and, in fact, is a subversion of the constitution as a high political crime of suppressing the inalienable right to elect its representatives. In fact, it is a criminal act against popular sovereignty, of the constitution, by any representative of the government, or public official. It is a high criminal (political) act that can only be remedied by the dismissal of the public office holding the culprit.

An intervention as such was observed in the 2016 election in which the GOP nominee Donald Trump was elected. The intelligence community positively tested Russia's intervention in this matter. Such intentions, decisions and actions are criminal acts that must be typified as high crimes against the constitution for cases of political dismissal.

Corruption is a chronic endemic in U.S. government and politics, and is a pandemic around the world, that eats together the structures of the Republican government, democracy and the Union. Corruption is a factor that gradually destroys the principles of the Union. Corruption is a crime that should be categorized as a high crime against, the constitution and national and popular sovereignty. During the time of the forty-first presidency of the United States, we observed several serious cases of political corruption and abuse of authority on the part of the president and several of his officers, violating the constitution. For example, the Trump administration has misrepresented constitutional principles, and the separation of powers from the state for personal benefits with the cooperation and involvement of the senate of the legislature. The (political case) dismissal of President Trump's charged with two counts of (1) Abuse of Presidential Power and (2) Obstruction of Congress. [ii][47] is by itself and action of abuse of power and or authority.

We saw another big case of political dismissal; it is that of President Richard Nixon, in 1973, which ended with Nixon's resignation from the position of president on August 8, 1974. Political corruption does not guarantee national peace of mind, nor does it promote general welfare. In both cases the evidence was blunt, but in Trump's case and by the complicity of Senate majority leader Mitch McConnell the accusation was virtually ignored (illegally?).

The abuse of power, although it is an act of corruption, deserves to be identified in its entirety, unique and separate, by the high damage it causes to the integrity, ethical and professional, of the government, in its three powers of the state, including the moral principles under which the Union of the United States of America was constituted. [iii]Rodney King was brutally beaten by cops in 1991. As the author writes reasons supporting constitutional reforms—beginning March 14, 2020—a white-race policeman assaulted George Floyd, a black man, and murdered him in eight minutes and forty-six seconds, in broad daylight and in the middle of the street, on May 25, 2020. Protest marches against police brutality (abuse of authority) began on the same day and have lasted for more than a hundred days.

We have seen the abuse of power at various levels of the government's structure from presidents to local police. The case chain is long; we can quickly list a dozen cases, such as George Floyd, Trayven Martin, Eric Garner, Michael Brown, Walter Sealt, Fred Gray, to mention a few.

Racial discrimination is a crime against the constitution, it is a violation of the precept that *"all men are created equal... with inalienable rights, endowed by the Creator, including Life, Freedom and the Pursuit of Happiness."*

---

[47] https://es.wikipedia.org/wiki/Proceso_de_destitución_de_Donald_Trump

Organized crime should be typified as a high crime for the purposes of political dismissal. The act of crime, or crime, organized includes the planning to commit therefore a criminal conspiracy against the order of the social, political and economic system of the Union. Each of these acts of criminal and corruption must be named in the context of an amendment to the constitution to serve as the basis for derived laws. [iv]

The spirit of the constitution

Within the situation there is a list of points that the people must study carefully with the intent to improve the fundamentals principles of the Union.

1. —The constitution lacks the text for the fundamental ideas of the Union expressed in the declaration of independence, specifically,
    1. *"All men are created equal, endowed by their Creator with certain inalienable rights among them (1) Life, (2)Freedom, and (3) Happiness."*

2. —The separation of the powers of the state.
    1. The choice of judges to the supreme court and federal courts should not be left to the discretion of the president, if we value the principle of strict separation of the powers of the state.

3. —It is necessary to enact in the constitution that the power of the central government, national sovereignty, derives from the power of the people, and only from the people, the popular sovereignty. Therefore, there is no power higher than the power of the people, the popular sovereignty.

4. — The right of the people to dismiss or change parts of the constitution, and or to establish a new government, *lays on principles and the organization of their powers as to them, will seem more likely than indeed their Security and Happiness.*

5. —We, the people, need to establish in the constitution the right of the people to choose the program of government which in their terms will seem more effective and guarantee their *inalienable rights endowed by their Creator.* This program of government of the people, by the people and for the people will be the requirements that candidates for president and vice president of political parties must use to propose their administrative plan. The people shall prepare its government plan through their state, based on a simultaneous participation of all the people of all states. No political party shall have the right to, nor responsibility to, propose, a program of government; but the parties and their candidates shall agree to comply with and satisfied the government plan the people specify for an election period. This reform is necessary to form a more efficient participatory democracy in accordance with the will of the people. Actually, it's the people who can best say what they need to receive from the government.

6. —The requirements for the office of President and Vice-President are not efficient. A reform is necessary to prevent anyone without the knowledge, skill, and experience the possibility of assuming the power and authority to manage the people's Life, Freedom, and Happiness. We need to establish requirements for the post of the presidency and vice presidency, like test of character, ethics and human capital (knowledge, skills and experience); each presidential candidate and vice president must present their credentials in advance. The alleged presidential candidate must present his or her credentials that meet the requirements of the position before entering the competition, and the vice president must present his credentials before being nominated by the president, credentials must be sent to the house of representatives for review and approval per set rules.

7. —The reasons for the political dismissal of government officials, including the president and vice-president, need to be clarified. This reform is necessary to clearly establish that no one is above the constitution and its rules of law.

8. —It is necessary to specify the powers, power and authority of the president of the executive branch to avoid misunderstandings and or misinterpretations; in particular of the power conferred on him by Article II, section two, which he says in its text (name) *"... Supreme Court Justices and all other Officials of the United States whose appointment does not otherwise provide this document and have been established by law..."* This power disrupts the separation of state powers and encourages the abuse of authority and the possibility of acting to favor a party's interests—which in fact is corruption or abuse of power.

9. —It must be clear that the president has no absolute powers, no powers to do what the president wants, even against the law or popular sovereignty, to avoid a misunderstanding. A reform should clarify the case in which an ex officio president of office may be dismissed and replaced by the active vice president.

10. —Reforms must improve the oath or promise before taking office. *"I solemnly swear (or promise) that I will be loyal to the office of President of the United States and that I will sustain, protect, and abide by the Constitution of the United States, to the fullest of my powers. And if I broke my oath and promise, I accept the consequence of political destitution, including the termination of my responsibilities as president."*

The weaknesses of the system suggest a need to change and reinforce and strengthen the fundamental principles of the constitution of the United States of America. The reader has the right to his/her own interpretation; however, it is prudent, fair and necessary to put together the criteria and submit them to the general public. Perhaps this can create a common interest in perfecting the Union. The concept of political parties' *de facto* divides the country. We must eliminate parties' influence by focusing on creating government platforms of the people that the parties must bid on.

Today's America, or for decades, is deeply divided. The government of the people, for the people and of the people, is the forum of political melees for controlling power for party benefits and not for the general welfare of the people. The cracks are so wide and deep that the Union may be in a state of terminal illness. The division of social classes still persists; —maybe overlapping—, on the one hand, white supremacy and on the other the colorful fur races. Economic gaps have erased, practically, equal opportunities. Although the founders created optimism based on that

> *... these truths are obvious, that all men are created equal, that are endowed by their Creator with certain inalienable rights, which include Life, Freedom and the Pursuit of Happiness.*

This statement *"... all men are created equal,"* rules out the differences between men, (women and men); but does not stipulate differences by skin color or give supremacy to men with white skin, nor does it declare inferiorities of men with dark skin. It does not state that females are of different class than male people. The declaration states that all men, –women and men and of all skin colors—, are endowed by their Creator with inalienable rights, such as Life, Freedom, and the pursuit of Happiness. However, it was a struggle to abolish the enslavement of black people, and another struggle to cede the right to vote to females. A white supremacy keeps the fight against people with dark skin whom they consider inferior.

Today, the hegemony of men rules, and women still do not receive equal pay for equal work. There are people who, because they are famous and have millions of dollars, can do anything, abuse women or shoot a person on New York's fifth avenue and no one would care. This is a failure of the constitution's legal regulations. On the other hand, corruption has already reached the electoral process and foreign nations intervene in favor of a candidate. The candidate allowed and the nation that help him and that nation get away with the crime, unpunished. On top of that, the house of representatives presses charges and the Senate exonerates him. Of course, there is evidence of corruption in the government suppressing the freedom of expression in the hands of the media; the media has exposed presidential intents in abundant details.

The capitalist system, free enterprise, and the free market created an economic rocker, accumulating capital in the hands of a few at the high extreme and poverty at the lower. Tribulations and suffering fall into the lower income communities. Obviously, the economic differences, the social gaps between those who have everything and those who have nothing becomes wider every day. And the shame is that the government supports that situation.

Journalists and reporters from major media outlets like Rachel Maddow and many others do not tire of raising the galloping theme of corruption, but the forces of evil do impose. The president says journalists are *"enemies of the people"*—*these* are words that come out of the mouths of strong men, autocrats, and dictators like Vladimir Putin or Adolf Hitler. Benjamin Franklin's words were wise in saying that every two hundred years governments become corrupt. The corruption here must be bigger than we see, for it's been forty-four years longer than the two hundred years Franklin predicted.

What Abraham Lincoln said in his speech, perhaps we establish one day, the government that is part of the dream of the citizens of the United States.

> ... of the people, by the people and for the people...

But this political state has not yet been given. For a few years now, perhaps since the beginning of the Union, the government has been the rulers, by the rulers and for the rulers, and with them for the rich, the private enterprise and the free market. They manipulate the people from the middle class down. The middle class is, has been, the demographic layer that, instigated and executed the greatest revolutions in the world, including the revolution that created the union of the United States of America. It is that demographic layer that should be valued, considered and seriously take the prognosis of Benjamin Franklin —*every two hundred years we need a Revolution.*

The objectives of the constitution focus on social, economic and political justice that reflect the will of the people under a true government of the people, by the people and for the people. The will of the people is "how the founders of the homeland designed it." But in reality, the government behaves in other ways.

The single and main article of the constitution, its preamble, does not define time of validity; its intention is in force and active as if it were written in the present time. The mandates and purposes sanctioned by the citizens of the English colonies of America at that time, is in the term "We", as if we had written them on any present day. In that article, they remain as duty, right and purpose, an end: ...to form a more perfect Union. The perfection of the Union has explicit specifications:

> *...establish justice, ensure national tranquility, tend to the common defense, promote general welfare and secure the benefits of freedom for us and for our posterity...*

It is obvious that our republic and our democracy are not fully fulfilling these objectives or the constitutional aim of *forming a more perfect Union*. Here, as Benjamin Franklin predicted, corruption invaded—and to some extent took over—the government; and has long threatened to destroy our democracy—popular sovereignty; we are no longer the people. Now it is the selfishness and greed of capitalism that controls and manipulates the government at will.

As long as these specifications are not met our republic and democracy will not be under national sovereignty, or the will of the people. It is under the dictatorship of the interests of mercantilism operating under the pseudonym of free enterprise in the free-market environment. That is the selfishness, greed, and ambition of rich and powerful people or groups. Legislative changes in recent years and the overlapping of the executive's action aided by the Senate is evidence of what Benjamin Franklin said about bicentennial corruption; therefore, there must be changes.

The exposure of the obsolescence of the constitution has an insinuating purpose that can awake citizens to realize these conditions. And the solution to chaos is not in the hands of the representatives elected by the people but in the hands of the people themselves because the right and duty to update their constitution and framework of laws is for the people—that is the exercise of popular sovereignty. It is true that no change should be arbitrary or partisan. It should not be done for the benefit of a political party, but in order *to form a more perfect union.* [and] *fostering general welfare*—.

Promoting general welfare is the spirit and strength that establishes and maintains our state of republic and democracy. The spirit and strength of the will of the people must establish Justice, ensuring inner tranquility and general welfare as the main goals. The government must provide for the common defense (social, economic, health and educational defense), that is the spirit and strength. The government must care to insure for us, and for our prosperity the benefits of freedom; that is the spirit and strength. Force is our national sovereignty or our popular sovereignty. By these principles, amendments to the constitution and changes to the rules of law are necessary. But the changes must be impartial and for the benefit of the people not political parties.

Let us consider the separation of the church and of current mercantilism. The changes should separate the government's function from the functions of free enterprise and the free market, as well as from the influence of the power of large capital in government and in the laws governing their existence. If private enterprise and the free market wish not to be regulated by the government, they should perform like any international enterprise operating in our nation. Domestic free enterprises in this country must operate supporting welfare, and national security by constitutional mandate. So, the citizens live free with liberty and justice, searching for their happiness. Free enterprises must not operate totally without restrictions, because the people will be neither free nor happy if they are kept as a consumer society—or as statistical numbers of mercantilism. No other way will the government of the United States of America be free and sovereign through time.

Abraham Lincoln's wise phrases live through the centuries, are eternal and vibrate in the souls of people who love freedom and general welfare above their personal interests. Listen to what he said, thinks, and follow his advice. Popular sovereignty is the will of each individual and national sovereignty is the collective will of citizens conferred on the government of their state. *"Always remember that your resolve to succeed is more important than anything else."* Your will prevails and this is over the intentions, decisions, and actions of the representatives you choose from your government. Franklin said, *"Fear not failure that will not make you weaker, but stronger."* After all, the changes you propose and demands are only intended to make this Union more perfect knowing that (Lincoln added), *"Democracy is the government of the people, by the people, for the people."* And this is the sole intention of fostering general welfare if you desire—your inalienable right—to achieve Happiness. *"The likelihood of losing in the fight should not deter us from supporting a cause that we believe is fair," Lincoln said.* And because no one knows if you could succeed if you don't fight, he added, *"In the end, what matters is not the people of life, but the life of the people."*

For today, many, but every action of the powers of the state, executive, legislative and judicial, tend to favor mercantilism, acting against the fundamental principle of the United States: the establishment and maintenance of a government of the people, by the people and for the people—popular sovereignty. The well-being, equitable prosperity, security and peace of the people depend directly on the changes that are enacted and implemented to update the constitution and its laws according to the demands of modern life and societies.

The constitution reforms are necessary, starting with the following issues.

1.   —Eliminate the militia and reform the national guard's objectives, strategy and mission.
2.   —Establish popular sovereignty and their right to directly elect their representatives in the government, in all three powers.
    2.1. —Establish the popular vote as the sole and final form of choice and election of President and Vice-President of the republic, allowing the system of the college of

voters to be the auditor and witness that the intention and integrity of the will of the people is preserved.

2.2. —Retake the people responsibility and the right to elect their representatives of magistrates to the supreme court of justice, and judges of federal courts. No representative of the people in a government power should have authority or right to appoint any official for the other two powers of the state. The president's current authority to appoint judges, including judges of the federal system, is a violation of the principle of separation of powers.

3. —Confirm the power of popular sovereignty to choose its governance program in accordance with the needs approved by each state. The people, and only the people, have the right and duty to formulate a government program and requirements that best suits their needs, for each presidential term, collected through state propositions and elections. The house of representatives of the congress has the responsibility of legislating the will of the people. The Senate Chamber has the responsibility to revise, propose amendments and approve the proposal of the government program. It is the responsibility of the House of Representatives to distribute to the public the government program that the people choose to implement, and to require from political parties and their official candidates' bid proposals of their plan satisfying the people's governing program. Similarly, the House of Representatives must assume responsibility for regulating the basis and procedures of how to define the political platforms for each election, as the people across their states desire.

4. —abolish the need for the militia. The militia is an outdated force of meaningless practice; it has neither organization, nor morality, nor training, nor definite purpose. The colonial-time militia has already fulfilled its mission and it is time to abolish it completely.

4.1 — Reform the national guard objectives of each state. The role of the national guard is responsible for the role of, training and maintaining the military militia to all citizens over the age of 18. Implement two continuous, mandatory, years in the service of the national guard or four years of training.

4.2 —The military reserve must integrate the popular militia into a single military corps, train in the use of weapons and combat procedures to each and every citizen.

4.3 — The military reserve must expand its scope and establish a mandatory two-year regime in service to all citizens, women and men, for military and vocational purposes. The purpose is to provide military training to citizens in preparation for being part of the militia in reserve, while at the same time training citizens in technology, production and services that are of benefit to the individual and society after leaving the military reserve.

5. —Amendment Article I, Section 2 of the Constitution. The absolute power to bring charges in political trials is broadly effective as necessary, without participation, obstruction or intervention of the investigative party, of any elected or unelected representative in the service of the people, including the president and vice president, by any method deemed appropriate by the representative chamber, including subpoenas, special counseling procedures. Establish that no representative under investigation shall have the right to refuse to declare or appeal to confidentiality privileges, when cited for that purpose, including the president and vice president (no one should be above the law).

When the House of Representatives submits a request for documents, the person or persons under investigation shall, without obstruction in the service of justice, submit the required, confidential or non-confidential documents. The investigative committee or special counsel shall agree on the date and time of the interrogation (for a limited time) with the person or persons under investigation so as not to disturb the work of that party. The investigation of any representative, on the sole ground, suspends any immunity power of the party under investigation. Once the investigation is complete, the chamber will be able to make the statement of proven indictments and open a grand jury to determine the constitutionality and legality provenance of the indictment. If applicable, the chamber prepares the formal charge of charges and crimes against the investigated party and will prosecute them in the Senate Chamber. The opinion of the judge or grand jury judges is evidence that must be admitted (be admitted as such) included attached to the indictment file.

6.   —Amendments Article I, Section 3 of the Constitution. This amendment modifies and promulgates that the accused party is not above the independent law of the Senate's ruling for or against the act of dismissal of the public office held by the accused. The Senate has no power to hold the accused for offences punishable by law, and therefore the accused party will nevertheless be subject to being charged, prosecuted and punished in accordance with the law when the accused party leaves his public office. That being the case, the constitution must clearly sanction or define the period or expiration of the time limit for making accusations.

7.   —Amendments Article I, Section 2 of the Constitution. As soon as this section delegates the responsibility of bringing political charges against representatives of the people in the government for treason, bribery, other felonies and misdemeanors" are typified: they will be major political crimes:

(1)   proven acts of association with any foreign government in order to alter, abolish or repeal, or change the republican form and democracy of the Union,

(2)   any act of the official with the intention of altering, abolishing or repealing, or changing the republican

form and democracy of the Union, whether this act is individually or in accordance with other persons, civil or public, national or foreign;

(3) to attack the justice system, by intimidation, bribery or corruption of the ethical integrity of the justice system, courts and judges in a corrupt manner, for personal or third-party benefits;

(4) to attack internal tranquility, whipping people inside or outside the country, whether or not citizens of the United States, to alter the social, political and economic order of the Union;

(5) intentionally undermine or weaken the common defense status, diluting or diminishing the knowledge, skill, and experience of members of the armed forces, putting U.S. military forces at a disadvantage, worldwide;

(6) Dismantle institutions and or weaken overall capacity, reducing the knowledge, skill, and experience installed in institutions that promote, protect, and maintain the overall welfare of the people of the United States;

(7) intentionally, explicitly or implicitly harass, deprive, and denigrate man's inalienable rights, including the right to life, Liberty and the pursuit of Happiness;

(8) embezzlement and diversion of the state's treasury of funds for personal gain.

(9) Minor offences shall be regarded as a cause of dismissal to the public office held by a representative, which the House of Representatives sanctions and establishes in these reforms.

Fallibility

What is fallibility? Fallibility is the possibility of wrong, failing or failing in an action. That is, the constitution and its laws derived from it may have errors. That seems to be it.

"The government and the democracy of the people has its weaknesses and vulnerabilities. Man's wickedness is constantly lurking, and the people put them in the hands of their representatives whenever they are elected them. This action is like throwing randomly the dice of possibilities for destroying their government and democracy. The people have had governments that tried or tried to seize the government and wealth of the nation, assembling a dictatorship, autocracy, monarchy, etc. Men of goodwill should reinforce and update them as soon as possible, and from time to time, adjust them to the reality of the evolution of citizens' thought, customs and behavior. Thus, we satisfy or fulfill with the primary purpose of the founders, *to form a more perfect Union*".

Approach

The people need to make serious studies of change—adjustments to our social, economic and political system—to maintain and satisfy the original and functional intention of the founders. The people must understand the foundations of the construction of this Union—state of mind and current knowledge to sanction the spirit of its principles, compatible with the conditions of the present.

1 —All men are created equal
2 —With inalienable rights endowed by the Creator
2.1 —Right to Life, Freedom and The Pursuit of Happiness
3 —Right to choose their government with powers derived from the consent of the people to ensure their security and happiness; —[it is the power of popular sovereignty].

The formation of the United States of America clearly defines the six points of the procedures— the same the constitution.

> 1 "Form a more perfect Union;
> 2 —Establish Justice;
> 3 —Ensure national tranquility;
> 4 —Provide for the common defense;
> 5 —Promote general welfare;
> 6 —Secure the benefits of freedom for the People.

These six mandates represent the popular sovereignty [of the people of the colonies] and constitute national sovereignty. These are the six great responsibilities—constitutional mandates—for the central Republican government. These mandates are the responsibilities of the three powers, Legislative, Executive and Judicial. And there are no more authorities for these three powers outside legal political scope written in the constitution. State constitutions and laws are responsible for strengthening these constitutional mandates and enacting their own state laws as long as they are within the spirit and letter of the constitution—laws detailing and expanding these six objectives. None of the three powers has the authority to alter, modify, or disobey these sanctioned responsibilities.

Evidence

The six mandates listed above have bases on recognized natural laws and can be summarized in rights inalienable, as irrefutable evidence.

—The declaration of independence specifies a point derived from popular sovereignty.

> 4. — Right to abolish and institute and provide new guards when such a government wants to reduce the people under absolute despotism.

The author considers that there are no higher political crimes, that the violation of the procedure and evidence, the sovereignty of the people listed above—this can be considered treason: acting against or attacking the principles of the constitution. These six points of action and the four fundamental evidences are irrefutable and necessary bases for the dismissal of any elected representative by electoral suffrage—the will of the people: their vote. And the constitution derives the rest of the legal regulations.

Warnings and consequences

The founding fathers were aware that corruption exists and is able to infiltrate the government. And the evidence is on the front lines of the declaration of independence, where they establish the right of a people to restore their governments to political and civil rights and their freedoms—*"... whenever any form of government becomes destructive to these purposes* [of the constitution]. It is the right of the people to *alter... and institute* [amend] *a new government..."* It is the people who delegate to the legislative branch (the house of their representatives), the responsibility not only to charge, to bring charges and to give cause an impeachment trial to the office held by the accused, but to build a standard procedure of how to conduct the trial.

Previous governments, and in particular Donald Trump's presidency, have failed to honor their oath to office. President Trump has sought to establish a government that works or operates exclusively for its personal interests in violation of the constitution, popular sovereignty. The Senate under the leadership of Mitch McConnell appears to have been corruptly involved with the president's criminal acting. The Senate denied the people the right to exercise that constitutional mandate *"to alter and institute a new government."* They say that doer and aider bare the same fault, and the case of President Trump's dismissal, both the president and the Senate have the same guilt.

Since the chambers of congress have the absolute authority to make and bring political charges (the House of Representatives) and to prosecute the accused (the house of senators) in law, the people expect the legislature to strictly abide and apply those six fundamental principles and four fundamental evidences (along with applicable derived laws) and bring into prosecution. And if the laws in force were not clear, and by such legal darkness, justice cannot be done, it is a duty of the legislative branch to propose, edit and enact reforms to the law, to serve due justice, according to the spirit and intent of the constitution. The manipulation of the judgment of complacent dismissal of the accused and the manipulation of the process for the convenience and benefit of a majority party, is consequently also a gross violation of the six fundamental principles and the four evidences mentioned above.

President D. Trump's case of political dismissal and the incomplete, justice-denied and rushed Senate process expose the weakness and vulnerability of the republic and democracy of the United States of America and expose overlapping and latent corruption.

Laws should make the standard procedure clear for the process of becoming a president and any other official in any of the government's powers, in an amendment to the section 2 of Article 1. At the same time, such an amendment must define the charges, —to this day obscured and subject to interpretations. Cases of political dismissal are serious cases and serious consequences, and have been seen to occur with some frequency; therefore, they must fall under the concept that no one should or may be above the constitution and its laws, including the president of the executive branch. The definition of crimes and consequences must be so clear that they serve as deterrent for civil servants, —so that they think twice— before acting. The amendment should lay down the grounds for prosecution and evidence necessary for the filing of charges. This amendment must suspend, eliminate and prevent resistance and rejection of the legal order imbued in the subpoena of appearance for all officials, elected or not, of the government.

The law should clarify the privilege of privacy, especially in cases of criminal investigation, as it should not give rights, to any person to be above the law. A law that provides the subject with gaps or tunnels of legal evasiveness, and facilitates many interpretations of enforcement is inefficient and ineffective, is not enacted law that *"establishes justice."* These legal weaknesses make the constitutional mandate a remedy of justice, giving a subject under investigation the possibility of manipulating the law in his favor, becoming immune or placing himself above the law.

Amendment five does not mention much less specifies the rights of the accused in political trials—those who are neither criminal nor civil—as is the case with charges of political dismissal. Trials by definition (political) the founders excluded from the criminal and civil proceedings ventilated in the courts. The constitution does not clearly define, let alone typifies political crimes. The constitution delegates to Article 1, Section 3 empowers the Senate to judge political judgments. However, it is also not defined here what the political trials referred to are, no judgments are specified, nor are the crimes and or charges that come from these trials listed or typified.

The author is sure that everyone involved in overlapping or covering up the alleged crimes will find excuses and supporting arguments; but the truth is one, and only one, and cannot be altered—at least for a long time. The case of the forty-fifth president in particular made it clear that it is possible for a dictator, monarchy or despotic and absolute government to take the government, when the combination of the three powers, or the executive and majority senate, of the state is favorable to a political party.

Need for Reform

Insure for the people
—sovereignty
—their rights and freedoms
—security and security
—Happiness

Following the guidelines set out in the declaration of independence and the preamble—unique article— of the constitution, and to satisfy the purposes of the Union, in accordance with the constitutional mandate of *"to form a more perfect Union..."*. In the present and future, the power legislation (the two chambers) should institute a law that promotes the five-year (or immediate emergency) revision of the constitution in relation to the evolution of the people's way of life) in line with technological advances, scientists, electronic social media (Internet) and the evolution of positions of the philosophical thinking of the people. Democracy, government, and laws cannot and should not be outdated or inept. For example, the regulation of social media on the Internet that violates personal privacy exposes individual and national security. The intervention of a foreign power in the sacred process of electoral suffrage highlights the vulnerability of national and popular sovereignty, as well as the righteousness and accuracy of the will of the people. Closing our eyes to these events is a crime against national sovereignty—it is an act of war against this nation. Legislative power must create and enact, seriously without evasiveness, laws that eliminate the vulnerability of the Union.

Causes

Any proposition of change or reforms should point to the aberration and or mirages that distort the founders' original intent and describe and recommend the remedy of the necessary change. For example, in the case of abuse of power, and or violation of the constitution.

> [Only] *"when a long train of abuse and usurpation, invariably chasing the same Object evidences a design to reduce them under absolute despotism,"* ...

Likewise, we should point out inconsistencies, deficiencies that violate Security, Happiness and the General Welfare of the People, and create merits of changes to maintain the state, but only when it is guaranteed, reinforcing the principles that originated the Union, the structure of the Republican government and its democratic system.

The text *"any form of government"* refers to any form, in whole or in part, and therefore includes etymologically the three powers of the state and not just the executive branch. Obviously, any of the three powers has the power to become destructive for the purposes of the Union.

The history of the United States—and many other countries—today show the typical case of this socio-economic, and political mirage in the world. The union of the English colonies in America stems from the oppression and greed of a reign that—by its wealth and power—usurped everything he saw and wanted.

This situation has not changed, and thinking clearly, we see the capitalism that was born with the concept of *fair price* at that time transformed into a mercantilism. And then it became autocratic capitalism where only a few are of the capitalist-supplier class (of products and services) and the rest ninety nine percent are the consumer class. The system is tied up to maintain that situation or economic condition and the government ignores it, is complicit in the strategy, or profits from the situation. This economic and financial situation does not contribute or comply with the constitutional provisions.

The desire to speculate or maximize profit with the least investment—i.e. the maximum return on investment–is the principle of excessive capitalization. Modern capitalism manipulates supply and consequently price, usurps everything it sees and desires, accumulating wealth in bags of a few individuals who oppresses, implicitly or explicitly, the consumer majority; "these are consumer societies, where consumers are held captive to induced and sublimated consumerism. In other words, capitalization is an absorbing machinery that sucks the scarce capital into the working and middle class—in any case, they make it reach their hands—to the coffers of powerful rich. Such actions undermine the great constitutional principle of promoting general welfare. The people must participate, it is their right, in the affairs of the government, creating merits to make changes or reforms to the constitution as soon as it becomes necessary.

The people have the (constitutional) right to alter and install a government that abides the constitutional foundations when the government becomes destructive to the ends of the Union, or when this government does not perform its functions (which is also destructive action). The government has, in fact, failed to legislate the legal form so that the people may exercise the constitutional right to change their government when it becomes destructive. Donald Trump's administration wears the "destructive" rating. The people have the right to require the legislature to create such procedures.

> ..."That every time any form of government becomes destructive to its purposes, it is the right of the people to alter it and institute [amend] a new Government, laying [reformed] its foundations on principles [the foundations] and the organization of its powers in such a way, as far as they are it will seem more likely that it will effectively affirm its security and happiness [welfare generates]. [But]…should not be changed for light and transient reasons;"

It is a failure of the state's three powers to allow or participate in any violation of the constitution and its rules of law. The relationship between the people's government and the economic system—capitalism, private enterprise, the free market—is neither included nor defined in the Constitution of the United States. And any law subsequently passed to the constitution and its original amendments are laws that are subject to the interpretation and judgment of the Supreme Court of Justice. Laws that are not within the constitutional framework cannot be imposed on the people, nor is it the duty of the citizen to abide by such erroneous laws that are included in the constitution; that right belongs to their states or their people. This point is a major failure of the government that does not fulfill the responsibility of ensuring general welfare and protecting the Safety and Happiness of the people.

After the discovery of the new continent, which they called America, in the name of an Italian navigator, Américo Vespucci, the torrent of migrants in sea caravans reached the shores of the Atlantic Sea in America and invaded these lands. American lands were land inhabited by other human beings with the right to use them, they were not wastelands. In fact, the settlers found cordiality from dozens of tribes with hundreds of Native Americans who intended to help the settlers. Perhaps Native Americans understood that the universe—particularly planet earth—is reserved, from its beginning, for all those beings that inhabit them, in addition to the inorganic things complementing each scenario. Existence did not designate the content of the universe for specific living beings—selfish individuals. The universe shares its content with everyone, without prejudice or preferences. Everything that encloses the universe is for everyone and for all, because existence promotes true equality in the universe. In these pre-established conditions the emigrants of the old continent found the lands of America. But the kingdom of England claimed—without any rights—the lands of the Atlantic coast, founding thirteen colonies, displacing its original inhabitants. Nor can the people of the colonies claim—they have no legal handle to validate such a claim—the ownership of these lands in the Americas, but it was through usurpation (vandalism).

This is the point; the equality of men is not owned by a particular race. For the sake of justice, the author notes that certain settlers negotiated and purchased native American land, implying that these settlers recognized the ownership (by eminent domain) of the natives. After the barbaric facts, and the *mea culpa* (the charge of conscience) the constitution states that Native Americans are exempt from contributing taxes. Of course, they do not pay more than that for the near extermination of these people—the true American citizens—nor do they want to pay for the usurpation of the territory of the United States the Native Americans owned by eminent domain; that is, property acquired by continued, unclaimed use, for more than twenty thousand years before Europeans invaded their lands.

The story called the Huns (like Tara Bulba's novel) barbaric, who left Asia, commanded by Attila—a legendary figure. These barbaric hordes invaded Europe at the time. Attila's law was his strength and cruelty that left in its wake destruction, shattered villages, women raped or kidnapped, while killing children and the elderly, indeed opposed to those who opposed it. Likewise, the European hordes invaded America and invaded the lands of the natives of America. The idiosyncrasies of Europeans were rigged by the customs and policies of the Middle Ages. [48]

Spain invaded, explored, looted, the lands of the new continent, America, from North America to Patagonia, except for a large territory—Brazil—that was taken by Portugal; and the territory of Canada that France took. France, England, Spain, and Portugal divided the Americas. England took the territorial strip along the Atlantic coast from Boston to Georgia. From this invasion on behalf of the king of England, as the Huns did, took over the lands later called the United States of America. From there the settlers expanded west to the Pacific Ocean, killing the natives to almost the point of extermination. In truth, it was a horrific and ill-intentioned genocide, and it is possible that the Indians were being said to attack the colonizers. I ask, what else could Native Americans do when they were invaded, and expropriated by armed aliens, if it was not to defend themselves and fight—with a lot of mental and technological disadvantage—for what by nature belonged to them? Perhaps the wealth they have in Europe today and now the United States may be because of all they plundered from the new continent. The new Americans gave the real Americans pieces of dry land, where they can't sow or go hunting. And then they were left alone independents with their own form of government, practically in a concentration camp from which they were forbidden to leave. This action does not fit with religious beliefs or moral values or principles that settlers intended to have.

---

[48] https://es.wikipedia.org/wiki/Atila

In America no one bought anything, they took over these lands and their contents by force. There are no titles, or transfer documents of ownership, from American Indians to Europeans, that attest to the legality of the acquisition of property—the Hun's method. Everything was usurped, except for acquisitions from Florida, Louisiana, Texas, and California, Alaska, etc., territories seized by other explorers in the name of other monarchies. That's the story of the beginning of America after 1942, in broad terms. Someone can say, *"dishonorable."* The author does not attempt to judge human behavior because he considers that the events were part of the evolution of man, acting with the knowledge and customs of that time; but the wrongdoing acts are evidently clear. All of the above is clear evidence that the settlers brought in their mental framework the idea of snatching other people's property as feudal monarchies did.

Photo from Internet. Source Bing (search)– photo of the colonies of USA/

CHAPTER 3

Human influences

Maybe we can see that mental framework analyzing the human influences of that time. In truth and it is clear that the value of a set is greater than the value of the parts—each taken separate. And so, the union is a multiplier applied on the sum of the values of the parts. The grandeur, extension and depth of the declaration of independence and the constitution of the United States of America is transcendent; it goes beyond the mental or intellectual framework of Europe in the 14th, 15th and 16th centuries. This greatness lies in the diversification of the thoughts of its people—so we can see their humanism.

The humanism that encloses the text of these two documents sums up the moral and philosophical thought of man of that time, transcending to this day and applicable in the same way. The sequence of events is accurate and clear; "is evidence of the law of cause and effect inaction." The Middle Ages and feudalism were just coming to an end, and humanism emerges intensely, and by coincidence, the fall of Constantinople reduces the power of the Byzantine empire. In addition, the Vatican, Rome, loses control of the new thinking man and the anthropocentric concept appears to challenge the concept of Theo centrism.

The Vatican is divided; Martin Luther, a German professor, presents a religious and political challenge to the Catholic Church of Rome and the authority of the Pope in the Vatican with a movement of Western Christianity in the sixteenth century, apparently raised by Martin Luther in a publication *"the ninety-five thesis"* in 1517. [49]Luther's theory exposed the abuse of the practice of clergy by selling plenary indulgence—i.e. certificates that were believed to reduce punishments in purgatory for faults committed by the purchaser of the certificate or by their loved ones. Martin Luther demands that Jesus Christ requires that forgiveness of sins be a repentance of the soul (inner spirit) rather than a simple solvency through an external sacramental confession.

Confusion increases with the separation of the Church of England from the Vatican, but this time not by Christian principles but by corruption and abuse of power of the King of England. There is theological confusion in the minds of Europeans and they seek peace to live their beliefs. Protestants are born from this and many of them migrated with their religious ideas (purity) to the new continent. So, people who come to American brought in their minds the painful experience that causes oppression, the restriction of freedoms, religious persecution, exploitation, autocratic, despotic governments, as well as absolute monarchies. The mental and intellectual framework aspired to freedoms to live a life according to its free will—which is that inalienable right of individual choice.

Existence prescribes its natural law of cause and effect—that is, everything has an origin and conditions trace a trajectory and intensity of the resulting event, a destination; this law defines the chain of events that brought the people of the colonies to the point of the declaration of independence. The conditions, situations, and circumstances define the causes every time—these three components are the bases and forces of causes. and because of this and this cause or causes events are born in the development of life. There begins another chain, according to the same natural law, with which the colonies, now independently, formulate their political constitution and form their government. Obviously, the term "equality and respect for their freedoms" lived in their minds.

The other law of existence is the law of chance, which includes independent events—random events—and isolated events that occur

---

[49] https://en.wikipedia.org/wiki/Ninety-five_Theses

unforeseen, affecting or disturbing the chains of causal events, although they do not change the fate of causality. These include unforeseen, existing conditions in latency that are not taken into account, in tracking causal condition chains. The declaration of independence, the establishment of the republic, and the creation of the constitution occurred because the conditions and circumstances were given for these events to happen. So, to understand what happened back then we must study these conditions and circumstances of that time; for example, the influences of the customs, thoughts and beliefs of other immigrants who came from other European nations.

Concepts behind independence

We cannot deny that the seventeenth century European thinking influenced the thoughts of the colonizer of the thirteen American states, even perhaps, the thinking of two centuries ago. Europe emerged from the Middle Ages to a renaissance, an era of illustration. It was the dawn of a new way of thinking and living— the modus vivendi. Nor can we say that it was totally and purely of a British nature —and by the year 1600 the illustration had begun. The sequence of events exhibited in chapter one shows the mixture of cultures, customs and objectives of Europe in those centuries. The colonization of America brought to the territory of the new continent, widely demonstrated, the tiredness of living under absolutist monarchies that restricted not only the choice and practice of religion but also freedom of action—social, political and commercial. Internal forces pressed on the minds and souls of the colonizers and almost naturally underpowered the conditions of a drastic, immediate and permanent change. This is how all the changes happen; first arise inhospitable conditions and restrictions in an environment ferment a reaction—the need for a change. The author believes that the laws of existence regulate the combinations and permutations of substances, beings, things, ideas, actions and forces that originate situations and conditions in an environment in accordance with the participation or contribution of each of them in the mixture. Most of the time, it is as Isaac Newton discovered that for every action there is a reaction—in the chain of cause and effect—and it was to be expected that the colonies would react against the oppression of the British Crown. The situation of the colonies was a pressure cooker about to burst; and actually erupted. We can see these concepts, at that time, in their own evolution.

The situation of Europe, 15th and 16th centuries

The migration to the new continent after 1942 creates new ideas of expansion, social, political and economic in Europe; there are joy and new hopes. It was the dream of being free, practicing your religious beliefs without persecution, restriction or stalking, working and producing for yourself and everyone—it was the dream of general welfare. That way of thinking was as a "live and let live" in individual freedom.

The most important thing of this era was the intellectual Renaissance, manifested by a genuine desire to achieve greater knowledge, including the humanist, scientific and artistic. The historical records indicates that Europe was going through a short age of food, services and artisanal products. A situation that could have been the cause of the many wars between the monarchies of those years, each seeking its financial and economic balance, in Europe. We have already mentioned the war of the seven years practically left the United Kingdom in a bankruptcy. And the discovery of America could have been a blessing in disguise—as religious believers can say. And it actually was. Immigrants knew what they had to do since before they reached the shores of North America. But they did not include in their minds the idea of returning to Europe. His mission was to get free life or die in the attempt.

Dutch Colonization of America

History records that explorations and raids of the Dutch in America appear around 1602; the English did not yet reach the new continent—eighteen years before the pilgrims—arrived. But he was an English navigator serving the Dutch West Indies company, which sailed through present-day New York in 1621, the Company had established trading points in the vicinity of the Delaware and Connecticut rivers as well as in New York and Albany. Trade frictions between Dutch and English for the rule of the territory of Connecticut ended up ceding to the English the eastern part of Long Island. Despite this concession, disputes continued until the war between the Netherlands and the United Kingdom erupted. As a result, the British obtained the New Netherlands, a colonial province of the Republic of the Seven United Provinces on the northeastern coast of North [50]America—from the Delmarva Peninsula to the southwestern tip of Cape Cod, now New York—New Jersey, Delaware, and Connecticut, as well as small areas of Pennsylvania and Rhode Island. After the capitulation of Fort Amsterdam in 1664 and the Second Anglo-Dutch War, at the end of the Third Anglo-Dutch War in 1674, and under the Treaty of Westminster, the Dutch finally ceded that area to the English. It should be noted that the descendants of the Dutch contributed to the Dutch culture of the Netherlands to the colonization of the United States, giving character to the region for about two centuries (the aforementioned regionalism). This region includes Albany, Hudson Valley, western part of Long Island, northwestern New Jersey and New York. The Dutch brought the new continent —especially the aforementioned region—the ideas of freedom and pluralism and these concepts became main pillars of the political and social life of the colonies in America.

The Enlightenment Era

Isaac Newton (1643-) thought and said *"for every action there is a reaction"*; and that *"for each force there is another force of equal intensity, but of opposite sense that leave a system of forces in balance"*. We do not know how long it took him to reach these conclusions, but in any way, they are laws of existence that govern the universe and have been present and active since before matter appeared in the universe. These conclusions are dynamic parts of the law of cause

---

[50] https://es.wikipedia.org/wiki/Colonizaciorn_neerlandesa_de_Amwasrich

and effect, so no event happens if there are no causes —conditions, situations and circumstances that generate it.

There are many thinkers and philosophers from the 15th to 17th centuries who can be considered agents of change. However, as a force, change causes friction, resistance, resentment and retaliation against such agents. The strength of change, apparently, is stronger than the strength of resistance and in the end the change is given by the general welfare. The author considers that there are no agents of change more intense than the conditions and circumstances that feed the causes of the resulting effects. Leaders are the breaststroke that ignites fire to the causes of change. Rulers must understand that there is no army stronger than a people's decision to defend their freedoms, natural rights, and existence. Evidence is shown with actions; all the revolutions in Europe and America that people did to achieve their independence.

The author believes that the United States is on the edge of growing social, political, and economic revolution; that is, it is reaching the brink of profound change. This book contrasts what led settlers to declare and implement their independence from the oppression of Britain in the 17th century with the current situation in the 21st century. There are great philosophers and thinkers who influence the mental framework of the Europeans of that time, who, for lack of space in this book, the author refers to the notes at the end.[v]

The independence of the thirteen English colonies in North America occurred by the causes—a chain or sequence of coincidental conditions and situations—that made it possible. The rebirth was a cultural movement in Europe from the 15th to the 17th centuries, resulting from the ideas of humanism—the new concept of man. The influence of the renaissance is spread throughout Europe and the world including America, in particular the English colonies of North-America.

The author finds an article about illustration interesting. According to this article, [51]*"illustration was a cultural and intellectual*

---

[51] https://es.wikipedia.org/wiki/Ilustración

movement, primarily European..." The people of Europe sought changes to the predominant status quo, and the movement was born and lasted a little less than a hundred years, from the mid-17th century (or earlier) to the early nineteenth century. In fact, it began as a result of the European renaissance. It was a change of thought or mental framework that transformed the way of life in Europe and influenced the social, political and economic formation of the union of the English colonies in America. That is why they said that *"their stated purpose of dispelling the darkness of human ignorance through the lights of knowledge and reason—The* ability of the human being *to think, reflect to come to a conclusion, or form judgments of a particular situation or thing."* Later, people symbolized this time of the eighteenth century as the "century of lights."

It was a correct concept that *"knowledge could change ignorance' superstition and tyranny to build a better world."* This is the great point; correctly true, that knowledge is the force that drives the evolution of man. And it is necessary to study the thoughts of those times— social, economic and political—in order to re-direct the current situation within those three terms. People were right, with modern thought, the author argues that knowledge, light, is the key to the evolution of man's idiosyncrasies and life. Knowledge is the basis of the social world, including progress, scientific advancement, cultural, political and social evolution of all eras. Knowledge, moreover, is the instrument by which sustained social uniqueness can be achieved, in the world of man, peace and security.

At the time, illustration—that is, study and education—was— available to the bourgeoisie, not the lower class or the working class, or women relegated to the background in business life, political relations, etc. In these modern times, it remains the same; education is so expensive that the middle and working class loses access to higher education. The best universities are almost reserved for the wealthy class. There is no denying, however, that the human mentality advances, albeit slowly, with the little knowledge that is filtered with socialization and rubbing, in daily life—news and dissemination, human contact—causes knowledge to pass, filter, to the unfortunate classes of that time and those of now. But human advancement can be accelerated by establishing free education [freedom of education as an inalienable natural right], as well as free enterprise, free market, and free religion. This is why the author argues that education should be free for all because the benefit of high education brings the knowledge that accelerates the evolution of man and societies in general; and so, the author says *"give knowledge to the people and they will build a better world for all."*

Today this phenomenon of illustration remains the same, maintaining the old social differences and creating new ones even more deep and wide. Perhaps it is that the minority holding power and wealth does not open the floodgates of the educational dam for fear of losing political, social and economic control; and employers also maintain control of the purchasing power of the working class at the level of poverty to eliminate the competition that would bring about the general boom—it sounds paradoxical, but it is often true. And with this, opportunities would eventually be equally given—and the Union's rise would grow at levels that are not seen before.

At that time, 17th to 18th centuries, the aristocracy debated political issues, education, literature, sciences and philosophy. And even though the direction of life at the time was in the hands of men, talented women appeared who contributed to change. These women include Madame Lafayette, Lady Mary Wortley Montagu, Olympe de Gouges, Mary Chudleigh, activist writers. Ms. De Gouges, for example, wrote and published "the Declaration of women's and citizenship rights in 1791 Under Quote 1). But instead of repeating the entirety of this important article, the author leaves the reader the task of studying this phenomenon of illustration on his own. He mentions that characters such as Immanuel Kant, Jean le Rond D'Alembert laid down critical principles of the thought of change of those years. D'Alembert, was an agent of change, exhausting everything, including (as the article says) *"he discussed, analyzed and waved everything, from the profane sciences to the foundations of revelation, from metaphysics to the subjects of taste, from music to morals, from the scholastic disputes of theologians to the objects of commerce, from the rights of princes to those of peoples, from natural law to the arbitrary laws of nations, in a word, from the issues that best concern us that concern us most weakly."*

The author considers that this *age of Reason,* was a process, revolutionary, sustained or continuous, to improve humanity, and not only to perfect the democratic system of the States of America. Political radicalization with efforts to implement certain party policies brings humanity back to the obscurantism of that time. For many autocratic or dictatorial rulers, ignorance is the ideal condition for dominating the people—in addition to fear under threat. It was a great step to achieve religious stability, ending the religious wars of that time, with the Peace of Westphalia. They were two peace treaties of "Osnabruck and Munster, signed on 24 October 1648, the latter in the Peace Hall of the city council of Munster.[52]

The Peace of Westphalia led to the first modern diplomatic congress and initiated a new order in Central Europe based on the concept of national sovereignty—The concept gives the power of the nation to the people. It is recorded in a constitution that cedes power to the state. Now the king becomes a mere ideological representative arising from liberal political theory. This same article defines the sovereignty in simple terms as follows. [53]

> [National sovereignty is] *"the supreme political power that corresponds to an independent state, without external interference. In political theory, sovereignty is a substantive term that designates the supreme authority that possesses ultimate and independent power over some system of government".*

In other words, there is no power higher than the power of the citizens of the nation [the people]. And the aspect of *"external interference"* is seen as a term that includes everything that is not in the power of the people or the government that represents it. The

---

[52] https://es.wikipedia.org/wiki/Paz_de_Westfalia
[53] https://es.wikipedia.org/wiki/Soberana_nacionala_nacional

nation is a system, and as such, has its balance—although transient is a balance sheet—while maintaining its six causes and four purposes mentioned above. So, if internal or external forces are applied to the nation, the nation inevitably reacts to restore its balance or gain another equally stable state. That is, the system, Nation, tolerates no other power other than the power of the people. This is the reason why any external power, independent, should not interfere with popular or national sovereignty.

Any power that is not, or wishes to be, subordinate to the power of the people cannot be a part, component or element of the nation, even though it is a necessarily complementary system in the operation of the nation. For example, the separation of church and state. That is, individual religious choice is a matter of conscience, and is not contingent on the state, government or sovereignty of the people. This issue represents two matters, the citizen, a right-to-right, in equal rights with the other members of the nation, and another who is not a subject or passive object of belonging to a political entity that is imposed on him; and opens national sovereignty translated into a representative regime, because the nation cannot govern itself directly. That is the point, therefore, the government exists by the will of the people and from which derives all its powers.

National and popular sovereignty are a social state and there can be nothing higher than the will of the people. Any other system is either subordinate to this sovereignty or is a system associated with sovereignty by advocating the constitutional principles of the Republican government and its democracy. If there is a complementary system that does not wish to subordinate itself to national sovereignty, such as religion, it should not participate in the administration of the nation's operation—which has only constitutional responsibility to manage the affairs and interests of the people. For this reason, the free market and private enterprise that claims its absolute freedom, self-determination and operational independence must be separated from the administrative efforts of the nation—the affairs of the people. Thus individuals, citizens of the people can form free businesses, and negotiate with each other without the intervention of the government, in the free markets according to their volition. However, the government representing the people has a single responsibility Constitutional.

1. —Form a more perfect Nation
2. —Establishing Justice
3. —Ensuring national welfare
4. —Tender common defense
5. —Encouraging general well-being
6. —Securing the benefits of freedom

The constitution clearly sanctions that such objectives are for us—free citizens—and for our posterity—the new citizens added in the future. But it does not explicitly or implicitly include any legal persons, whether of one or more natural persons. This is why the government is of the people, by the people and for the people. And the people are regarded as created by the Creator endowed with inalienable natural rights that legal persons (created by consent and by common agreement of natural persons) cannot do or have for themselves. So, the government must ensure the welfare and tranquility of the people by regulating the private enterprise and the free market so that they take no advantage of the user or consumer people of products and services that the free market offers. This point is a major issue that the government, and in particular the legislative branch must reform in order to fulfil the Union's objectives set out in the preamble to its constitution.

Therefore, as well as the church, it is autonomous and independent, private enterprise and the free market must depart from the operation and management of the republican government, and abide by the privileges, permits and regulations that the nation—the will of the people—wishes to grant to its operation and relationship with the people of the nation. That is, the republican government under its democratic system is under the will of the people and is responsible for fulfilling the will of the people. Therefore, the duty of the government is solely to enforce the constitution and its rules of law to ensure the benefits of freedom for the people. So, the economic or commercial system that affects general welfare or internal tranquility is against national sovereignty and violates popular sovereignty.

The economic situation of citizens is paramount and is about the interests of private enterprise in free trade. The free market and private enterprise must not claim national rights of the nation and at the same time invoke and claim freedom to operate without the nation's regulations. This claim violates the fundamental spirit of the constitution—the will of the people and popular sovereignty. Therefore, it should be considered as a foreign entity licensed to operate within the nation without affecting the interests of the people. Just as freedom of worship is promoted and protected and the nation puts in the hands of religions the choice of the beliefs of the nation's people, the protection of the same people against consumer abuse and the mercantilist attitudes of suppliers must also be rigorously established. The constitution of the United States excludes the exploitation of man by man—a reason for the declaration of independence and concept of the constitution. But the government's duty to fulfill the will of it by ensuring general well-being should not be considered interventionism. Every company within the national territory is one, or more than one, property of the people. But the commercial activity of products or services, of one or more members of that commercial entity, does not change the individual right of the owner or owners of the company.

The concept of giving personality to an entity of the private company is to accept that the owners of that company, de facto, acquire double rights, as a natural person and as a legal person, which is contrary to the concept that all men are created equal. The will of an entrepreneur as a private enterprise does not rise above the will of all the people, popular sovereignty. It is clear that any business, or company, must be licensed to operate within the United States or within any state, anyway.

The author considers that the simple majority of the people do not represent the will of the nation, when the nation includes all the people. This is a matter that should be clarified when legislatures are established applicable to the behavior of the people and should be subject to the consent of the minority. This is why the term of the people's power must be clearly defined. Similarly, every subterfuge, system or mechanism, which depends on human intelligence, is not a human entity and consequently and cannot, and should not, hold the rights of a natural person. The operational freedom of private companies (corporations) does not imply freedom to abuse or cause harm to the consumer people, because it violates the general welfare, justice, national tranquility and undermines the general welfare of the people. Within these concepts the company can operate in a free market, as long as the government protects small businesses that compete with large companies.

The free market (a means) and free enterprise (a method) are commercial resources (or tools) aimed at the commercial relationship of men, but they are not men themselves. The will of the people through their government establishes the rules of behavior and commercial relationship of the free market and private enterprise in the internal domain. The government is responsible for ensuring the general welfare of the people with a duty to prevent and prevent a system from intentionally behaving by taking advantage of the people. And in this case, it must also ensure the competition and benefits of local companies operating in international markets. A company owned by citizens of this Union installed in a foreign country and operating outside the country does not belong to the United States and must therefore be treated as a foreign company trading with the United States. Therefore, such companies operating within a global association, if it wants to be free and autonomous, must be separated and operated externally, complying with the policies of the general will of the people, delegated to their government.

Religious controversies also reached the English colonies in America. An example of the consequences of these controversies was the expulsion of Roger Williams from the Massachusetts Bay Colony for his religious beliefs. Roger Williams was a Puritan minister, theologian and author who founded the Plantations de Providence settlement, which became the colony of Rhode Island. He was a staunch defender of religious freedom, the separation of church and state, and fair dealings with American Indians, and was one of the first abolitionists. [54]

Society and economy in the 13 colonies [55]

Industrial production was not yet arriving, and agricultural production occupied settlers' time, but Europe felt the power of the north American colony boom, while becoming Europe's boom. There were the big plantations, the cultivation of tobacco, and cotton. Once the colonies consolidated their settlement and defense in the early 17th century the population grew unexpectedly, even though Britain filtered trade, import and export.

What was going on stirred the thinking of free enterprise and the free market. Perhaps it was desirable to separate the business function in the constitution of the function of the government, in particular to prevent capitalist tendencies to operate in a mercantilist manner by exploiting the people—in order to maximize profit by minimizing investment. Their idea is increasing their return on investment without limits decreasing their investment to zero (if possible). For this purpose, banking, services, production and commerce, reject government regulations, accusing it of interventionist. The wealth of the American continent, a virtually unspoiled territory, offered all the raw material, and more, for a massive economic explosion, which was actually already occurring in agriculture, plantations and tobacco treatment. One of the impediments to faster economic development was the UK's policy of not granting manufacturing licenses. The production was massive because of the tireless work of the settlers. At the beginning of independence, the thirteen colonies dined about two and a half million inhabitants. According to historical notes, growth was due more to mass immigration from European countries, mostly from England, than to the birth rate.

---

[54] https://en.wikipedia.org/wiki/Roger_Williams
[55] https://elnacimientodeclio.wordpress.com/2013/04/27/sociedad-y-economia-en-las-13-colonias-inglesas-de-norteamerica/

Economic aspect

During the 15th century, after the discovery of America and continuing in the 16th century, Europe entered a stage of prosperity and economic growth. [56]This expansion concerns the population growth that brings the need to accelerate the supply and supply of products, services and information, balancing growing demand. Europe experiences expansive and innovative societies, overlapping the transition from feudalism to modern capitalism. The concept of currency becomes the driving instrument of the new economy. With the development of colonization on the new continent by the Netherlands, France, England and Spain—and on a smaller scale, Scotland and Ireland, trade which at the time was only in the European territory, opens up intercontinental trade. This new form of trade requires a new system. Prosperity or boom begins with the colonization of the new continent by Europeans and for Europe. Native Americans did not receive anything in return; only European culture and religions—in addition to ruthless looters.

Private enterprise: is it above the constitution and popular or national sovereignty? No, it is not above the Union and the legal framework that allows them to operate. Capitalism is reborn in Europe under the idea of Fair Price; i.e. the price of goods and services was the cost to the point of consumption plus a reasonable and fair percentage of net profits.

The renaissance imposed on man the unease and need to acquire capital, tending to profit under the spirit of business and commerce companies. In reality, the spirit of private business in the trading is in substance and forms only procedures and is actually the freedom of owners who want to act free of regulations—regardless of the harm they cause to the people.

In the time of the colonies, the prosperity in Europe opens new horizons, and people who like to dress well and adorn themselves with jewelry, live in maximum convenience and comfort, laziness and pompous parties give way to mercantilism. Capitalism then

---

[56] https://www.slideshare.net/dianaluciavesgapascitto/economia-del-renacimiento

transfigures its fair *price* form to maximum *utility (maximum return on investment)*, i.e. increases the price because demand increases when the cost of the product or service remains constant, taking advantage of the growing purchasing power of money and the abundance of raw materials and products. This is the point or time when the government fails to promote and protect the general welfare and prosperity of the people, abandoning them to mercantilist greed. We must reform the constitution to protect the consumer, the people.

At that time capitalism began with a clear concept; the *fair price* theory considered that the value of the products and services depended on their usefulness. It is natural and acceptable that manufacturing a product or preparing a service and bringing them to the point of consumption adds costs to the cost of obtaining the raw material. In addition, the supplier wishes to obtain a satisfactory gain that encourages the supplier to carry out the process of producing or serving the consumer. Such a gain must be higher than the normal interest that the bank pays for the money in a savings account. Profitability is the difference between the value obtained and the value of the investment. And the ratio of this difference and the value of the total investment is the return on investment.

The author finds the above natural and positive. But the practice of earning a return greater than 1.20 times the value of the product or service is unsatisfactory, incorrect, and unfair. And the government will always be responsible for ensuring general welfare and ensuring justice must protect the people (the consumer). That is, the government must set the limit of profitability and or return on investment applicable to products and services. The government is of the people by the people for the people; it's not of rich, by rich and for the rich. The government was inclined to work for the long-known, famous and powerful, seriously making the Union's conscience seriously ill. And the greed and selfishness of the rich became the cancer of society by gradually destroying national tranquility, justice, the pursuit of happiness and general welfare—the fundamental objectives of the Union's constitution.

image borrowed from the Internet

The economic model of price based on supply and demand is neither fair nor equitable as supply is manipulated creating fictitious shortages to increase the price of sustained demand. Educated consumption also affects demand so that demand decreases with product selection. The renaissance awakens a different economic policy at the end of medieval time. There is also a perspective that includes not only the decreasing authority of the Pope, but the growing dependence and authority of science. For matters of justice and perhaps intellectual property, the renaissance is mostly due to Italian thought—for it was in Italy that global renewal, art and science, production and commerce began. We should mention that in Florence the large bank of the House of Medici was the latest in banking and financial procedures and management systems that invented formal accounting.

It is important to note that the movement was the product of a few scholars and not a general popular development. So, with the influx comes also expansion and social power accompanied by claims for the expansion of freedoms. We have seen that the oppression of the less affluent classes leads the people to explode in rebellion—the rebellion of the masses. The expression of discontent is not abrupt but gradual and sequential without reverse. Social differences created in a period of abundance create wealthy people, extremely rich, poor and extremely poor. Social resentment over social and economic gaps has the inevitable consequences. Social resentment and the claim of

Author created image

civil liberties include middle-business and working class. Governments are guilty because they tolerate the enrichment of the few who exploit the people.

Mercantilism[57]

(Mercantilism) It consisted of a series of measures that focused on three areas: the relations between political power and economic activity; state intervention in the latter; and currency control. Thus, they tended to state regulation of the economy, the unification of the domestic market, population growth, the increase in own production—controlling natural resources and foreign and domestic markets, protecting local production from foreign competition, subsidizing private enterprises and creating privileged monopolies—the imposition of tariffs on foreign products and the increase in monetary supply—through the prohibition of the export of precious metals and inflationary minting—always with a view to the multiplication of tax revenues. These actions were aimed at the ultimate formation of nation-state as strongly as possible.

---

[57] Fuente: https://es.wikipedia.org/wiki/Mercantilismo

Of course, in those days mercantilism focused on concepts (the policies) of state intervention in the economy, but concurrent with the absolutism of kings. The article in footnote 57 in its first paragraph says, mercantilism " [1] *It consisted of measures… focused on three areas: the relations between political power and economic activity;* [2] *State intervention in the latter; and* [3] *control of the currency. Thus, they tended to state regulation of the economy, the unification of the domestic market, population growth, the increase in own production—controlling natural resources and foreign and domestic markets, protecting local production from foreign competition, subsidizing private enterprises and creating privileged monopolies—the imposition of tariffs on foreign products and the increase in monetary supply—through the prohibition of the export of precious metals and inflationary minting—always with a view to the multiplication of tax revenues. These actions were ultimately aimed at the formation of nation-state as strongly as possible.* "

Of course, this is not what the founding fathers dreamed of for the union of the colonies. I think private enterprise is a right of citizens to form and run their own businesses with freedom of action. However, national sovereignty is based on what the constitution prescribes as the power and authority of the government protecting the life, freedom and happiness of the people, but also the general welfare. Within the general welfare is the economic life of citizens; therefore, the government must promote, channel, protect and maintain the economic system that the people choose. But private enterprise must respect the requirements and conditions of constitutional mandates.

Reforms to the constitution must clearly sanction the scope of the freedom of private enterprise on the market so that it does not infringe on the inalienable rights of citizens.

Physiocracy

It should also be noted that when the environment squeezes man, his mind works tirelessly looking for how to achieve the minimum endurance step for his life, and always finds solutions to the situation. Perhaps the situation of the Middle Ages opened the door to the rebirth, period of illustration, as a solution for Europe. One of the concepts applicable to the situation—the mentality—of the settlers is the physiocracy. [58] It's an economic way of thinking, or maybe it was a school. It was a thought that opened to private and public debate the idea that the world is endowed with an inviolable natural law—a Greek term that promoted the idea that nature has an executive authority—and this authority commands that all other natural or human rules must abide by natural laws.

The author reviewed the concept of physiocracy and found that life is a natural action of existence in which man, in general, does not participate in that creative decision of his life; but it's really not an economic think but a fact that the immediate environment doesn't fully meet the needs of each individual. Seeing this council from the point of view of economics, the physiocracy, is literally the innate regulation (mandate) of nature that specifies that what can be acquired or in fact acquired has a specific price equivalent to the sum of the acquisition costs. Everything that existence put in the universe for the benefit of life has no specific assignment for a particular life but in a uniform and equal distribution for all lives. But if everything can be acquired the price is the total costs of the acquisition. This is the *"fair price"* that Europeans gave to the products and services of nascent capitalism in the age of illustration.

The author believes human needs defines the products and services that man requires to promote and maintain life. Then a natural sequence is born that includes the mental and physical effort of how to acquire, the raw material, process it, and deliver finished products and services to the people who need them. The way they need them is also an intrinsic part of that innate regulation of nature—the physiocracy. The capital-money risked in that sequence is included in the price of the product and service delivered to purchasers. The fair price of a product or service originally conceived according to its usefulness should include standard interest plus a small profit. Therefore, the individual by natural law seeks and exchanges, something for something, with other individuals, to meet

---

[58] https://es.wikipedia.org/wiki/Fisiocracia

their needs. This exchange is part of the natural process in existence that keeps the balance of life. So, everything man needs to protect, promote, and maintain his life is part of life. This is where the need to exchange products and services with equivalent values is born.

Reading the history of Native American life in the Americas, we see that the so (wrongly) so-called Indians had their way of changing (value for value) products and services. The Mayans, for example, created a type of currency represented by cocoa seeds with which they bought products and services on the indigenous market, so

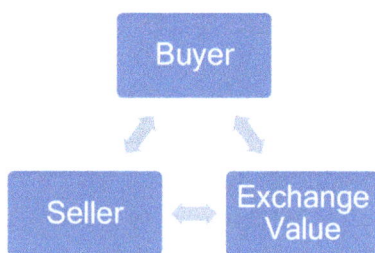
Author created image

many cocoa seeds for something they needed. In its natural form the value to the buyer and seller is the intrinsic principle of the exchange not the type of currency. The value of the coin is the value of the support (in gold, for example).

Another idea is that the product obtained from resources used in the preparation of the product must have a value greater than the sum of the input values; therefore the ”*plus value* “ of the product generated, is the economic surplus. It is clear that ideas such as physiocracy arise from the —intellectual— reaction of producers to interventionist actions, or mercantilism, of governments. Instead, freedom under physiocracy increased prosperity. The concept seems to be very valid, the freedom of production of products and services, was the solution to the economic impasse of that time. Thus, it tended to replace mercantilism with free trade. However, as we will see below, this book shows, incompatibilities with capitalism and the relationship of democratic politics—especially when the weakness of governments allows excessive capital influences over the management of the state's three powers. Actually, the latter is an attack on the constitution and popular sovereignty.

Autonomism

Autonomy is a social, economic or political attitude under which an entity, natural or legal, proposes to have the power to self-govern its behavior and or operation without the intervention of another or other external forces. [59] There are several examples of autonomous institutions in the governance structure of the United States of *America—for* example, the management of national mail, declared in the constitution, and national intelligence *institutions*.

Autonomy implies the independence, of other powers, or rather the elimination of subsidiary links or dependence on other entities, over which the executive branch should not intervene or influence. But autonomous bodies or independent agencies in the United States, while constitutionally part of the executive branch, are outside the authority of the president and are largely influenced by whims, games of interest, politicians, or personal interests of the executive. The autonomy agencies have their own characteristics and administrative organizations different from the government departments. According to their approved statutes you can say that they have their own internal constitution or operational regulations. The president should not have the authority to appoint, as in fact does, commissioners of the boards of directors of the autonomous bodies, and the president should not appoint the chairman of those boards.

From Benjamin Franklin's point of view, corruption grows and takes over the government. As we can see, presidents have the opportunity to accommodate directives in a way that favors their ideal or political parting, or their personal interests, through conditional appointments. Typical cases have been, for example, the dismissals of directors of the Federal Intelligence Agency (FBI) during the presidency of Donald Trump. The dismissal was apparently political and to cover personal interests in the president's behavior.

---

[59] https://conceptodefinicion.de/autonomia/

That is the existing danger emanating from the power and authority that the president has or self-grants, capable of modifying and or reducing to inefficient levels or even removing them from the system of government, without the other two powers being able to intervene in executive action. President Trump has managed to substantially destroy some autonomous entities, as well as has tried to eliminate or privatize the mail institution, the United States of America; it has also intervened in the structures of other autonomous institutions such as those in the intelligence community, dismissing or replacing senior officials of those institutions. These officials include James Comey, director of the federal investigative agency (FBI). The list of acts of likely abuse of authority and power is long.

Autonomism was an international movement in Europe. Records show that, in Spain, *"Autonomism is a central element of Spanish politics since the democratic transition. Autonomism exists de facto and applies to the 17 regions of the country. There are however sovereign movements in several regions, especially in historical nationalities: Aragon, Catalonia, Valencia, Basque Country, Andalusia and Galicia."*

While in France, *"Regional autonomism in France is known as decentralization, and does not arise from nationalist or independent aspirations but from the application of the Principle of Subsidiarity. The nationalist movements in Corsica, Brittany, Provence (Occitanic), and autonomists/regionalists in Alsace and Flanders have failed to change the configuration of the French state."* According to this article, decentralization in France *"transfer competences and responsibilities to new institutions. An example of institutional decentralization is the transfer of monetary policy from the Finance Minister to an independent central bank; The transfer of executive powers at the level of the prefect's departments to the departmental council, [including] primary education and vocational training. [and functionally] the transfer of a central government competence to a local government entity."*

Closer, here in the United States, Republican party governments have tried hard to privatize, a form of decentralization, the health of the people, trying to dismantle what is called, The Costly Care Act (ACA)—Obama Care Health Plans ("Obamacare"). The constitution must sanction the full independence of the autonomous entity and thus prevent the infiltration of corruption for party and or personal purposes of presidents.

Subsidiarity

On the other hand, the principle of subsidiarity implies that the authorities closer to the point-of-origin must resolve all cases, objects or problems that arise there. It is a guideline that establishes the responsibility of a central government and the rights of the states that make up the Union. However, subsidiarity does not relieve the central government of the responsibility of creating and implementing standard measures that apply to states. This is the case with the COVID-19 pandemic in 2020, when the central government did not perform or abandon its federal responsibility by not giving the guidelines to follow the states. On the one hand, the government failed, ignoring the seriousness of the impact on national health and economics—that is, social welfare and national peace of mind. The management of the cause-and-effect relationship of these matters, object or problem can—and should—be handled by the authorities close to the place where these causes occur to counteract the effect. But the central government has a responsibility to provide standard procedures to combat the problems and issues that attack the nation in a common way for states. [60]

The problem of subsidiarity is the etymological origin of the term, which entails a factor of ownership, permit and dependence, as was the case with the thirteen English colonies in America. And it was a factor of the feudalism of the Middle Ages. At that time the lords (Lords) subsidized the land in exchange for loyalty, labor, protection, and services to the Lord. In the present time you can see this concept where the authority person grants a government job or position in exchange for unconditional loyalty, and execution of tasks that benefit the representative. The employee owes the representative a favor and is engaged to the representative for that favor. On the other hand, in organizations, although the central government derives its

---

[60] https://es.wikipedia.org/wiki/Principio_de_subsidiariedad

power from the consent of the member states of the federation, the central federation assumes the supremacy of authority over the states, forgetting the origin of their power—popular sovereignty. In this case there should be no federal subsidiarity but only the power of representation of the states granted to the central government—without surrendering their legal, civil and natural rights. Remnants of this personal and political behavior were noted in Donald Trump administration when after his public announcements and dismissing the Attorney General by replacing him with another, William Barr, who gave him full loyalty and support, as his personal lawyer.

This principle of subsidiarity promotes a hierarchical social order with a higher and lower groups. Here is the anomaly of the allocation of power of governments. Under this principle, the total delegation of power of members of a federation violates natural law, putting excessive authority in the hands of the central government. In this case, the people should reduce the size of the central government to functions serving local governments' common interests. The warning of subsidiarity is its conflicting duality between its obligation and its authority. That is, the central government has an obligation to cooperate with states, and the limitations of their authority. So, it has no right to intervene in issues, problems and situations that local governments must resolve on their own—only if the states ask for. For example, the president has no right or authority to mobilize the national guard to reduce or eliminate demonstrations or popular demonstrations in states.

Principles of order

There really is no subsidiarity; if we consider that a central government is formed by the consent of the members of its union receiving the power of representation of the union. This notion is confirmed with the limited time of his function in office—neither long term or permanent. Contrary to this principle, it is not the central government that assigns the responsibilities of the members but the will of the members of the union, coming from popular sovereignty, who assigns the functions of the central government through the constitution of the union.

Separation of powers

In this theory, Montesquieu proposed a model of government that divides the powers of the state into three independent powers so that these branches of powers do not enter into conflicts or interfere with the authority and functions of the other branches of power. The typical division proposes three powers, a legislature, an executive power, and a judiciary—that is, the political triad. This division is contrary to the merger of powers in a parliament, where the legislative and executive branch overlap. The separation of powers prevents the concentration of these three powers, promoting oversight and balance of the executive power. That's the mirage of the concept of a republican government: the integrity of its three powers. It is chimeric because it depends on the honesty of the representatives that the people choose in electoral suffrage. As Benjamin Franklin warned, corruption takes power from the government and destroys the Union's constitutional intent every two hundred years. And the government of this Union has already had that situation. [61]

But let's go over the story of the colonization for another moment. Over the years the discovery of America by Christopher Colon, Aristotle, nearly the middle of the fifteenth century announced the idea of mixed governments in his writing *"politics."* He suggested different constitutional forms for cities and states. At the same time as Aristotle, John Calvin said Democracy. *"It is an invaluable gift if God allows a people to choose their own government and magistrates."* On this point, he suggested setting up a number of complementary political institutions that control each other within a system of supervision and balance sheets. It was obvious that Calvin did not tolerate absolutist politics and preferred the power of the people. And it is good to note that the pilgrim parents installed a tripartite democratic system of government in the Colony of Plymouth in North America.

---

[61] https://en.wikipedia.org/wiki/Separation_of_powers

"Free men" chose the general court, functioning as legislative and judicial power, and this power, in turn, elects the governor, and together with his seven assistants, constituted executive power. The other colonies, Massachusetts, Rhode Island, Connecticut, New Jersey, and Pennsylvania installed similar democratic systems. But the colonies of Plymouth and Massachusetts added freedom of worship.

Montesquieu maintained in his philosophy and by inference it can be concluded that if a power has the authority to elect members of another power the separation of power ceases to exist. For this reason, a democratic system must lay down effective rules that eliminate the application of the concept "divide and command" proposed by Niccolò di Bernardo die Machiavelli—supposedly the father of philosophy and political science. The principle of oversight and balance in a government implies stability and self-control of power. Supervision and balance sheeting mandates that each branch of government have power and authority to limit or supervise the other two, creating the balance of power in all three branches. Therefore, the equitable power of each branch prevents any branch from becoming supreme and absolute. Unfortunately, Montesquieu did not include in theory the influence of corruption, and Machiavelli triumph. It is not that dishonesty is uncontrollable, but that the system is not perfected to reduce, eliminate and ensure that corruption is resorted to in governments. That is why the founders said they form a more perfect Union, implying that this Union is exposed to corruption and it is necessary to seal the entrances through which rats enter.

Discourse on inequality

According to the author, every condition of inequality between men is born of the decomposition of the soul and the evil attitudes of their egos—as well as selfishness, egocentrism, or egotist. But the author interprets the philosophy that Rousseau (Jean Jacques) established in his *discourse on the origin and foundations of inequality among men.* According to his discourse, all social problems and ills are first and for all due to the gaps or inequalities of men founded on a single cause from the state of sociability. Rousseau considered that "the structure and image of man is always the same, vague and wild", primitively. Rousseau proposed that "the distinction of animals as free has the capacity to morally perfect itself." Rousseau thought that man is endowed with a natural feeling, piety; therefore, it is not a perverse or evil body, being that it lends itself to helping and succoring the sufferer. Thus, man originally lived in harmony with nature until the property pandemic infected his mind; according to Rousseau, when the man said *"this is mine,"* the concept of ownership first appears, and man founds civil society—the author agrees with this precept. And from there, the race to guard, increase without limits, all *"what is mine"* began. And consequently, the notion of imposition and dominion over others is born—the concept of power. Even more so in the desires to protect what's *"mine"* are born with agreements and commitments, alliances and joint activities, giving way to the creation of civil society and the laws that regulate human behavior, guaranteeing the right over what is mine. Inequality is born from all this—the difference between weak and strong; and man's natural freedom. Disputes with the definition of property both generate the need to maintain peace and social cordiality and the concept of agreements. Consequently, this anthropological and philosophical thought, Rousseau conforms to his theory of social contract.

Social Contract

The author's research finds a wealth of information on the Internet; and reads and analyzes several articles of public information. While working as the ambassador's secretary in Venice, Italy, in 1743, Rousseau began writing a book on the subject of freedom and equality. Meanwhile, the colonies remained involved in their development and controversies with the impositions of the English crown. A summary of Rousseau's work appears in 1762, entitled *"The Social Contract or Principles of Political Law".* [62] This book deals with political philosophy, covering the theme of freedom and equality. Rousseau's philosophy considered that the individual is

---

[62] https://es.wikipedia.org/wiki/El_contrato_social

fundamental within the social convivial, and therefore the harmony of the conviviality is in function of the general will. Rousseau does not finish writing that book, but composes a summary of what was his work of the social contract in four volumes. In the first volume, he writes that man is born free by nature, *"Man is born free, and yet everywhere he is chained;"* and on the other hand, he adds that *"family is the first model of political society."* Rousseau opposes the right of the strongest and says, *"Let us therefore agree that force is not a right, and that it is only obliged to obey legitimate powers."*

The author agrees with this philosophy and maintains that this is the case of autocratic rulers or dictators, who usurp the power of the people and subdue them by military force and corrupt political dominance they maintain. In his second tome Rousseau exposes, on the one hand, the idea that the people seek abundance and peace; he thought freedom is up to an equality; *"it is precisely because the strength of things always tends to destroy equality, so that the force of legislation must always maintain it."* Perhaps we can understand that force can be nothing more than the government's abuse of power, and therefore the legal framework must protect the right of the people to maintain equality; so, if the laws are not enforced or are not done for this purpose the government becomes a tyranny, a dictatorship or a monarchy. In the third volume, Rousseau believes that democracy is such a perfect form of government that it never occurs in its pure form; the gods are governed democratically, *"but such a perfect government is not typical of men."* The author differs in this, and even if true, he thinks that the deviation at first is not to have a well-defined cause and a serious and enforceable rule of law for man to follow the norm. On the other hand, this attitude is dictatorial and taxable; when in reality what is required is for man to work for the common cause by his own volition. The author thinks that man will work for the common cause when the benefit is just and equal. This is the point of reforming the constitution, that in order to make a Union more perfect, it is necessary to draft and sanction laws guaranteeing the six objectives (or mandates) and the four fundamental evidence presented in the paragraph of Chapter 2.

The perfection of democracy depends on the perfection of man, rather his ego, and it is greed and human selfishness that causes the imperfection of democracy. For seeing this case from a contributory point of view, it can be established that the rise, the welfare and total peace of a society is the sum of the boom, welfare and individual peace. So as long as that state of boom, welfare and general peace is not achieved, social differences will always cause nonconformances, social rifts and discord policy. For example, the following.

1.– "The more the state grows, the more freedom decreases.
2.– "The government to be good, must be relatively stronger as the people become more numerous.
3.– The more numerous the magistrates, the weaker the government.
4.– The resolution of cases becomes slower as more people are taken care of.

Rousseau presents these phrases alluding to nonconformism and social differences, giving points of arithmetic. It is obvious to the author that the larger the state—the organized sum of all its elements, population, territory, power, government and law—freedom is reduced by respect for the right of others. Then for a government to be a good government, it must consolidate its functions more effectively and efficiently as the population grows in number. It is also clear that the efficiency of the government is not in the bureaucracy because it returns to the inefficient government. And on the other hand, the greater the number of decision-making authorities, the greater the number of opinions, and the weaker the decisive process. and the slow resolution of government affairs is slower.

Rousseau writes in his fourth book *that kind men righteously need few laws.* This is true because these men who belong to a class who respect other people's right of their own truly do not need additional legal obligations to behave responsibly. The ideal is that the will of these simple men be the general and sustained will of all members of the state. The author already mentioned that man acts as he is treated or mistreated, and when the benefit of the common cause is equal, man works for general welfare. We must reform the constitution to institute, promote, care for, and maintain the country's social, political and economic equality.

The author finds an information in an article on the Internet. This article dates back to another of the great thinkers in the field of political issues—John Locke—who writes about political philosophy. Locke, in addition to his attack on patriarchalism, focuses his thinking on the theory of political or civil society, published in 1689, based on natural rights and the social contract. Locke writes two treatises, according to the article in footnote 64. The first Treaty Locke challenges the divine right of kings—treated upon the government to its challenge. In his first treatise, Locke introduces a blunt theory of political or civil society. In the second treaty he presents his theory of state, focusing on natural rights and social contract. [63, 64]

Causes and consequences of separation

From all that we have read in the prologue and in this chapter one, we can summarize the causes and consequences of the resentment of the inhabitants of the colonies of North America. The territorial wars of Europe's powers economically weaken the great monarchies—as can be seen with the outcome of the seven-year war. The end of the Middle Ages and feudalism was another important factor. But the intellectual awakening of Europeans with the rebirth and period of enlightenment gave these people a new perspective on life. With this perspective came the anthropocentric concept. With this new thinking the individual recognizes the importance of his presence in the universe, discovering that only knowledge can, and actually advances, humanity—humanism. An in-depth review of what happened at the time reveals certain interesting and influential aspects to the mental framework of North American settlers. Rural

[63] https://es.wikipedia.org/wiki/Dos_tratados_sobre_el_gobierno_civil
[64] https://en.wikipedia.org/wiki/John_Locke

nobility and feudalism declines in the face of the concept of real power, giving way to authoritarian monarchies of urban character. Cities are born and the bourgeoisie emerges as a social class involved in artisanal, industrial and commercial activities.

Life changes; and the concept of money comes out of the need for immediate exchange—that is, the value of change. And not only this, the move from rural to urban awakens the intellectual unease driven by the demand for services. And with this comes scientific curiosity, too. People's mindset expands and critical thinking awakens. This critical thinking develops the urgency of gaining more and more knowledge, reading and studying. And inventions flourish, including printing, facilitating the spread of new ideas. And for the first time, schools—literacy, schools, and universities—emerge. The motion of illustration takes man beyond his physical existence; it pushes him to understand that he is a more extensive person than his anatomical and biological being. And art and admiration of aesthetic pleasure flourishes, including literature and poetry. It seems that the discovery of America not only confirms the sphericity of the earth but throws scientific thought to study what surrounds the earth—such as astronomy, physics, chemistry, etc. Geographical boundaries expand and trade develops. But England welcomes this age of illustration until almost the end of the 16th century, when in the middle of this century the English colonies of North America barely asserted their settlements. There were great thinkers and philosophers in that period such as Charles Louis Montesquieu, Jean Jacques Rousseau. The first creates the theory of separation of powers and wrote the *Spirit of laws;* [65, 66] and the second writes the discourse of inequality and proposes the social contract and confections.[67]

[65] https://en.wikipedia.org/wiki/Montesquieu
[66] https://en.wikipedia.org/wiki/Jean-Jacques_Rousseau
[67] https://es.wikipedia.org/wiki/El_espritu_de_las_leyesritu_de_las_leyes

The Spirit of the Law

It is a treatise on public theory and comparative law, published in 1748 (28 years before the independence of English colonies in North America). This theory suggests points of great importance, for example, Montesquieu states that *"executive, legislative and judicial powers should not concentrate on the same hands."* The author praises Montesquieu's theory that *"every power counteracts and balances the other two."* However, the author finds certain weaknesses in theory, such as the origin of the social *organization* and the virtue of compliance with their *respective principles of government.* Both the social organization and the complying with principles of government may have flaws in its conception, in its implementation, and in its implementation, and not to represent the will of popular sovereignty—therefore, the system fails. A potential danger has already been presented, such as the concentration of the three powers in the hands of only one of the three powers—which comes to be practically an autocracy, dictatorship or tyranny. Montesquieu takes the conceptualization of three types of government (1) aristocrat, (2) democracy, and (3) monarchy to classify governments into three classes and proposed (1) the [aristocratic and democratic] republican government, (2) monarchical, and (3) despotic. For Montesquieu's reasons that power should not be concentrated in the same hands, the need for the president of the United States to not have the power or authority to nominate supreme court judges, federal judges, or power over independent agencies, is emphasized. Nor should he have powers to place him above the rules of law and have the power to go over court decisions forgiving people sentenced for their crimes. This authority and power fosters corruption and destroys constitutional principles.

The author does not find the logic of change—the proposal is like having bananas of three sizes, and then grouping them into three groups by weight range; they will always be the same bananas. On the other hand, classification by the nature of each government, based on who has power and how it executes it is more feasible. Montesquieu describes his classification in three main government categories.

1.- The republican government where the people, or a part of it, retain sovereign power (democracy or aristocracy) and the people are responsible for making the laws.

2.- The monarchical government where the king holds power and exercises it under a structure of fixed and established laws.

3.- The despotic government where a person holds power and exercises them without fixed laws imposing his personal whims.

Of course, of the three options above, the first is the one that the founding fathers chose for the Union. We have seen that the colonies formed their own government in a similar way. We have also seen, and it is the subject of this book, that the Government of the Union has its flaws and is exposed to corruption and abuse of the powers by politicians for purposes that are not of the people. The author believes that republican government and democracy is not enough. In other words, popular sovereignty is not just the voting period (the day). Nor does the vote mean the granting of a very general power to the president and other public officials in the government. Nor is it a license to stand above the law and to abuse the power and authority that the people grant to elected and nominated representatives. A fourth version of government is a higher democracy, where the people are the sovereign state, which elects all representatives in the three powers by their will and popular vote, and reviews the laws that the legislature makes before passing into law in force. A democracy where the citizens claim their independence, freedom, and rights with one voice to govern their elected government.

"--What, to secure these rights, governments are instituted among men, deriving their just powers from the consent of the governed, --That whenever any form of government becomes destructive to these purposes, it is the right of the people to alter or abolish it, and to institute a new government, laying its foundations on principles and the organization of their powers in such a way, in that they will seem more likely to indeed seem

> to be their security and happiness." "... and, consequently, every experience has sown, that humanity is more willing to suffer, while evils are suffering, than to straighten themselves by abolishing the forms to which they are accustomed. But when a long train of abuse and usurpation, invariably pursuing the same Object, evidences a design for reducing them under absolute despotism, it is their right, it is their duty to discard that government, and provide new guards for their future security."

It is clear that the constitution considers the possibility for its representatives to abuse the powers and authorities they receive from the people. Therefore, they also established in the letter and spirit of that document the solution to the situation in the quotation, saying *"discarding that government, and providing new guards for their future security."* Consequently, when the people publicly express their discontent and demand a form and thorough substitution of their government, they do so with the explicit right that the constitution sanctions. This is the sovereign right of the people and we cannot categorize it by any qualifying adjective other than the exercise of their natural right—the management of their Life and Destiny. However, the legislative branch has failed to establish a constitutional process that aims to dissever the government and propose new guardians when it fails or violates constitutional mandates.

Natural rights

Locke was aware from the moment he conceived his argument that any new system is always exposed to political corruption. And he resolves by proposing that a constitutional king that is subordinate to civil power (of parliament) is more than enough. He then adds that a state must have a political trichotomy; raised in three powers that prevent political corruption. He meant (1) a legislative power, (2) an executive power, and (3) the federal power (the house of representatives today). The interesting thing about his political philosophy is that he was thinking (at all times) of national sovereignty (or popular sovereignty). Locke has certain cracks in his philosophy, because he entrusts the authority to choose , after being elected by the people–to members of the executive branch, in addition to making the laws. This proposition is incorrect and dangerous, as evidenced by the actions of governments. It is also not true that these three powers eliminate political corruption because the system itself is subject to the influence of corruption—as history demonstrates. It was therefore not the solution sought for a more perfect democracy. There is no denying, however, the greatness of John Locke's thought. Nor can Locke's influence in the enlightened and American thoughts be denied. In the mind of the author of this book, "Reforms," American democracy has a long way to go. And of course, the evidence of the impact of John Locke's political philosophy leaps into reality in proclaiming the independence of the English colonies in America. The political model of the separation of powers, as a spirit, was introduced in the drafting of the constitution of the United States of America. The author notes that Locke's approach does not define natural law, nor popular sovereignty, explicitly, although he speaks of human natural rights.

John Locke (August. 29, 1632 – October. 28, 1704)

image borrowed from the Internet

English philosopher and physician, widely regarded as one of the most influential of Enlightenment thinkers and commonly known as the «Father of Liberalism."

image borrowed from the Internet

From left to right: John *Adams, George Washington, Thomas Jefferson, Benjamin Franklin, and Alexander Hamilton.*

We, the people, owe them the power and glory of life with rights in *"... a nation under God, indivisible, with freedom and justice for all,"* designed under the concept that all men are created equally.

CHAPTER 4

Fundamental Principles

We cannot cling to a single strong and pure demographic line, when by the 1500 the cultural mix—social, education, politics and economics—was the result of the influences of new thoughts of the people in the European nations of those times, in particular Spain and France. So, we cannot insist that the independence movement was an English movement, isolated and without the influence of external international forces or thoughts. The age of illustration had already permeated in the minds of settlers even before reaching the colonies of North America. The settlers already brought their principles based on philosophical thoughts of freedom, self-determination and national or popular sovereignty. It is then appropriate to carefully review the main progressive thoughts that influenced the settlers' thinking and decision in 1776. Although all social, economic and political issues influenced the thinking of the people of the American colonies, there are certain issues that stand out for their influence in the formulation of the democratic republic of the United States of America.

Pluralism

Pluralism is a form of diversification of the concept of participation in social, economic, and political life. This concept refers to the presence of multiple interest groups, possibly consolidated within a social, economic or political system; and those interests influence decision-making in general. Pluralism accepts the participation of all members of the group. [68] In reality, it is the basis of democracy, from which the sovereign power of the people is derived. In homogeneous societies where all people are of a single culture, political thinking, customs and cults pluralism comes down to—becoming—monism.

The case of the thirteen colonies is different from the beginning of their settlements. And we have quickly seen the influences exerted on the colonies with settlers from various nations in Europe. This is why the factor of pluralism becomes important, both in the social, economic, and of course political aspects. Perhaps from this pluralistic concept the application of the concept of Union is born, confirmed with the Latin phrase that says *"e pluribus unum"* or the phrase "union makes *strength*". Either way, demographic diversity had to act as a homogeneous mass to realize the common dream. But in addition to the above, the challenge of pluralism, social, religious, political thinking, and economic theories to heterogeneous peoples is the form of integration into a union. Integration needs the forces that bind plurality stronger than the ideological differences that separate them. In other words, the sum of the positive and negative forces plus the benefits of the union is zero (they are in balance). The benefits of freedom are the difference between positive and negative forces, where positive forces are greater than negative ones. Then peoples come together in a common cause (the American dream): To form a more perfect Union (every day) with justice, tranquility, security, and general welfare, which ensures the benefit of freedom for all, the people. The key to uniting different interests, beliefs, philosophies is in the common benefits for every member of society. That is, the benefits obtained must be greater than the sacrifices made to obtain those benefits. This was the situation of the colonies, and the union offered them the opportunity to achieve these benefits—those that are summed up in the concept of general welfare. They rolled the dice; luck was cast.

---

[68] https://es.wikipedia.org/wiki/Pluralismo

The Natural Law

What is "natural law"? The author considers natural law is the representation of the truth of the reality of existence—in this case, human. It is the logical truth of life, not only of man but of all living beings. An article on the internet defines this term as follows.

Natural Law is a moral theory of jurisprudence that maintains that the law must be based on morality and ethics. The Natural Law argues that the law is based on what is "right." The Natural Law is "discovered" by humans through the use of reason and choosing between good and evil. Therefore, the power of the Natural Law lies in discovering certain universal standards of morality and ethics.[69]

The greatness of the concept quoted above is to accept that existence has a standard of ethical and moral behavior, which humans must abide by. And government decisions must be not out of necessity but because it is right to do so. In reality, natural law is a quality of the feeling, of the soul, or of the jurisprudence of human conscience that judges what is good or bad, right or wrong, just or unjust and also—why not—the pleasant or unpleasant. And the quotation in conclusion says, *Finally, where does the law come from? The Natural Law Theory maintains that certain moral laws transcend time, culture, and government. There are universal standards that apply to all humanity throughout all times. These universal moral standards are inherent and recognizable by all of us, and form the basis of a just society.* The author adds that existence gives a pattern of behavior for living beings—particularly for humans—composed of tranquility, satisfaction, and gratitude. It is the ethical and moral channel that exists alongside popular sovereignty. Popular sovereignty is a mirage if man does not abide by the natural laws. People must not allow representatives elected to public offices to hold their positions for personal benefits, in any form, or method. Man is born free, free to move within his environment and choose from the resources of that environment what is necessary for his subsistence; free to think and shout to the wind how hw feels and thinks; free to associate

---

[69] https://www.allaboutphilosophy.org/spanish/ley-natural.htm

with one or more humans, and to form societies, communities, nations; free to create and establish governments that ensure the just and equitable relationship between all men, the people: this is the popular sovereignty.

Liberalism [70]

Liberalism is a thought of liberality. Natural law and popular sovereignty point to the path of liberalism. [71] That is, liberalism is the idea that each individual *brings the freedom of the individual and the minimum intervention of the state in social and economic life.* This is where free enterprise and the free market are born. This liberalism was the condition that the colonizers of America wished to obtain for the development of trade and social and economic welfare of their colonies. Therefore, the government, representing the people, is responsible for ensuring the interests of the people. It should not allow the free enterprise to abuse the naivety of the people. Even though an enterprise is private choice, part of life. It must not endanger the general welfare of the people. That is, since the government is responsible for the six constitutional mandates and its four-evidence presented above, it should not allow the free enterprise to exploit, deceive, abuse and impede the constitutional rights of the people, allowing the right of fair competition.

According to Wikipedia Liberalism [72] *"is a political, economic and social doctrine that defends individual freedom, equality before the law and a reduction of the power of the state... it generally defends individual rights (mainly freedom of expression, freedom of the press and religious freedom), the free market, secularism, gender equality and racial equality, capitalism, private property, democracy, the rule of law, open society and internationalism...* [and also] *opposes absolutism, and conservatism."*

---

[70] http://etimologias.dechile.net/?liberalismo
[71] https://en.wikipedia.org/wiki/History_of_liberalism
[72] https://es.wikipedia.org/wiki/Liberalismo

Conservatism

What is conservatism? Quote 74, defines conservatism as *"In politics, the set of doctrines, currents, opinions and positions, usually of center right and right, that favor traditions and that are opposed to radical political, social or economic changes, opposing progressivism, is called conservatism".* [73]

The political inclination of conservatism is to keep the status quo, opposing progressivism. In other words, conservatism supports the preservation of traditions, rejects radical changes, although it protects moral, religious rights in society. Conservatism does not allow economic progress. The author finds in another quotation a definition that says *"Conservatism is a term that refers to all those doctrines, tendencies or opinions that are based on belief in an order, law or natural right, and, consequently, adhere to traditions or customs while resisting political changes; that is, they intend to preserve"* the status quo. *Therefore, conservatism often opposes progressive policies".* [74]

It is clear that the foundation, bases, of the declaration of independence of the American colonies should be clearly defined to create, establish and perpetuate a political, economic social balance favoring the people of the new American nation. Liberal and conservative political currents existed before the first problems with the absolutism of the British reign. As can be read in the writings of the different characters participating in the independence process of America.

In 1789, the French tired of so many years of absolute monarchy sought popular sovereignty with freedom and fraternity. It was a political, social, economic and military movement, which overthrew the absolutist monarchy that until then had ruled France, leading to the establishment of a democratic republican government. The causes that gave rise to the French Revolution were: Monarchical absolutism, characterized by the boundless power of the King, whose authority was not subject to any control: Social, political and

---

[73] https://www.significados.com/conservadurismo
[74] https://es.wikipedia.org/wiki/Conservadurismo

economic inequality; lack of freedoms and rights. To these causes we must add an important factor: the powerful influence of new ideas. Perhaps it is necessary to know the philosophical and moral thinking of the founders in order to understand the foundations of the United States Union. Reading the phrases of the declaration of independence we listen the philosophy of the founders and the thought of all who agreed to the letter of the declaration. For example

"... the separate and egalitarian station to which the laws of Nature and the God of Nature gives them rights..."

"that all men are created equal, that they are endowed by their Creator with certain inalienable rights..."

This is the intrinsic foundation of the nation that the founders created. They clearly publicly stated that nature exists, (existence or universe) and has laws applicable to human life. The integrated thinking of the founders evidently accepted that, under these laws, the Creator's intention is to create all men equally and give them rights that no man can break, reduce, alter, or eliminate, they are inalienable rights. Moreover, the founders explicitly state that among these rights the Creator confers on men the right *to life, Freedom and the pursuit of Happiness.* That is, the Creator of Nature grants Life, freedom and opportunities to seek Happiness. Attributes that no man can deny. Then the founders expanded their interpretation of the Creator's will, and declared that by these rights they together decide to *"form a more perfect Union, establish justice, ensure national tranquility, tend to the common defense, promote general well-being and ensure the benefits of freedom for us and for our posterity";* and this commitment was only to protect those three rights, Life, Freedom, and the pursuit of Happiness.

Popular sovereignty

The feeling of the colonizers of the thirteen colonies in America was controversial. Were they truly free from the English crown or do they live forever subordinate to Britain and its Parliament? There are precedents elsewhere.

The highlight of the French Revolution of 1789 is the idea of the ownership of the sovereignty of a nation, a monarch, a ruler, a political party or the people. With all the right and accuracy of thought scholars such as, Thomas Hobbes, John Locke and Jean-Jacques Rousseau, and also Benjamin Franklin. And this philosophy spreads to the rest of the world. But the seed of the concept of "popular sovereignty" was part of the concepts included in the foundations of the independence of the thirteen American colonies.

According to this article on the Internet; *"The term popular sovereignty was coined against that of national sovereignty, which was interpreted narrowly as sovereignty resident in the nation, a difficult definition that can be more difficultly identified and restricted in its effective representation to the highest layers of society (universal suffrage); while the principle of popular sovereignty is born with constitutional rights and guarantees. The theoretical principle on which all conceptions of democracy are based and which today has virtually universal acceptance as the source of all power and authority. As a modern political doctrine, it comes from Rousseau. People are a historical unity of common customs and habits of life; whose members agree to form a state to govern itself better in a sovereign way (without another power above it). The people constitute the state, and then control and change it if it deems it appropriate. The people owe nothing to their rulers, who are servants, scribes, or messengers of the popular will. At the same time, the people have great power over individuals, only compensated for by the reciprocity of their situation"*. [75]

Within this concept of *"popular sovereignty"*, the rulers are servants, scribes or messengers of the popular will; The people owe nothing to their rulers. But their rulers owe the people honesty, loyalty, and efficiency in the administration of the people's affairs and businesses. The concept of popular sovereignty and natural laws do not particularize a class of men, it is general, conclusive and collective. It applies to all the people of the world. And as far as a government is concerned, the point that *"a government can only exist with the consent of the people"* necessarily implies that its government

---

[75] https://es.wikipedia.org/wiki/Soberanía_popular

does so through its representatives, chosen in free and popular vote who must abide by the will of the people. The expression of the will of the people, democracy—the power of the people.

The framework of laws

There are two kinds of laws in existence, the laws enacted and the Nature. The laws (positive) enacted are fallible while natural laws are infallible. The former is flawed and vulnerable and susceptible to human selfishness, ill-intention, hidden agendas and personal interests. Natural laws apply justice with proportional consequences applied in due course—often immediate—without the possibility of forgiveness. In reality, no, forgiveness of sins does not exist and is always paid under the justice of natural laws. This degree of justice does not exist in the laws enacted; and the application of laws and punishments are articles at auctions of human mercantilism. In this mercantilism the rich, famous and the power of the rich buy and sell the justice of the laws enacted. Justice is often exchanged with or favors that those who sell justice receive favors, loyalty or economic. Presidential pardon could be in this category. The situation is different for the poor or those who cannot afford the price of justice at auction. The manipulation of the laws enacted is an immediate consequence of the nature of the corrupt man. The founding fathers of the United States of America knew of this situation and with knowledge of cause publicly stated.

> 1— *"We consider these truths to be evident, that all men are created equal, that they are endowed by their Creator with certain inalienable rights, which include life, liberty, and the pursuit of Happiness."* And so, they say more.
>
> 2— *"When in the course of human events, it is necessary for a people to dissolve the political bands that have connected them with another, and to assume among the powers of the earth, the separate and egalitarian station to which the Laws of Nature and the God of Nature gives them the right, a decent respect for the opinions of humanity requires them to declare*

the causes that drive them to separation." Consequently, also according to natural laws claimed are the rights that the God of Nature conferred upon them to execute an end, a purpose.

3— *"in order to form a more perfect Union, establish Justice, ensure inner peace of mind, provide for common defense, promote general well-being, and secure for us and our prosperity the benefits of Freedom, establish and sanction this Constitution for the United States of America."*

Moreover, and with the sole idea that the United States of America represents a geographical territory, individuals, the inhabitants, who have the capacity for opinion and vote, of the thirteen colonies declare the unity of citizens; and the founders incorporated in their banners, emblems and stamps, the Latin expressions "e *pluribus unum (all in one)"*, under the great concept of *Novus Ordo Decorum* (a New Order of the Centuries). So, the new government is a stable order over time; and only natural people enter the union. Thus, legal persons, created by laws enacted, not having the characteristics, attributes and capacities, of natural persons, created equal by the Creator, do not fall into or belong to the category of natural persons that make up the Union—the United States of America. Only natural persons for natural rights have the right to participate in the efforts of their government, which is of the people, for the people and for the people—the people composed of natural people.

Neither the declaration of independence nor the constitution grants any right of participation inherent in the government to any economic, social, religious or political system. But they clearly state that *"Religious Testing will never be required as a condition of any public office or mandate depending of the United States."* That is, the constitution does not discriminate against any person because of his religious inclination to hold a public office.

And the founders of the Union established that *"We, the People [of the colonies], established and sanctioned this Constitution for the United States of America—the* people of the colonies consent. The phrase at the end of the quote, *"this constitution for the United States*

153

of America" suggests or implies *"We the People"* and no one but the people, natural people.

The founders clearly established, in the text of the declaration of independence, that the power of their governments is born of the power of the people, saying *"—That, in order to secure these rights,* [of the people], *governments are instituted among men, deriving their righteous powers from the consent of the governed."* That is, not of legal persons because they are the property of natural persons, and cannot and should not assume or take equal rights to natural persons to which the legal personhood belongs. Legal person is a concept entailing a double participation, as the owner and as that entity; one is a natural person and another is property of the legal person—If we recognize both persons implies giving double representation to a natural person in all affairs, unfair for the rest of people.

On the other hand, the laws that Congress issues must adhere to the constitution of the United States of America, according to the manifesto, *"This Constitution, and the Laws of the United States issued under it;"* The author interprets the phrase *"The United States will guarantee every state of this Union a form of republican government,…"* —which implies that the United States government is republican. The idea is according to the intrinsic definition being that certain representatives chosen by the people in electoral suffrage represent the people in the management of their government—the representatives. But what defines the government as a republican is the structuring of power that derives from the people in three branches (executive power, legislative power, and judiciary) under the constitution. However, for the reason that the founders left in the hands of the people the sovereignty of the Union and the right of the people to elect their rulers the political system is a democracy.

Then the government of the United States of America has a republican structure governed by a democratic system, —the power of the people. Therefore, the three powers of the State, established by the will of the people, with representatives elected by choice of the people, are subordinated to the will of the people. And the people reserve their right to *"… form a more perfect Union, establish justice, ensure inner peace of mind, provide for the common defense, promote general well-being and ensure for us and for our prosperity the benefits of freedom."* It is clear that this right includes reforming its constitution with amendments for those purposes where necessary. There have already been sufficiently serious developments demonstrating the weakness and vulnerability of the established constitution and form of government; for example, during the administrations of Andrew Jackson, Richard Nixon, Bill Clinton and Donald Trump. The political process of dismissal has been different in these three cases; although they somehow present a pattern of corruption in the executive power of the constitutionalized republican government. The action of attorney general William Barr is clear evidence of the rampant corruption and intent to prostitute the principles of the government, constitution and democracy of the United States of America, acting as President Donald Trump's personal lawyer. The founders anticipated this vulnerability and the tendency to corruption that some representative of the people may practice as the president of the republic. And to protect the democratic system they included in the constitution a process of political impeachment with which a representative can be removed from his political post. The House of Representatives has *"the absolute power to bring dismissal charges in Political Trials"* [Art. 1, Sec. 2].

Likewise, the founders prevented the process of dismissal from being done by hidden agendas instigated by political reasons or party interests, clarifying this point in the declaration of independence; *" "Prudence, in fact, will dictate that long-established governments should not be changed for light and transitional reasons; and, consequently, every experience has sown, that humanity is more willing to suffer, while evils are suffering, than to straighten themselves by abolishing the forms to which they are accustomed"* [Middle of the Second Paragraph] of the Declaration of Independence]. However, they clearly sanctioned the condition or conditions by which the process of dismissal can be executed; that is *"...when a long train of abuse and usurpation, invariably pursuing the same Object evidences a design to reduce them under absolute despotism, it is their right, it is their duty, to discard that government, and to provide new guards for their future security"* [End of the Second Paragraph] of the Declaration of Independence. However, governments (their three powers), present and past, have ignored the mandate to *"form a more perfect Union"* in this regard. That is, it is not yet constitutionally or legally clear what *"a long train of abuse" is,* but President Donald Trump's behavior is clear and leaves the historical evidence of pursuing *"invariably the Same Object evidences a design to reduce them* [the people] *under absolute despotism..."* But, to do so, the senate by its majority leader in Trump's time, concealed the president's performance. The constitution must be reformed so that situations like these do not happen again in the future. Thus, we fulfill the constitutional mandate "in order to form a more *perfect Union, establish Justice, ensure inner tranquility, provide for the common defense, promote general welfare and ensure for us and for our prosperity the benefits of Freedom."* The government fails to serve these six terms.

The legal basis was established on the basis of the declaration of cause and effect that support independence and in the constitution that forms the superlative law of the legal framework of the United States of America. And there is no law higher than this constitution, after popular sovereignty; and all laws enacted must be settled in accordance with that supreme law. The founders sanctioned the responsibility to understand all disputes, both law and equity, arising as a result of that constitution, of the laws of the United States. The judiciary will be under the eminent danger of party politicization and personal benefits that may corrupt the fundamental intent of the founders. This is with regard to the process of nominating candidates to the Supreme Court of Justice by the president of the republic. The nomination is weak and vulnerable to the party forces. History has already recorded some cases of nomination and approval rigged and manipulated by the interests of a political party occupying a majority of the Senate. There is a high probability of corruption that a magistrate is obliged to pay the favor of being nominated and approved with another and other favors to those who approve the appointment. Obviously, this train of actions corrupts democracy, steals the sovereignty of the people, violates the constitution, destroys the fundamental separation of powers from the republic. These cases certainly fall into the abuses that the declaration of independence seeks to prevent and consequently the facts, consensual and beneficiaries are subject to the process of political dismissal. The constitution and the framework of laws must be amended, covered and sealed by these loopholes.

Obedience to the Rules of Law

We have already seen the point of civil and political rights in this chapter the harmonious social coexistence with the members of a group or community, satisfied with the respect for the Life, Freedom and quest for the Happiness of the other members of the group. Therefore, individual peace and security in participation in the community and people depends on such respect and obedience to the legal regime approved by the people.

Humanism [76]

Humanist philosophy brings to man a new way of thinking; and takes the mind to a higher plane where human value assumes the concept of anthropocentrism, abandoning the old concept of Theo centrism. The awakening of thought redirecting to reason during the European renaissance and the period of illustration. Man conceives of his true value as a human being, concluding that he is the main factor in the world; adding that it is, *"the center of all things—the absolute end of creation."* The ability to acquire knowledge and the ability to think and reason clearly puts it on that higher plane above all living beings. The founders drafted the constitution with obvious humanitarian aspects that say *"all men are created equal, which are endowed by their Creator with certain inalienable rights..."* This is the beauty included in the spirit and letter of the declaration of independence. Among these humanitarian aspects, they considered the civil freedom of all.

Man conceives his true value as a human being concluding that he is the main factor in the world; adding that it is, *"the center of all things—the absolute end of creation."* The ability to acquire knowledge

---

[76] https://es.wikipedia.org/wiki/Humanismo_renacentista

and the ability to think and reason clearly puts it on that higher plane above all living beings.

Civil Freedom. [77]

Civil freedom is a natural right that gives man unrestricted access, if he so wishes, to lawful situations framed by the legal framework of that civil freedom. So, any right that is not sanctioned by a legal regulation must be considered, and in fact, a natural right.

The concept of total freedom is a mirage, individual or group, political and social—and even economic—but always related to the human being. Even in the case of individual isolation in any environment—that is, in its natural state—man is always limited, mentally and physically. Man's freedom exists only in his freedom of choice—free will—, thinking and acting, involving movement, to his taste within his natural environment. This natural (environmental) freedom is reduced in direct proportion to the number of people who enter to live in the same environment. This is the point; the entire environment and resources of the environment that were only of the first man who lived alone, are now shared among each and every one and other individuals who inhabit that environment—as a group, society or *community*. The concept of individual law is born and demands reciprocal respect from each individual towards others. And with this respect also comes the need to agree among all the rules (laws) of the movement within, and the use of the resources of the environment. There is no initial charter; the resources of the environment are owned by all men in the environment, and the use and usufruct of such resources are also the property of all men. So, the added value, for the work of extracting, processing and manufacturing such resources in usable products, plus the distribution effort are costs that the producer has the right to recover, in addition to a profit rate that the state establishes. But not the cost of raw material unless the government imposes tariffs on the use of that raw material.

---

[77] http://www.enciclopedia-juridica.com/d/libertad-civil/libertad-civil.htm

This is why the concept of freedom is a social mirage. In other words, man's civil freedom is limited by the right of others, and respect for the right of others contributes to the general welfare of the social group. From this point of view, in any social relationship there is no individual freedom, there is only freedom (agreed) of the social group. The issue of individual freedom quickly becomes a matter of comparative law for members of the social group. Then peace is relative and depends on the equitable allocation of the right for each and every member of the group, community, state or nation, where the link is the ratified agreement of those rights. Finally, free choice loses breadth from the moment men decide and accept to live in groups or in community; However, what is lost should be the same for everyone, naturally, without privileges or preferences for any member of the group or community. Likewise, what is gained from the grouping or association— as a people—must be egalitarian. Laws such as the constitution order must protect and preserve this status of equality in all humanitarian and social aspects. Likewise, every individual retains, without restrictions of any kind, the freedom to think, decide and act on anything that does not affect, restrict or limit the right of others, individual or group. The limit of the freedom that the individual yields depends on the nature of the individual—the nature defined by the capacity of the common environment. Likewise, this natural capacity creates a trichotomy of rights, social, political and economic. But leaving social law aside for a moment let's look at the other two for now.

Civil and political rights [78]

"In general, they are rights that protect individual freedoms from illegal breach (repression) by power (whether governments or any other public or private political agent), and guarantee the ability of the citizen to participate in the civil and political life of the State on an equal footing, and without discrimination. [These] *are the* [rights] recognized by all citizens by *law; and in this they distinguish themselves from human*

---

[78] https://es.wikipedia.org/wiki/Derechos_civiles_y_políticos

rights and natural rights. Civil rights are granted within a State, whereas natural rights or human rights are international [universal], *and, you have, either by the fact of being born, according to the theory of iusnaturalism, or by the constitution of society, according to this theory (iuspositivism, which separates morality and law, does not raise the existence of natural rights)". Jean Jacques Rousseau.*

The Social Contract

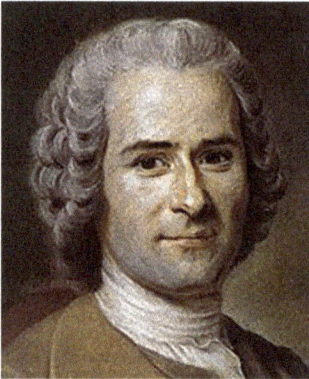

image borrowed from the Internet

Jean Jacques Rousseau provides decisive concepts in his book *"Social Contract (1762)"* to give foundation to the idea of democracy and replace the notion of "will of the king or monarch" that founded the monarchy. [79] It also includes the will of an autocratic, despotic and or dictatorial government that abuses its position, granted by the people, to destroy popular sovereignty or the power of the people.

In reality, there is no contract between the citizens of a nation and the state or government that they define for the management of their affairs and businesses. This is because the people being the popular sovereignty from which a government derives its authority, the people are not subordinate to their government but to the legal framework that regulates the general behavior. In other words, the supremacy of power always belongs to the citizens of the nation and never becomes a property or a right of their representatives in government, as in a monarchy, an autocratic or dictatorial government. It is interesting to note that the social contract elucidated much of liberal philosophy, or liberalism, *"because of its philosophical vision of the individual as fundamental, which then decides to live in society so that it needs the rule of law that secures freedoms in order to live together,"* as seen in the same article.

---

[79] https://es.wikipedia.org/wiki/Voluntad_general

The social contract is indeed the rule of law, derived from the constitution approved by the people and abided by each of the citizens, including any person who occupies or is elected to a public service office—this subordination to the rule of law includes the president of the nation, since no one is above the law—.

The theory of the Social Contract, originally set out by Rousseau, *"refers to the agreement that takes place within a group of individuals, assuming that all members are in favor of what is agreed, and agree to submit to common rules and recognizing the existence of an authority regulating order".* The people use this theory of social contract to explain the origin of the state. Human beings, with the intention of living in society, implicitly establish a social contract that gives them certain rights, but which in return requires them to set aside the freedom they would have if they lived in a natural state since they must submit to the laws. The clauses of the social contract thus establish the rights and obligations of citizens, with the State being the institution that individuals agree to create to ensure compliance with the pact in question. [80] The reader can read the rest of this article in footnote 80 to broaden his understanding of this term. The author finds traces of other influential philosophical thoughts in the formation of the Union of American States; for example.

Libertarianism

Civil liberties

All rights are based on natural rights considered in natural law; Europeans had already discovered with illustration at the end of the Middle Ages. The purpose of civil and political liberties was to protect individual freedoms, avoiding any illegal *breaches*—such as repression—of monarchs and governments representing the king. This concept was soon extended to include any government, or political, public or private agent. Its objective was (and should be) to guarantee the rights of the citizen to have a participatory

---

[80] https://definicion.de/contrato-social/

life—[social], civil and political in the State— equally and without discrimination in any way. [81]

Interventionism

Interventionism: a government policy or practice of doing things to directly influence the country's economy or the political affairs of another country. [82]

Interventionism is a political attitude, an interference, premeditated of a government in its internal economy affairs, or control, and in the domestic politics of other countries. As a result of this attitude is the resentment of citizens, internal reaction, and the defensive measures of a government intervened against an interventionist government. The interference of the state and its administrative agencies has a particular purpose. The intention of the interventionist government is to monitor the economic and commercial activities of companies and the private market and, of course, to manipulate the operational management of the private sector—*as is the case in a targeted economy.* [83] The immediate effect is observed in decrees regulating the savings and consumption of the people restricting the levels of production and marketing of products and services. Interventionism has countless phases and or scales, which are obviously expressed with regulations. But among some they can manifest themselves to the public as fiscal and monetary policies, tariffs, customs, etc. The internal reaction of the private sector in the local economy is one of rejection, resistance and repudiation against the public sector. Signs of interventionism are decrees or regulations that directly affect the private sector; between these signals contracts and working conditions, price manipulation, etc. Interventionism may include fiscal policies such as tax enforcement and business subsidies.

In a democratic government, interventionism has no place. It must also be understood that within free will each person has the

---

[81] https://es.wikipedia.org/wiki/Derechos_civiles_y_politicos

[82] https://www.merriam-Webster.com/dictionary/interventionism

[83] https://economipedia.com/definiciones/intervencionismo.html

inalienable right of Life and to live life as he sees his well-being and happiness. Participation in or of a private company, as well as interactive activity in the free market, is also part of how to live life led by your right to free choice. Interacting with, inside and outside the private enterprise and the free market is a personal decision that is not detailed in the constitution; therefore, it is a libertarian and or right that falls on the individual. This is why democratic government cannot and should not intervene in the behavior of the economic life of the people. As a matter of the case, the government cannot and should not interfere, influence, or intervene in the activities of private enterprise or the free market. Considering these two separate sectors, autonomous and independent of government, local or central. The constitution must make it clear that it is the choice of the individual citizen, or the whole people, has the right to choose their economic way of life—just as they are free to choose and practice their preferred religion. However, the government is and will be responsible for fulfilling and enforcing the Union's six objectives: to form a more perfect Union, to establish Justice, to ensure national tranquility, to serve the common defense, to promote general welfare, and to ensure the benefits of freedom for all of us, the people.

And the question is latent, is there justification for interventionism? No, there isn't. In a nation with a democratic and capitalist government, the economic system is governed by the free market beyond the control of the government. This is why the author contemplates certain conditions that by his approach may look like interventionism, for example, protection of life, health, general well-being, happiness. The government cannot abandon the fundamental principles of the Union in order to promote the economic system, it is not the government's function.

In both cases the government has taken funds from the village to get out of the problem or financially assist the private company with possible ruin. The Obama administration having inherited the Bush recession save General Motors from bankruptcy and then become the big company it is again. The author asks and challenges that, if private enterprise and the free market are autonomous and independent, why do the people have to pay for their economic failures? Is it fair? No, it is not. The government does not help us when they foreclose our house.

Speaking of other areas, the government must act in saneness to protect the public property of the people according to the six constitutional objectives set out in its preamble, including all of the following: General Health; Welfare; Equality; Tranquility; Public resources; Environment; Happiness; and the like.

These public goods include, but are not limited to, education, drinking water, fresh and healthy air, the road system and natural resources within its territory—these are heritage of the people. The failures of capitalism, such as the economic collapse during George W Bush's presidency (43) and during Donald J. Trump's presidency (45), affects us all, the people, directly but not a cause of the Union or the people.

The government was not established for promoting free enterprises, the free market, and or to promote the economic system. It is not the government's function to do what is not sanctioned in the constitution, although there may be subsidiary laws that do this exactly. In fact, how to run our lives is not ruled by the constitution. If such laws exist, they are unconstitutional, null and invalid. The capitalist system as a private thing belongs to natural people and must abide by constitutional provisions. the government must *"promote equality of citizens* and greater social *welfare, by making efficient allocation of available resources without producing large gaps in inequality in the population,"* according to the article.

There is another fundamental principle that we must review; is next.

Laissez-faire

Let us make a brief exposition of this concept, Laissez-Faire originated in France at the time of illustration in the XVI century. It is an economic system where commercial, stock exchange, production and services activities are beyond the reach and control, regulations and subsidies of state power. The concept declares [84] *"... the individual is the basic unit of society and has a natural right to freedom; that the physical order of nature is a harmonious and self-regulating system; and that corporations are creatures of the state and therefore citizens must monitor them closely because of their propensity to disrupt spontaneous order."* [85] This concept is what we have mentioned before, excepting that (1) corporations are created by one or more individuals but not by the state, and (2) that due to the corruption of man being able to affect the six constitutional mandates established in the preamble, the government must closely monitor that they do not violate the constitution of the people. The Laissez-Faire principle states that markets must be competitive, maximizing freedom for markets to self-regulate. Spontaneous order is a power of nature to self-regulate and sway and thus emerge from chaos. In a large way, this is the natural principle of balancing physical and chemical systems, etc., which states that when a system in balance is disturbed by internal or external forces in a way that causes it to lose its balance, the system reacts to seek its original balance or to mobilize through quasi-balances until another stable balance is achieved. Social, political and economic systems do not exactly follow this equilibrium principle. The certainty of this phenomenon is that the system loses something, but also gains something, even if the displaced system does not retain its characteristics which it had in the previous stable balance.

Civil rights

The author cites the following article published in wikipedia. org/wiki which reads the following.

"Rights included.- Civil rights include the guarantee of physical integrity (right to life) and moral (right to honor)and the security of persons, **domiciles** *and communications; the right to equality* **and protection** *against discrimination arising in any personal or social condition (age, sexual orientation,* physical or mental *disability,*

---

[84]   https://en.wikipedia.org/wiki/Laissez-faire
[85]   https://en.wikipedia.org/wiki/Spontaneous_order

economic or social *marginalization,* religious or other *beliefs, ethnic status), designated as "race" or otherwise-* and individual *rights, among which are property* and a large list of rights *and freedoms:* freedom of *thought, expression,* press *and printing,* freedom *of worship,* freedom *of movement and residence; together with rights of participation in civil and political life, such as the* right of *suffrage, the* right *of petition, the* right of assembly and *manifestation,* the right of *association, etc. Political rights include natural justice or procedural fairness, expressed in the rights of the parties* and *inmates or accused persons and in the right to a* fair *trial with* procedural *safeguards (due process),including guarantees against* unlawful *detention, the right to know the indictment and the accuser, the right to contest accusations, the* right to *assistance,* representation and *legal defense, not to testify, the absence of torture, habeas corpus, the presumption of innocence, the non-retroactivity of sanctioning laws, the proportionality of penalties, the right to* procedural *recourse, to obtain redress, etc."* [86]

Political rights [87]

In reality, the legal regulation of these rights is not necessary because they are understood to be innate rights of individuals in a social relationship. But the government must understand the policies of the relationship to execute the intent of the agreement to the sanctioned in the magna letter of the relationship, as well as the limits of its authority and implementing power. People have the right to participate in administrative management since the government is of the people, by the people and for the people (through their representatives).

Capitalism

What is capitalism? Different people have different versions in their minds, but they are all similar. it doesn't really deserve to

---

[86] https://es.wikipedia.org/wiki/Derechos_civiles_y_políticos
[87] https://conceptodefinicion.de/derechos-politicos

discuss the philosophy of their differences. The author recognizes that there are other economic and social systems, but he does not compare them to capitalism. The nature and idiosyncrasies of the people of the United States—in fact, the people of the world—have their attachments to free, independent, and natural activities, as choosing their ways of life. And attitude includes how to relate to others in joint activities of mutual and reciprocal benefits in their environment. All this is within your natural and inalienable right to Life. Socialism, for example, is the social, political and economic idea that considers the means of production to be collective property and therefore its administration is the responsibility of a central government of the people.

Socialism

This system assumes that such an administration creates the equal balance of wealth. Obviously, this concept violates the inalienable right of free choice that Nature and the God of Nature gives to man. In such a case the government manages the wealth and distribution of it consequently manages the way of life of man. Socialism associated with the corruption of rulers actually entails an unjust society.

Communism

This system on the other hand, is a social, political and economic system that conceives a state of equality of the social classes. And it bases on the elimination of means of production, land and industry, as private property. Their approach considers the means of production to be common property and their administration is centralized by the government. This concept, like socialism, also violates the inalienable right of free choice that Nature and the God of Nature gives to man.

The author argues that the natural order of creation is harmonious, balanced and permanently self-regulated, or

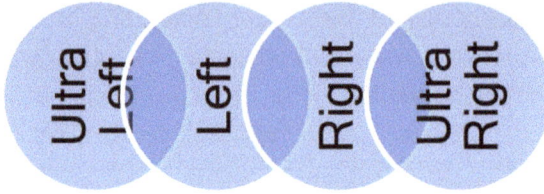

image borrowed from the Internet

doesn't exist. He considers that the categorization of the spectrum of social, political and economic tendencies does not represent Life, as it was designed for species, especially humans. Nature and the God of Nature created and arranged uniform equality in the universe; every system exists in a sustained balance in this arrangement. The God of Nature created a state of tranquility, satisfaction, and gratitude, particular and unique, for all species. Any system that directly or indirectly constrains or restricts this state is unnatural, undesirable, not acceptable.

Perhaps, we must clarify that from the beginning man needs to satisfy his needs. Man strives to live peacefully, satisfied, and perhaps thanking the goodness of nature. The Creator gives life to man offering everything in his surroundings to maintain Life, but does not give it in the way man desires—ready for use or consumption. For this reason, from the time of cavemen man has the notion of giving and receiving things and or help in exchange for his things; and this help have equal benefit and convenience for others. This is the natural and reciprocal exchange that is born with man. This is the natural way to live in social charitable relationship with other men. This is the natural way of living as an evidently natural condition of existence, considering that the resources of the environment and the environment do not belong to or are owned by any particular man—the content of the universe belong to the environment and destined by the Creator for the benefit and usufruct of all men. And the respect for man's right to live Life in his own way brings the notion of exchange products and services in social equality.

The author uses two references to the definition of capitalism; One from Wikipedia and one from Economipedia. And he focuses his discourse first on the definition of capitalism with the analysis of that definition and then focuses on the history of capitalism. He follows this sequence because of the impact that capitalism has on the constitution, government, and democracy of a people. [88]

According to footnote 88, capitalism is a free economic system based on private ownership of the means of production. The concept is the definition in (1) means of production, and (2) market and capital. However, the concept of private ownership is not exclusive to the exchange of products and services to the consumer. Communities have common properties, which belong to the whole community, run by its government. For example, natural resources belong to all people; resources that the company can use not as a right but as a government concession and for which the private express must pay the price of such resources. This price should include the damage that the private company causes to the environment due to the extraction and processing of natural resources (the raw material), including the restoration of the environment to the sustained safe condition. Likewise, there is no law restricting the government's ability to become a provider of products and services that the people can buy. In fact, there is a history that proves such a possibility; for example, the mail service (USPS).

Capitalism is also a social system, besides being economic, because it belongs to the way of life of the social man. But it is not social from the point of view of sharing the benefits of their freedom with the rest the consumer people. It is by this nature that capitalism is an individual egotistic attitude, a relative private property with regard to the processes of serving and producing. But the system is public as soon as that methodology is available to the use of the whole people. Certain resources such as the raw material extracted from nature is not private property, but belongs to the nation representing the people, the raw material, as a natural element, is not a resulting element of Production. Production acquires it and integrates the productive medium as a necessary element to produce a service or finished product. Likewise, human capital is the property of every individual that exists outside of capitalism, carried by the

---

[88] https://economipedia.com/definiciones/capitalismo.html

individual in the form of man's knowledge, experience and skills even if capitalism did not exist. Human capital has prime resource characteristics, in its finished form. In other words, human capital and raw material exist independently of capitalism before it appeared any production system. Then we can define that the means of production as intrinsic and extrinsic. And raw material and human capital are medium extrinsic.

The other elements are specific or intrinsic to a production process, processes, and resources, or are the necessary integrated production elements to create products and services.

The failure of capitalism

Systems that man make are imperfect due to the imperfection of his knowledge, failures of thought and logical reasoning. In addition, the lives of men are limited, and thought, logical reasoning is different among men at different times. Man's systems almost always have flaws that are often unforeseen. The capitalist system in the United States does not escape man's faults. The founders knew that and thus expressed the end of *"... make a union more perfect...".* Benjamin Franklin anticipated the nature of man and mentioned the possible influence of corruption on the government and the need for a revolution every two hundred years to heal the nation.

Capitalism began with "fair price" based on the usefulness (its effective use) of products or services at the time of the illustration of Europe in the 15th to 17th century. That concept quickly shifted to the concept of "maximum-benefit" to maximize their profits with the boom or prosperity and productivity of people in the Americas. In fact, we, the people, live in an "autocratic capitalism." The author defines this capitalism as an economic, selfish and greedy political system, where a few individuals have hoarded and enjoyed wealth for centuries.

That is, the thought of original capitalism based on freedom and equality was a passing chimera and the reality is that *"the rich becomes richer and the poor becomes poorer",* but not by the choice of the people but by the selfishness and greed of those few mentioned above. The government failed and continues to fail allowing this form of exploitation of man by man. In addition, the government is complicit and co-authored by the economic differences creating social divides, poverty including social (homeless) displaced people living on the streets or under a bridge.

The model of autocratic capitalism is linear is not circular that opens and closes at the same point. For example, the capitalist invests in the acquisition of human capital and raw materials, invests in the production of services and products, in marketing and sale, recovers the invested capital when the equilibrium point arrives and begins to accumulate the profit on (the risk of) the investment according to the business plan. The business plan is calculated so that the probability of losing is minimal, ensuring investment.

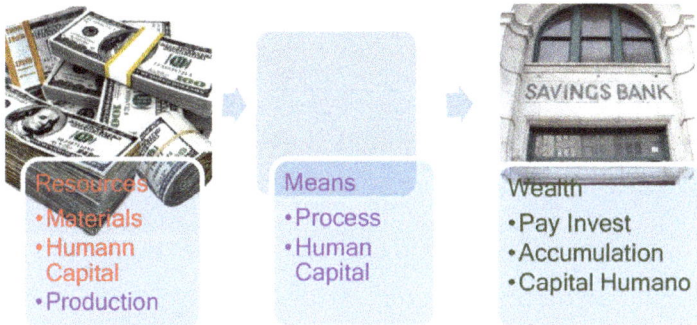

Resources
• Materials
• Humann Capital
• Production

Means
• Process
• Human Capital

Wealth
• Pay Invest
• Accumulation
• Capital Humano

SAVINGS BANK

images borrowed from the Internet, author's collage

Human capital is present in all the details of production and production phases. Human capital like money capital is not a mean of production, these capitals are generators of wealth not considered of equal importance. It is clear that capitalism does not regard human capital as a generator of wealth but as a mere resource of production. This is the point and reason why human capital is devalued and salary, is considered a benefit, royalty, or a privilege and or blessing of receiving the job. In this sense and by the idea that business is business, capitalism is despotic and autocratic. Private enterprise conspires to keep human capital below its real value, and the government is reluctant to see that reality.

But by studying the linear model of capitalism we see that capital-money and human capital are invested at the beginning of the production process, they go through the production phase and in the end only the owner of the capital-money receives the benefit of wealth. From the point of general welfare, human capital must be a partner of monetary capital in the product and service generation consortium. The author's vision is in the future when private individuals awaken and understand they can form human capital banks to lend, give in lease, facilitating knowledge, skills, and experience, to generate wealth, just like any current savings and loan bank. The owner of the human capital has the right to add to its price the cost of acquiring human capital and a percentage (interest) for providing that capital. There are precedents for this alternative; we had the Job-Shop companies not so long ago.

In other words, human capital need to have a return on investment. The capitalist thinks that the compensation of human capital is well paid with a compensation, wage or salary, the individual receives for his work; working is considered a privilege rather than a right. In reality, this thinking is not fair, it is not equal, it does not promote general welfare, it is an overlapping way of exploiting the worker, diminishing constitutional equality. The author defines autocratic capitalism as follows.

Autocratic capitalism: It is a private and exclusive economic system, an extension of basic capitalism, which controls and monopolizes resources, capital-money, means of production and services; tends to disappear when it falls in debts; capital accumulates at one end of the property spectrum. This system plunges the majority (the workers) into poverty as a small minority accumulates wealth. Wealth accumulation is progressive, eliminates honest competition by any means that justify this end, and decreases opportunities for most. This system rejects any regulations that tend to control their operation.

Capital-money

Always hangs the question about the mind of philosophers, is money the engine of world societies or the destruction of the world? It depends on the perspectives with which the symbol theme and the symbolized object are analyzed. And in terms of products and services in relation to the concept of value, appreciation comes with the need that must be met on a basis of time. The above is so true that the money symbol must be backed with something tangible, of equivalent value, and must be convertible and acquirable, as are the gold and silver that the state keeps in its coffers. Without that backing money it is worthless. The backing of the U.S. dollar is gold. An ounce of gold backs approximately $1,542.09. So, if you were given that amount in bills and coins, you should think that the federal bank backs it up with an ounce of gold that it has stored in Fort Knox, Kentucky, or at West Point, or in Denver, Colorado. The United States has an estimated quantity of 8,133.5 tons of physical gold.

Human Capital

> The human capital is the source of human advancement and of all changes promoting that advancement. Human capital is a primary generator of products and services, culture, social advancement and human evolution. Nothing really moves or changes without human capital. It deserves to have its real value in social, economic and political worlds.

In short, this human capital is the knowledge, skills, and experience that each person accumulates through academic and empirical studies. Human capital has an acquisition cost. The sum of the human capital of the individuals of a society is the general knowledge and total value of the societies of the world. This general knowledge and total value of a society derives from the cultural and intellectual value of society. The evolution of the world depends on human capital. I mean, nothing moves, really, without human capital. The clearest evidence was the 2020 COVID-19 pandemic. States ordered people to stay at home, privately held close to economic and produce products and services. Monetary capital cannot generate products or services, nor capital-real estate, or capital equipment and machinery, and others, without the presence of human capital. Unemployment rose to levels of the U.S. depression, the exchange of banking, and the economy collapsed completely. That is, without human capital there is no private enterprise or free market.

The government has failed and is failing to establish human capital as an exchangeable product and service in the free consumer market of the private company. Companies must establish human capital loan banks and marketable on the free market. The right to life, equality, general well-being and the pursuit of happiness includes the right to choose how to live your life. In this, the right includes the freedom of individuals to incorporate companies free of human capital.

A constitution reform should sanction free university education and the commercialization of human capital in an amendment that eliminates the problem of minimum wages, equal wages and salaries, claims, arguments, and legal processes of labor unions. Human capital banks would regulate social and economic differences and the boom would be greater than under autocratic capitalism.

Capitalism, your story [89]

The God of Nature allows the birth of man on an equal footing, but that does not mean that men are equal. There are differences, mental and physical, that make them different. Nature clearly shows that everything belongs to everyone equally, without specifying who can get more from them. Likewise, Nature establishes, at the same

---

[89] https://es.wikipedia.org/wiki/Historia_del_capitalismo

time, that living beings will obtain what they seek with their own efforts—effort is an added value to the intrinsic value of the resource that is obtained.

This is a principle of existence, with a meaning and intention, that cannot be understood in any other way than love for life. Therefore, everything, and total reality, tangible and intangible, is equally for every living creature. We must understand the history of man demonstrates a trajectory that goes from ignorance to general wisdom, from individualism to collectivism, from selfishness to altruism. Evidence shows that forms of government travel from despotic and absolute monarchies to perfect democracies. Man came out of the Middle Ages, through long periods of illustration and rebirth and in the 14th to 17th centuries. Man recognizes his identity and begins to realize the purpose of existence. And as the world's population increases, the consumption of nature's resources decreases, so these resources tend to be extinguished and scarce. The evidence is found in the attitudes of European monarchies in those centuries, manifested by the wars that unfold in those centuries driven by the intention to accumulate wealth, land, gold, silver, and resources of recognized values. These monarchs clearly saw that the accumulation of wealth brings the power they needed to control their empire and manipulate neighboring nations. That's why when Christopher Columbus discovers the Americas, and the exploitation of America begins, Europe emerges from its long economic impasse in which it is submerged. Then capitalism was born from the need to expedite the business relationship, with equitable values, among men.

The situation of living on pay or wages—from week to week—impedes the society growth and promotes economic gaps, creating possible disgusts, resentments, anger, and possible wars in the world.

The profile of the founders

We do not have an explicit list of names of all who could be the parents of this American nation—the United States of America.

But the author is sure that there are more people who deserve to receive that honorable credit and title. The result is the greatest thing to expect, as this nation's success truly demonstrates not only in its economic greatness but also in the greatness of its moral character based on solid principles of equality.

The success of independence depended on the set of knowledge, experience and skill—a human capital—sufficient to formulate a new nation with a new order from the leaders of the colonies. This human capital of the colonies in general included knowledge, experience and skills in governmental systems; the leaders were jurists, lawyers, politicians, journalists, rulers, educators, experts in communal affairs, self-governance, economics, financial statesmen, trade, banking experts, military and others. And it was, in truth, the value of human capital that made the difference to transform the subjugated colonies into independent free states, consolidated in the Union of the United States of America.

There is no doubt that the result embodied in the declaration of independence and then the national constitution would be prepared with legitimacy and precision. Among these leaders are seven characters—mainly—who are considered founding fathers. No one can ever judge persons' intentions by the words they express; intent is automatically defined by the action that follows their words. That is why we must listen to the phrases of the founding fathers and compare their actions in the reality of life.

John Adams. – [as quoted] (constitutional lawyer) to think puritanical; who *believe in life according to the Bible.* From his teens John Adams shows his humanism, free thinking, and rebellious thinking; at that early age he opposed his father's wishes, a farmer, a religious fanatic who wanted John to be a clergyman—John's mind was not the ecclesiastical, he saw his future in politics and in law. He was a natural writer and for this gift, John worked as a contributor to several national

image borrowed from the Internet

newspapers, thus opening up a broad perspective on the political and social landscape of those times. A lover of justice and truth; that in his early publications he writes his complaint against the laws of stamp that violated the economic well-being of settlers in North America. As early as his career, Adams drafted a writing that became the Massachusetts constitution, which serves as the basis for the constitution of the United States of America.

John regarded the Puritans as *"carriers of freedom, a cause that still had a sacred urgency. For Puritan dogmas they were a system of values in which I believed, and a heroic model in which they wanted to live up."* [90] John Adams was another of the three characters who signed the Treaty of Paris of 1783. I've had some of John Adams' lines.

"There are two ways to conquer and enslave a nation. One is through the sword and another is through debt."

In truth, the people, perhaps half the middle class down, which is the vast majority of people, are indebted. The ease of buying credit through credit cards makes it easy for them to put their rope around their necks for their own economic suicide. These people live on their long-term wages and salaries. Consequently, they lose the possibility of saving and achieving their economic independence. It is a macabre plan, orchestrated or not, that results in the impossibility of competing with those who accumulate wealth.

"Power always believes that he has a great soul and is acting in the service of God when it is violating all his laws."

The author considers that it is not that they believe, but that they think that they make people believe that they are generous, kind, always thinking for the good of the people, when in truth is the sweet that they serve to exploit it.

"Always stand on your principles even if you're alone."

---

[90] https://es.wikipedia.org/wiki/John_Adams

"(A) government is instituted for the common good: for the protection, security, prosperity and happiness of the people; and not for the benefit, honor or private interest of any man, family or class of men: Therefore, only the people have an incontestable, inalienable and unviable right to reform, alter or change the same thing when their protection, security, prosperity and happiness require it."

Franklin is right. The people have the power to exercise the right to alter, modify, and even change the government that does not comply with their oath or does not work for the general welfare, life and happiness of the people.

Benjamin Franklin. - [as quoted] he was a politician, polymath, scientist, and inventor... newspaper editor; his thinking about practical values included hard work, education, community spirit, self-governing institutions, opposition

image borrowed from the Internet

to political and religious authoritarianism, with scientific inclination. Benjamin Franklin was another character who signed the 1783 Treaty of Paris. Among his famous sentences that show his solidarity with human feeling these. [91]

"After freedom is reflected in a constitution, there is no way to change it. Freedom, once lost, never returns. Therefore, it is imperative to preserve it, to defend it." Letter from John Adams to his wife Abigail Adams. So, if the form of government and democracy that the founders sanctioned for the people of the United States is lost, a monarchy or dictatorship or an autocracy will take power and eliminate freedom and the rights of the citizens, of all the people.

"We need a revolution every 200 years because all governments become obsolete and corrupt after that time."

The time of that revolution is upon us, the evidence is in the public eye, in the despotic act of president Trump and in the complicity of the senate and the republican party. History records and

---

[91] https://es.wikipedia.org/wiki/Benjamin_Franklin

tells the facts and the truth will light the way back to the American dream.

"Don't trade health for wealth, or freedom for power."

These are Franklin's words; and we see the president and others trying to sell our health and mail system to the private sector, covertly handing over our national sovereignty. Our lives mean nothing in the hands of corrupt officials.

"War is when the government tells you who the bad guy is. Revolution is when you decide for yourself."

"Security without freedom is called prison."

"Tricks and betrayal are the practice of fools, who do not have enough intelligence to be honest."

"He who is good at making excuses is rarely good for anything else."

"That few are the ones who have enough courage to own their own faults, or resolve enough to amend them."

image borrowed from the Internet

Alexander Hamilton. – Through a poor and fighting life, protected by certain benefactors Alexander achieves his triumph, studies law and becomes a lawyer, establishes a law office and enters public service. In 1786 Alexander represented his state in the Assembly of Annapolis where he recommended a Constitutional Assembly. [citation] economist, statist, politician, writer lawyer... founder of the nation's financial system... His vision included a strong central government led by a vigorous executive branch, a strong commercial economy, with a national bank and support for manufacturing, plus a [92] powerful army... lead author of George Washington administration's economic policies...[93]

Let us listen to Hamilton's thoughts by reading his words and deduce from them the intellectual and moral contribution he gave

---

[92] https://www.archives.gov/espanol/dia-de-la-constitucion/alexander-hamilton
[93] https://es.wikipedia.org/wiki/Alexander_Hamilton

to the intention of the declaration of independence of the United States.

"State governments have inherent advantages, which will once give them influence and ancestry over the National Government, and will forever prevent the possibility of federal invasions. That their freedoms, in fact, can be subverted by the federal chief, is repugnant to all rules of political calculation."

This means of course that the states of the Union have hierarchical superiority over central government. The central government cannot conduct federal invasions in any state. It is also from this sentence, that the federal government should not subvert the freedom of action of states, with any political scheme or plan. President Trump's actions to send federal troops to a state is a gross violation and abuse of power against the people's popular sovereignty. Hamilton keeps saying.

"Given human nature, exercising power over a man's livelihood is tantamount to exercising power over his will."

No government, let alone a representative of the people in the government, has the authority and power to speculate, manipulate, or master the basic and critical needs of the people's lives, such as health, food, air and water, among all those elements that support and maintain their lives.

"Why has the government been instituted? For men's passions do not conform to the dictates of reason and justice without a coercive force."

The need to institute a government is not to exploit or subjugate the people under a despot regime, but to manage their social, political and economic affairs while the people focus on managing their lives the best they can. The government has a responsibility to guard, protect, and improve the overall well-being of the people.

Federalist Documents (1787-1788), Context: There is no position that depends on clearer principles, than an act of a delegated authority; contrary to the wording of the commission under which it is exercised, it is void. Therefore, no legislative act, contrary to the constitution, can be valid. To deny this, would be to say, that the Member is taller than his director; that the servant is superior to his master; that the People's Representatives are above the People himself; that men who act by virtue of their powers can do not only what these powers authorize, but what they forbid. If the legislative body is said to be in itself the constitutional judges of his own powers; and that the construction that makes them is conclusive for the other departments, it can be answered, that such judgment cannot be the natural presumption, where it should not be taken from any particular provision of the Constitution. There is no way that the Constitution may intend to allow the People's Representatives to replace their will with that of their constituents. It is much more rational to assume that the Courts were designed to be an intermediate body between the People and the Legislature, in order, inter alia, to keep the latter within the limits assigned to its authority. The interpretation of laws is the proper and peculiar suitability of the Courts. A Constitution is, in fact, and should be considered by the Judges as the fundamental law. It is therefore for them to determine their meaning, as well as the meaning of any particular act that comes from the legislative body. If there is an irreconcilable variation between the two, the one with the higher obligation and validity should, of course, be preferred; or, in other words, the Constitution must be preferred to the law, the intention of the people, to the intention of its agents. Nor does this conclusion imply in any way a superiority of the Judiciary over the Legislative Power. It only assumes that the power of the People is superior to both; and that when the will of the Legislature, declared in its statutes, opposes that of the people, declared in the Constitution, the Judges should be governed by the second instead of opting for the first. They should regulate their decisions by fundamental laws, not by those that are not fundamental. [...] every time a particular statute contravenes the Constitution, it will be the duty of the judicial courts to accede to the second and ignore the first.

This statement embodied in the constitution is blunt and precise; the will of the people is above the rest. As a fundamental law and expression of their legal intention. No power, of the three constitutional powers, is superlative to the power of the people declared in the constitution. In truth, no personal interest, like no one is above the law, no public official at the service of the people is above the people, because the state is the people and the constitution is the will of the people, embodied in the laws derived from the fundamental law that gives way to the establishment of government. Any action by any public official, elected by the people or not, subordinates to popular sovereignty. So, any attempt to subvert this order is a hold against popular sovereignty, the will of the people and their constitution—and should be regarded as a high crime for the purpose of a process of political dismissal of the office held by the official.

John Jay. —The son of a wealthy merchant, he grew up under the tutelage of his mother until she sent him to study under Pierre Rochelle, an Anglican priest. After studying at the King's School, he pursued a career in law, finishing his studies in 1768. [94] He was a politician, lawyer, statesman and diplomat, jurist, proponent of a centralized, abolitionist government, who negotiated the Paris treaty of 1783. [95] This treaty seals the end of the war between Britain and the United States of America, in the time of George III. One of the signatories to this treaty was John Jay. He was the first president of the United States Supreme Court. Let's read what John Jay thought and said.

image borrowed from the Internet

"Distrust naturally creates mistrust, and goodwill and kind behavior change, more quickly, for nothing (more) than, by envious jealousy and dishonest accusations, whether express or implied."

Any president, not just President Donald Trump, can try to use power for his personal interests and benefits. With this desire, he abuses the power conferred by the people for their purposes. In the process, presidents do not mind dividing the people to achieve their purpose. That is the meaning of *"the medium justifies the end"*.

1770, to Lindley Murray (1774), Context: Among the strange things of this [96] *world, nothing seems [more] that men who pursue happiness must knowingly leave the right and take the wrong path, and often do what their judgments neither approve nor prefer. However, so is the fact; and this fact strongly points to the need for us to be healed, or*

---

[94] https://www.lhistoria.com/biografias/john-jay
[95] https://es.wikipedia.org/wiki/Tratado_de_París_(1783)
[96] https://citas.in/autores/john-jay/?o=new

restored, or regenerated by a more energetic power than any of those who properly belong to the human mind. We perceive that a great violation has been made in moral and physical systems through the introduction of moral and physical evil; how or why, we don't know; so, however, it is, and it certainly seems appropriate that this violation should be closed and order restored. To this end, only one suitable plan has appeared in the world, and that is Christian dispensation. In this plan I have full faith. Man, in his present state, appears to be a degraded creature; their best gold is mixed with slag, and their best motifs are far from pure and free from earth and impurity. [97]

To which John referred it doesn't really matter; the point is that *"a violation of the moral and physical system by the introduction of moral and physical evil... must be closed and order restored."*. This thinking applies to situations that the people are going through in Donald Trump's presidency. And the solution according to John Jay is to restore order. Jay keeps saying.

"This country and this people seem to have been made for each other, and it seems as if it were the design of Providence, that such an appropriate and convenient legacy for a band of brothers, united together by the strongest bonds, should never be divided into a series of antisocial, jealous and foreign sovereignty."

"No power over the earth has the right to take away our property without our consent."

There is no stronger or more determined statement than the previous sentence, stating that the consequences would be final if someone tried to take that right away from them.

"With the same pleasure I have taken note, that Providence has had the pleasure of giving this connected country, to a united people; a people descended from the same ancestors, speaking the same language, professing the same religion, attached to the same principles of government, very similar in their manners and customs, and who, by their joint advice,

---

[97] Letter (August 22, 1774), published in The Life of John Jay (1833) by William Jay, Vol. 2, p. 345."

weapons and efforts, fighting side by side throughout a long and bloody war, have nobly established their general freedom and independence. [98]

"Americans are the first people heaven has favored with the opportunity to deliberate and choose forms of government under which they must live."

Apparently, it refers to living under the precepts of the constitution.

image borrowed from the Internet

Thomas Jefferson. – author of the declaration of independence of 1776... known for his promotion of the ideals of republicanism in the United States. He anticipated the vision of the United States of America as the backing of a great "freedom empire" that promoted democracy and the fight against British imperialism... political philosopher... He idealized the small independent owner farmer as an example of Republican virtues, distrusted cities and financiers, favored state rights, and a strictly limited federal government... supported the separation of Church and State... Jefferson offered the radical idea that settlers had the natural right to govern themselves [this is the concept of popular sovereignty discussed below]. He argued that Parliament was Britain's legislator alone and had no legislative authority in the colonies. [99] It is obvious that Thomas Jefferson seriously considered in the distribution of power between states and a central government; Jefferson believed that the central government should have limited power while states should have greater powers than central government.

Jefferson was right, and the evidence that the power of a central government stems from the will of a united people who draft the limit of power for their central government in the constitution. And

[98] *John Jay, Federalist Documents of 1780, Federalist Documents, Federalists No. 2 (1787).*

[99] https://es.wikipedia.org/wiki/Thomas_Jefferson

even if it is understood that unwritten freedoms and rights in that constitution belong to the states or their peoples, it is necessary to have clarification in the constitution to stop those having intentions, and so acting to destroy the government, the constitution itself and its democracy. Jefferson adds to his thought.

"I believe that banks are more dangerous to our freedoms than all permanent armies. If the American people allow a day for private banks to control their currency, private banks, and all the entities that flourish around them, they would deprive citizens of what belongs to them, first with inflation and later with the recession, until their children wake up, penniless and homeless, on the land their parents conquered."

The situation Jefferson alludes to in this quote is already given. Private enterprise, the free market, and capital control are in the hands of a few who control and manipulate the fate of the people, their lives and choices. The people live in debt by design of the great capital, wages are reduced to a minimum, the opportunities to achieve individual economic independence are scarce or simply do not exist. The rich, powerful and famous, have every opportunity, the best education and the power to eliminate competition. As Jefferson said, the vast majority of the people are deprived of what belongs to them, with inflation, the incompatibility of income based on the cost of living, inflation and recession, with the great difficulty of acquiring a roof. Jefferson's wise words still resonate in the modern echo as if he said them today in his public expressions. Read.

"A little rebellion from time to time is a good thing."

"It is neither wealth nor splendor; but the tranquility and the occupation give you happiness."

"The course of history shows that when a government grows, freedoms diminish."

"Only those in situations of confronting the facts know with the lies of the day they can know how far that state of misinformation goes."

"When injustice becomes law, rebellion becomes a duty."

With these phrases it seems that Jefferson paints the face of the inner being of politicians who has played with the laws and dignity of the people. Lawmakers are obliged to legislate to form a more perfect Union, as the founders soared.

image borrowed from the Internet

James Madison. - political theorist... At first, he believed that the best would be a strong central government while in the end he came to support the idea that states should have more power than central government. At the end of his life he came to accept a balanced idea in which states and the federal government share equal power... writer of the first 10 amendments of the U.S. Constitution, which are known as the Bill of Rights. Let's hear Madison's main thoughts that say.

"The accumulation of all legislative, executive and judicial powers in the same hands, whether of one person, a few or many, and whether hereditary, self-proclaimed or elective, can be presented with all fairness as the very definition of tyranny."

President Trump's actions indicate that his intention is to be a monarch or an autocrat dictator in the United States of America. Today, the obvious behavior of the undercover executive branch by the legislative branch, the Senate to be exact, has executive and legislative power in their hands. We've seen the Republican Senate close its lines behind President Trump, also the Republican Party, and in a lightning trial and rigged to find guilty in the political destitution trial. This is what Madison predicted in the previous sentence. Madison keeps talking.

"Freedom can be jeopardized by the abuse of freedom, but also by the abuse of power."

"It is a universal truth that the loss of freedom at home must be carried out by provisions against the danger, real or supposed, of the foreigner."

"In the republics, the great danger is that most do not sufficiently respect the rights of the minority."

"The essence of government is power; and power, presented as it should be in the hands of man, will again be susceptible to misuse."

All of Madison's phrases accurately point to the state of government and calamities of the people that have been brewing since 2016, gaining intensity in 2020.

George Washington.–Great strata and military commander... is considered the father of the homeland. And his military career led the colonies to independence... he began winning decorations by arming troops from the Virginia colony to support the British Empire during the Franco-Indigenous War (1754–1763), a conflict he inadvertently helped initiate. And their victories in several battles were necessary to independent the colonies and put them in the passage of the union of the 13 states.

If these celebrated honest men existed and we heard all those phrases for the first time in a single speech, obviously, we would say that they are addressed to the governments of the last presidencies, in particular the presidency of Donald J. Trump. In the minds of these seven scholars was all necessary to resolve the situation of the colonies and the formation of a new nation. But also, in their minds is also the solution to form a more perfect Union — at this time. The general European philosophy shone at the time, especially in France. The yearning for economic freedom where the worker —the people— could work and trade their products without the government intervening in its productive and commercial operations. From these comes the concept of laissez faire, free enterprise, and free market. And in those concepts flying around they drew the future of a great nation. But it is necessary to study other aspects of philosophy and concepts that served as the basis for the formulation of the great nation. Let's read other phrases from the founders.[100] [101] [102]

"If freedom of expression is removed, then mute and silent we can be guided, like sheep to the slaughterhouse."

"Freedom, when it begins to take root, is a fast-growing plant."

---

[100] https://en.wikipedia.org/wiki/Laissez-faire
[101] https://es.wikipedia.org/wiki/Libre_empresa
[102] https://es.wikipedia.org/wiki/Mercado_libre

"Government is not a reason, nor is it eloquence, it is force. It operates like fire: he is a dangerous servant and a fearsome master; at no time should irresponsible hands be allowed to control it."

"Laws dictated by common consent should not be trampled on by individuals."

"Keep against the impostures of so-called patriotism."

"The effective way to preserve peace is to be prepared for war."

Benjamin Franklin said that every two hundred years a revolution becomes necessary because governments become corrupt.

The intangible thinking of each of the founders of the homeland was clear, precise and the being tangible consistent with their actions. The author's intention is to lay solid foundations that support the concept of change, which is rather a commitment to restore the precepts of the original constitution and democracy, including, of course, the reform necessary to perfect the legal framework under that fundamental law. For this purpose or purpose, we must study the concepts that served as the basis for the declaration of independence and the structuring of the constitution and form of government. Indeed, it is necessary to follow in the footsteps of the settlers in order to legitimize reforms to the constitution of the Union.

CHAPTER 5

Genesis of the UNION

> ... adopt *"among the powers of the Earth the equal and separate station to which the Laws of Nature and Divine Nature give it the right". Thomas Jefferson*

Before the declaration of independence

The English colonies adopted forms of similar governments. They were governments composed of an executive branch assigned to a governor of the colony, a colonial council acting as the upper house of the legislative branch, a legislative assembly, with its variants. The governor was appointed by the English crown and represented the king. These governments had some interesting differences; for example, the legislature was elected in the Rhode Island colonies, and Connecticut—two adjoining colonies in the northeast of the United States. It convened and dissolved the public assembly.

The American Dream

We, citizens, don't need to have completed a PhD in philosophy, in political science, sociology to interpret the thought, purpose and achievements achieved by the people of the thirteen English colonies in America. The founders actually described the summary of the American dream in just two documents. The declaration of independence and the constitution of the United States are those two documents that include the definition of the American dream. A dream that we can tell in simple form of ordinary language.

Once upon a time in a distant nation there was a despotic and absolute monarch who persecuted and eliminated all those who opposed him or rejected his arbitrary mandates and the church of his reign; he demanded absolute allegiance to his crown. Desperate people didn't know where to go. One day a group escaped from that reign and set out to distant lands never to return, but the shadow of the sovereign's power haunted them, like a cruel ghost, mercilessly and continued to control their lives. The God of Nature appeared in their minds and put them all to sleep, in those new lands, at the same time. And everyone dreamed the same dream, at the same time. They dreamed of getting rid of that precarious situation and the absolute, despotic king who was chasing them. But the king controlled all his thoughts, and actions, choice of religion, production and commerce. Then the God of Nature appeared, and enlighten them and taught them the way of truth; and men understood that God created them equal; and God gave them inalienable rights such as life, freedom; and God said unto them, seek the Happiness to which I give you absolute right to possess. These rights are inalienable and no one, absolutely, no one can take them away from you. And God said to them, unite, "and *pluribus unum (all in one)*" because human events against you, my people, in the present time, make it necessary for you to untie the ropes that bind you to harmful forces. Assume the powers I have given you in a separate scenario under my laws, the natural laws, that protect you; and express the just reasons for claiming and regaining the form of your destiny and departing from the causes of your afflictions and tribulations. And with those rights I have given you, institute your government—your government, for you—only with your consent—and no other—that ensures your peace of mind I offer you and then annuit coeptis (approve the decisions and actions already initiated). And that government will be a Novus Ordo Seclorum (a New Order of the Centuries).

I tell you that there is no power over the earth in any nation than the power I have given you (my people), I also give you the right to change the representatives you choose to the posts of your government when this government, whatever it may be, as well as any of your representatives, becomes destructive and acts against the will of all of you (my people) or breaks the foundations of the principles you endure or violate against your Security and Happiness. Do not forget, or ignore, that the power of any government you institute derives from the power I have given you (my people); then, you have the right, it is your duty, to discard that government, and to provide new guards for your future security—when in the course of human events, it becomes necessary for you, my people, to dissolve that autocratic government and to repopulate it for another one that fulfills your will. Use those inalienable rights I give you to do good things as you agree with Prudence. And all the men awoke full of energy, determined to realize that dream with the determination of a simple plan of action.

1 – form a union and perfect it over time
2 – establish justice for all
3 – ensure national tranquility (of all people equally)
4 – lay the common defense
5 – promote well-being for general well-being
6 – ensuring freedom for us and our posterity
7 – implement and respect the natural right, to have the freedom to declare the reasons to choose to separate or dissolve that connects them with that despotic monarchy.

And so, it was, the people of the villages told each other their dreams, but it was the same dream. And more excited than frightened, glad that the God of Nature had opened their minds in their sleep and awoke them to a new day, the beginning of the struggle to execute what they had seen in the dream. Then people took to the streets, making demonstrations and for five months against the abuse of power of the king. The monarch broke in furiously and commanded his troops against the thirteen villages. But the alerted people rose in arms, fought to the death and defeated the forces of the monarch tyrant.

Declaration of Independence of the United States

The Cause and Effect Act mandates that there are no events (or effects) if there is no cause (or more) that generate it. But the causes are the conditions and circumstances that ferment over time—not necessarily instantaneous—and are given as the basis of the expected event. And the character or nature of the resulting event is defined by those conditions and circumstances. The economic situation of the United Kingdom created the conditions—restrictive and despotic—for the colonies. The settlers listed their reasons, as supporting causes of their final action—the declaration of independence. At the author's discretion, it is appropriate to repeat these supporting documents in this book.

Supporting causes

One of the solid arguments of the declaration of independence is the concept of *"natural law"*, under which any government can only exist by and with the consent of the people. It is the answer to the famous question, who comes first, the people or the government that represents the people? And the people have no duty to bow or obey orders from an autocratic governor, a dictator, or a monarch. The relationship of men in societies must be based on fundamental principles of equality and self-determination. The legal bases must adhere to the "obvious truths" for which no evidence is required. The same declaration of independence of the English colonies in America summarizes or synthesizes the arguments on which they based their independence. The precedent is written in the declaration of rights, acts considered fair and legal to dethrone James II. The declaration of independence says so. [103]

---

[103] https://es.wikipedia.org/wiki/Declaración_de_Independencia_de_los_Estados_Unidos

image borrowed from the Internet

In Congress, July 4, 1776.

The unanimous declaration of the thirteen United States of America,

When in the course of human events, it becomes necessary for a people to dissolve the political bands that have connected them with another, and assume among the powers of the earth, the separate and egalitarian station to which the Laws of Nature and the God of Nature gives them the right, a decent respect for the opinions of humanity requires them to declare the causes that drive them to separation.

We consider these truths to be obvious, that all men are created equal, that they are endowed by their Creator with certain inalienable rights, which include Life, Freedom and the pursuit of Happiness.--That to secure these rights, governments are instituted among men, deriving their righteous powers from the consent of the governed, --That whenever any form of government becomes destructive to these purposes, is the right of the people to alter or abolish it, and to establish a new Government, laying its foundations on principles and the organization of their powers in such a way, as far as they are to do, they will seem more likely than indeed their Security and Happiness. Prudence, in fact, will dictate that long-established governments should not be changed for light and transitional reasons; and, consequently, every experience has sown, that humanity is more willing to suffer, while evils are suffering, than to straighten themselves by abolishing the forms to which they are accustomed. But when a long train of abuse and usurpation, invariably pursuing the same Object, evidences a design for reducing them under absolute despotism, it is their right, it is their duty to discard that government, and provide new guards for their future security. "Such has been the patient suffering of these colonies; and such is now the need for them to alter their former Government Systems...

****

It is a mandate of popular sovereignty to *"alter or abolish it, and to institute a new government, laying its foundations on principles and the organization of its powers in such a way, as far as they will surely seem more likely than indeed their Security and Happiness. whenever any form of government becomes destructive., to ensure these rights..."* Violation of this. mandate, and rights involved in the son major crimes that must be criminalized as such in the charges against any official representative of the people—No one, absolutely no one, is above the constitution (approved or ratified by the people).

An Article on the Internet presents a list of causes that the author repeats in this book. The primary cause of the declaration of independence of the American English colonies includes, but is not limited to the following. [104]

1.   —*The unfair treatment by Britain for the colonies. Such injustices bring the settlers to the point of no return - the declaration of their independence - regardless of the consequences.*

2.   —*The interference of the Parliament of England creates severe unrest in the lives of the settlers.*

2.1 —*The annulment of laws enacted by the colonies of South Carolina and Virginia.*

2.2 —*Increased control over courts of justice and judicial authorization to the customs authority to enter warehouses and homes suspected of smuggling.*

2.3 —*Military establishment in the Appalachian mountain ranges in order to eliminate trade between settlers and Native Americans.*

---

[104] https://www.aboutespanol.com/las-causas-de-la-independencia-de-estados-unidos-1772391

3. —*the arbitrary establishment of the Sugar Act, with the intention of forcing the colonies to contribute to the expenditure of the imperial bureaucracy. The settlers resisted paying taxes without representation in the government of England. This law was extended to the trade in wines, coffee, potassium, silk, iron in addition to sugar.*

4. —*The imposition of taxes on all kinds of printed material, an action known as the Stamp Act, with which they charged advertisements in newspapers, legal contracts, etc.*

5. —*The imposition of another law passed in 1766 confirming the authority of the kingdom and to which the colonies were obliged to subordinate themselves to Britain - a law known as the declaratory law.*

6. —*Another tax collection law on paper, glass, lead, paints and tea issued by Parliament. England simultaneously created customs breaks to force the colonies to comply with this law.*

The settlers' resentment of all these outrages and abuses publicly rebelled against the English on 5 March 1770 when the English shot and killed about five settlers. The incident was called the *Boston Massacre*. England did not lift any imposed laws, although they authorized the British East India company to sell directly in the colonies. The English strategy did not work for the English, because the settlers calculated long-term inconvenience. And in December they boarded some English boats and threw into the sea the load of tea they found in them. This event was called the *tea party*. This is the point of no return; luck was cast and there was no turning back. Then in 1774 with the Continental Congress the revolution began and continued without pause until the creation of the United States in 1776.

In this year or 2020 after the assassination of George Floyd the people of all races, colors and social conditions took to the streets to protest against racism, injustice, and equality of man. After five months people still take to the streets in expression of repudiation against the political system and justice. Interestingly, the settlers marched in the streets protesting for about five months.

image borrowed from the Internet

The Constitution of the United States.[vi]

The war of independence. [105]

The United Kingdom unleashes its fury against the colonies and war breaks out and passes between 1775 and 1783 -thirteen years of clashes between unequal forces.

France supported and assisted the colonies with infantry troops under Rochambeau and Marques de la Fayette, and sailors commanding Guichen, DeGrasse and d'Estaing. Spain, through Bernardo de Galvez clandestinely, helps the colonies at the beginning and openly since the Battle of Saratoga, provided weapons supplies carried on ships of the merchant Diego de Gardoqui, to the southern front. Of course, both Spain and France helped the settlers because they saw an opportunity to take advantage of England. And while the end comes with the Battle of Yorktown and peace and recognition comes in the Paris Treaty negotiations, it doesn't end in a happy ending. The distribution of territories did not bring complete happiness for all, but it brought the end of a long war and peace in America. In the Treaty of Paris of 1873 England recognized the independence of

---

[105] https://es.wikipedia.org/wiki/Guerra_de_Independencia_de_los_Estados_ Unidos

the colonies and dissevered the territory of the thirteen colonies. In this treatise the territorial cake was generously distributed, and they all won. The end of the war concludes with the migration of around seventy thousand pro-British loyalists from the colonies that were built Canadian territory.

image borrowed from the Internet

The constitution

Political philosophy controversies of how to set up a central government were issues of daily discussions. Not everyone agreed on everything; it was a complicated situation, but goodwill and knowledge that they were free and wanting to form a strong and serious nation kept the founders forging the best idea. Some representatives gathered in Philadelphia in 1787 and began their work. They created a federal government with a president, a house of representatives and a senatorial chamber. The constitution was inspired by the French illustrators based on the principle of equality and freedom. The magna letter embraced the principles of political liberalism, establishing a republican and democratic regime.

A few years later the people came together in one or one voice, agreed to adopt their form of government of the people, by the people, and for the people. And they lived happily ever after for many years. Interesting to note that the third part, "by the people" deciphers a delegated governorate through elected representatives of people of the same people.

Supporting causes

Perhaps the laws of man—particularly when a monarch, or a dictator has the power—are restricted to man's natural right to his free choice (or free will), the right of his life and the management of it as he sees fit, and the Natural right to freedom. Existence gives all men (of the world) these rights—Life, Freedom, and The Pursuit of Happiness—equally. Life is to live it with love. Freedom is to choose (the free will) that best suits: freedom of action and mobilization. And the search for happiness is to find the sustained state of tranquility, satisfaction and gratitude to the Creator who endowed us with these inalienable natural rights. That state is equivalent to Nirvana. For this reason, the declaration of independence is naturally legal and necessary—and will always be for all people, in all nations, of the world.

But in a monarchy, where, including the life of the subjects, people belong to the monarch, a declaration of independence is a rebellion against the will and the absolute power of the monarch. Many law scholars have discussed the concept of illegality or legality of independence. Obviously, in a monarchy—or in an autocratic or dictatorial government—, popular sovereignty is a betrayal of the monarch or ruler. And it was on this subject that, in the summer of 1776, members of the second continental congress in North America met in Philadelphia. [106] The matter was mainly coincidentally the absolute power of British sovereignty. There Thomas Jefferson submitted a document, which was approved, listing the grievances suffered, and for which independence was just and necessary. And as the article in quote 8 says, it was *"a call to war, freedom and the founding of a new empire." And according to the lawyers gathered there "it was totally illegitimate and illegal."* At the end of the debate

---

[106] https://www.bbc.com/mundo/noticias/2011/10/111021_independencia_estados_unidos_legal_il

and having analyzed the legal basis for dethroning James II, according to the account of this quotation. The citation goes on to state that *the declaration of independence is undoubtedly 'legal'* and adds that *"under the basic principles of natural law, a government can only exist with the consent of the people and there comes a time when there is no need for loyalty in the face of tyranny."* This is the key point—the natural law that grants equality and the inalienable right of self-determination.

What has happened in the United States between 2016 and 2020 seems to be a doubling, similarly, albeit on another scale, of what happened about two hundred and forty-four years ago. At that time the despot power was the monarchy of James II. The pro-independence fringes presented a list of supporting causes to prove the legality of the declaration of their independence. This list contains points applicable to the situation of recent decades, especially in the last four years—during Donald Trump's presidency. The points referred to are, for example. The irony of life is that a despot and autocratic monarch does not present evidence of his rights to the life, production, trade and economy of all, the people.

1 —The government fails to make the equality of the citizens of the people prevail. His action neglects the obvious truth that all men are created equally with inalienable rights endowed by the Creator such as Life, Freedom, and the pursuit of Happiness. Racism is an unfair treatment for citizens, especially dark-skinned, brown and black men. And the pretense of doing white America again is a coup, an attack on the constitution, the Republican government, and the democracy of the United States of America. This is a high crime sufficient for a political dismissal.

2 —The Complicity of the Senate in the hands of republicans covering up the authoritarian, arbitrary, autocratic, and dictatorial behavior of republican President Donald Trump who assumes he is a monarch with absolute powers above the constitution and its derived laws. In fact, they got away with manipulating the process of political dismissal to the position of president raised by the House of representatives held by

democrats. The senate formulated its rules of judgment in a manner that limits or stalks the process by preventing material and suitable evidence and witnesses from being presented in this trial. The result that came out of a rigged vote was that the senate did not find President Donald Trump guilty (but not exonerated) of the crimes charged. These charges are based on the accusatory document filed by the House of Representatives. There are other doubtful crimes resulting from the investigation (May 2017 to March 2019) documented by a special counsel, Robert Mueller. People in positions close to President Trump's administration were formally charged, prosecuted, found guilty and sentenced to several years in prison, but not the president. And the popular question is, and why don't they prosecute the president? The justice department has the policy that a president in office cannot be prosecuted. This policy obviously puts the president above the law.

3 —Abuse of authority and power –

No person is above the law, and for this reason every person should answer in the courts for their dismantling, sins and crimes. It is prudent not to prosecute a president in charge of dismantling, crime and or crimes while performing his duties. But it is the author's opinion that research and processes of political destitution must follow their courses without any impediment or legal subterfuge. In the case of President Richard Nixon, the abuse of authority and power was evident. In the case of President Donald J. Trump, the abuse of power was and remains apparent and public. The president challenges the separation of powers from the state on the assumption that he has absolute power to do what he thinks he is to do. And he therefore rejected and ruled out the constitutional responsibility granted to the House of Representatives to investigate and question the president under subpoenas. The House of Representatives was unable to exercise that constitutional function and duties, so investigations into President Trump's political dismissal case did not get to the bottom. This is an abuse of power and authority not sanctioned in the constitution. Abuse of authority and power is quickly complicated by the authoritarian and despotic behavior of an official, not just the president. For example.

4 —Position above the law.

There is no law higher than the supreme law, the constitution, representing the will of popular sovereignty constituted in national sovereignty. And the power and authority of the three powers is limited as the spirit and letter of the constitution sanctions it. Any power and or authority not included or described in the constitution remains the power and authority of each state or its people. Any action by any official, elected or not, that goes further, or attempts to achieve greater control, than the constitution includes is outside the law; therefore, it is placed, without or with intent, above the law. In this context, when the action is intentional, or not but the damage is probable, the official violates the constitution and national and popular sovereignty—commits a high crime against the state.

5 —Obstruction of justice.

A simple definition of the destruction of justice is based on obstacles in the place between prosecutors and investigators, or other government officials to find or uncover the truth. The consequence is that justice is not done or delivered because those actions create such obstructions; and the damage is obviously the point; justice ignores harm when it does not find or can prove intent. The reality is that, if the crime is committed with or without intent and there are consequences, the defense claims that there was no corrupt intent. But intention, corrupt or not, yields the consequence that always leaves grievances. Alleging ignorance of the law and therefore there was no intention is not, or should not be, justification for the facts. The experience of defense advisers has many tools to confuse intent and blind justice ends up closing the case. Thus, works the righteousness of man; and many culprits walk innocent people with experience to commit other similar crimes. You can't formally charge, or prosecute without evidence, or eyewitnesses to anyone. Apparently, this situation is a great failure of justice, especially when there is another requirement to the argument and evidence. In other words, in addition to the above, prosecutors and investigators must prove beyond the doubts that obstruction of justice has or comes from corrupt intent. Jurisprudence fails, but the argument also because the offender cannot appeal to ignorance of the law at the time of taking an action that may not be legal. That is, that person is obliged to understand the law and know that the action he is about to take is illegal; specially when that person is a president.

Any action that hinders, prevents, hides evidence, threatens and intimidates witnesses ready to testify, the investigation, impedes the service of justice. Misrepresenting the truth when communicating with the public, verbal or written, in any way confuses people's understanding. Also bribe potential witnesses relevant in the case directly or indirectly, destroy evidence, lie to confuse investigators. All of this is obstruction of justice—to a lesser or greater degree.

6 —Use of power for personal gain.

The use of power and or authority conferred on officials, elected or not, to public positions in the administration of the government and or its autonomous institutions is a factor of Corruption. Political corruption includes, but is not limited to, criminal acts, influences on others, whether intentional or not, to embezzle the state's monetary and/or human resources; to achieve illegitimately, to satisfy hidden agendas and personal interests, for profit. The people have had real experiences with their government in recent decades. The most serious and dangerous we have seen in the presidency of Donald Trump. For example, after several attempts, he found, nominee and was approved a general prosecutor who serves the president as his personal lawyer and not as the position he holds requires the people to serve the people in the application of justice. [107]

---

[107] https://es.wikipedia.org/wiki/Corrupción_política

The general concept is that political corruption applies only to public officials, however, the state of corruption is spread across all areas, public and private, such as a net or spider web laid out over government, private enterprise, the free market in autonomous authorities and the general people. In truth, Benjamin Franklin announced that corruption could reach the tolerance limit every two hundred years, but it has been two hundred and forty-four years since that time. The Franklin revolution spoke then is necessarily. But not an armed uprising, but a recognition of that state and the application of a new illustration that supports the decision to reform and strengthen the constitution and its laws derived from it.

7 —Mishandling of the public purse.

This is the diversion of funds outside the allocation of expenses. According to the constitution, public funds are allocated to specific accounts and destinations that the executive cannot handle or change as they please, whims and purposes without the authorization of Congress. Such action is to ignore the functions separated from the three powers of the state, which, as constitutional mandates, the careful action to modify them is an attack or attack on the constitution. This must also be regarded as a high crime, to attack the constitutional order. The president should not take from one account to cover the responsibilities of another or other accounts.

8 —Own Governments.

From the beginning and before the declaration of independence, the colonies formed their own governments—very similar among them—that included the three powers of states we know today.

CHAPTER 6

The Constitution

By the Providence of existence and its laws and the goodness of nature (the universe) all men are born free with the right to life. [108], [109] And within this freedom is his choice to move to his liking across the planet and to choose his way of living, to believe in what she or he want, to live alone or as a group, and the freedom to seek the best way to survive. Work is a right of life. This is popular sovereignty. People's freedoms, or rights, are inalienable and come with the life that Providence gives us. These freedoms and natural rights had existed since before man appeared, they are thus true and inalienable.

Nature classifies and groups each thing and species by its characteristics, nature or idiosyncrasies. So, man belongs to one of those pre-established classes—the human race. Man learns that association with other men has benefits that are non-existent in his solitary life. The association facilitates the life of man by sharing thoughts and actions; and the product of these ideas and actions together improve the way they live. But the association results in the limitation of individual natural freedoms, accepting that the association has its form perspectives of reality. Every association requires the rules, duties and rights of each individual voluntarily united in the group; groups of any kind until they become a people

---

[108] https://es.wikipedia.org/wiki/Prembulo_de_la_Constituciorn_de_los_Estados_Unidos

[109] https://en.wikipedia.org/wiki/Constitution_of_the_United_States

or nation. The association of humans is not a natural right; it is a choice that stems from the freedom to join a group or society. The association is born from the exercise of his will. The common behavior rules and purposes of partners represent the will of the group. The supreme authority of the people derives from the will of each individual; and each individual derives his will from the natural rights that existence bestows upon every citizen of the people.

In accordance with the above, the rules of general conduct of a society do not restrict, deny or eliminate the freedoms of individuals not affiliated with the association. Nor does it prevent the members of the union from carrying out acts or actions which are not governed by the agreement of the company provided that such acts or actions do not affect the functional and operational behavior of the association.

The structure of freedoms makes it clear that the sovereignty of the Union derives from the sovereignty of states, and the sovereignty of states derives from the popular sovereignty that depends on the will of individuals derived from their inalienable rights that their Creator grants them. So, the rules that unite men in a society, a nation, or a union of nations is the popular sovereign that may become a national sovereignty; and national sovereignty comes from popular sovereignty. Therefore, popular sovereignty is above national sovereignty and over the constitution and its rules of law. Just as the people wrote their constitution and laws, they can rewrite it to perfect it with amendments. Amendments to the constitution are necessary as conditions change over time. They are necessary and fair; they're not extravagances.

The constitution could not be real or in force without the approval and ratification of the contents of this constitution by each of the states. Four states argued that the constitution was unclear and demanded amendments to improve the Union. Finally, Rhode Island ratified the United States Human Rights Charter in twelve amendments of which only ten were attached to the original constitution. Historical evidence shows that full ratification occurred when the ninth state ratified the articles of the Confederacy— and entered into force. And the constitution was fully ratified by these ten amendments on 29 May 1790. That was the work of the popular will (sovereignty), from which the constitution derives. The people demonstrated their sovereignty by accepting and approving the Constitution of the United States in September 1788. The Republican government and democracy of the United States was born out of popular sovereignty, the will and consent of the citizens of each colony or state.

The last amendment—Amendment No 27—to the constitution was proposed on 25 September 1789 and was ratified (two hundred and three years later) in 1992. The constitution still presents darkness that provokes misinterpretations, bringing it to the brink of serious crises. As has been the case with the presidency of Donald J. Trump. The U.S. legal framework mandates that no one can claim ignorance of the law, including the president. President Trump's administrative behavior has run up to the edge of a constitutional crisis that he provokes. Situations like these should not happen because the nation faces the risk of losing its government, democracy, the Union and the rights and freedoms obtained with its independence.

It is time to reform the constitution and adopt or reject the pending amendments altogether, perhaps amend existing ones and add new ones that make this Union more perfect. So, let's study the constitution to interpret and understand its content.

It is clear that the people of the thirteen colonies considered, approved the commitment to, *"AnnuitC'ptis",* to be the people of the United States (until then known as English colonies in America), integrated into a single group, called themselves "We", never more separate individuals—we are the people. And now the popular will is transfigured into the national sovereignty of the United States of America, Novus Ordo Seclorum, the new order forever after.

Preamble

> *We, the people of the United States, in order to form a more perfect Union, establish justice, ensure national tranquility, tend to the common defense, promote general welfare and secure*

the benefits of freedom for us and for our posterity, we hereby promulgate and establish this Constitution for the United States of America.

Together we stand with a single purpose "to form a more perfect Union" through the years. What interpretation can we give to the content of that phrase other than the will to work continuously seeking the perfection of the Union? It is clear that after so long—centuries—under despotic absolutism of European monarchies, they had no other vehement desires to establish and ensure permanent justice aimed at ensuring the tranquility of the people. It was the dream, seen as impossible, of living in peace and freedom, owning his own destiny. That's the American dream. The dream is to eliminate fear, terror of being persecuted for their religious beliefs, and to live to manage their lives, caring for one another after a perfect union. This was not possible under the absolute power of a despotic king or queen. That is why they decided to unite, *"E Pluribus Unum"*, [many in one], and establish a common defense, where all citizens, protect or protect each other. And in that state of tranquility and security promote the general welfare of the people, ensuring the benefits of freedom for us, *"We, the people and our posterity"*.

In reality, none of the people who came to North America had the right to be American citizens, just, and only, the native Americans. And if the Europeans took that citizen category all other people were entitled to the same, including people subjected to slavery. That is, at the time of the declaration of independence, all Europeans assumed the status of American citizens just because they lived on this continent. Consequently, and by the intention of the declaration of independence, the preamble and text of the constitution all the residents of the colonies become, in fact, also American citizens, with all the same rights as any other person. There is nothing in the constitution that sanctions otherwise. In addition, every person born in the territory (now American) is by birth American citizen; therefore, all the children of slaves were

American citizens, from that time on. So, the thirteenth amendment was not necessary. And the fourteenth amendment is nothing more than a clarification of an obvious fact included in the constitution. In fact, from the moment of the declaration of independence slavery was abolished all people held in slavery and their children became citizens of the United States of America. The constitution must be reformed to clarify this anomaly.

For the author the word "encourage" implies the continuous action of promoting and encouraging the effort to establish, maintain and improve the overall welfare for all (the people). Welfare means a state of all citizens whose physical and mental conditions provide a feeling of satisfaction and tranquility. And the term "we and our posterity" is an association or society, which made the agreement to found the Union. The benefits of freedom are for everyone, it's a social function. The author points out that promoting general welfare is not socialism or socialist action. This democratic republic does not protect the idea of nationalizing ownership and or the management of means of production by putting them in the hands of workers. The constitution promulgates that all men are equal at the will of the Creator, recognizing equal rights, duties and opportunities. It is equality that partly states that no one is above the law and all are equal before the law, as is sanctioned in the civil rights enacted in the first amendments to the [110],[111] constitution—in particular Amendment Fourteen: Civil Rights.

The author suggests that the people reserve their right to study, understand and interpret the meaning of the words included in the text of the constitution and to clarify the intention of the text referred to. The author understands the term "We" as "the people of the United States", implying and considering the people of the states and beyond each state—rather the conglomeration or all of the people of all states in the American Union—including future citizens. The author also interprets that the preamble does not represent a particular state but the totality of the thirteen English colonies in North America, united

---

[110] Definition of well-being:
[111] Definition of Socialism

by unanimous and voluntary consent, a Union or nation called the United States of America.

The phrase "... *in order to form a more perfect* Union," implies (1) that there was already a union of the people of the thirteen colonies, and that union is of the people who must now perfect it in something more formal and permanent, implying, that the improvement of the Union is a continuous process, defined by the phrase" ... *more perfect* [because it is not yet perfect]; this being the first objective (purpose) established by its hierarchical importance over the other objectives listed in this preamble. So, the name America represents, and indeed does and legally includes, the people of all thirteen colonies as if they were each of them at the same time, including people in slavery, at that time. Moreover, the Colony Union or the Nation that now represents them has a responsibility or duty to perfect this Union, insinuating that the original union is not yet perfect and follows a process of improvement over time. Actually, "... *form a more perfect Union...* "is more than a goal, it is rather an inevitable mandate, falling within the responsibilities of the legislative branch [the two chambers]. This purpose is explicit and expands to include, and indeed includes perfecting the mandates of, (1) *establishing justice,* (2) ensure *national tranquility,* (3) to provide for *common defense,* (4) to *promote national tranquility, and* (5) to *ensure the benefits of freedom for us*—the people of the colonies—where these goals are for the people of all colonies, without excluding any, of the now citizens of the United States; and extending these goals to their descendants, and the descendants of their descendants without limit of time. Thus, for this purpose the preamble promulgates and lays the foundations for a constitution of this union of states, the United States of America. In addition, the term *"we"* does not specify any distinction—or discrimination of people by any physical or mental characteristics, skin color, language, or religion—of the people of the colonies, and in fact includes all the people in these states who reside at the time of the establishment of the constitution and all who willingly adhere and agree to abide by and work on the improvement of these objectives.

On the other hand, the text implies that the objectives of Justice, tranquility, defense, well-being, and freedom are offered, and indeed, given to all citizens of the thirteen states equally and unconditionally. Likewise, the aim of forming a more perfect Union, as well as establishing those purposes, is an objective or task not only of the nation as a unit, but of "We, the people" and of each of the citizens of the thirteen states. The extension to "our posterity" involves not only the immediate descendants of the original population of the colonies but all new people who become citizens of the United States of America.

The term", *"promote general welfare"* implies a decision and action whose purpose and result is to create, maintain and improve people's physical and mental conditions within a state of satisfaction and tranquility. That is to say that anything that breaks, disturbs the balance of that state is against it and attacks the target in question. Of course, this principle applies to natural people who have the capacity for that feeling of satisfaction and tranquility; so that it does not

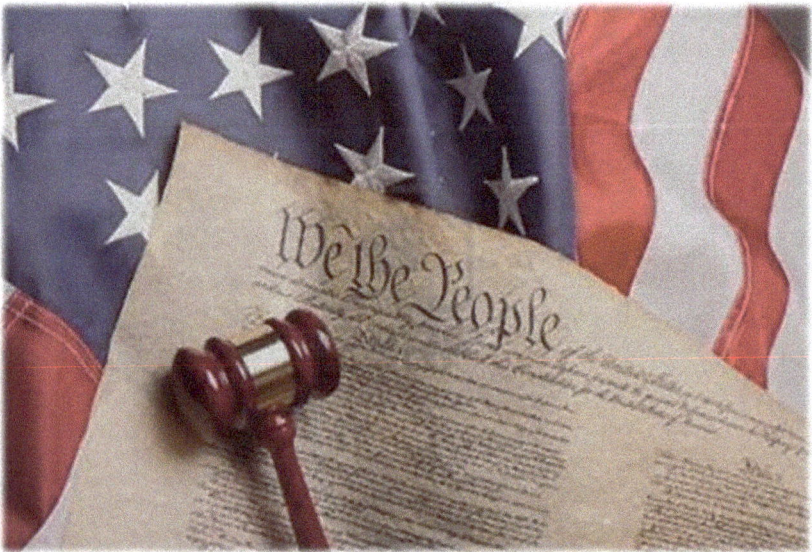

image borrowed from the Internet

include any legal or legal persons. On the other hand, *"... ensuring the benefits of freedom for us and for our posterity" implies the natural or natural persons of the people"* and does not mention fictitious people of that time or any other time. Finally, people enacted and established the Constitution for the United States of America, claiming the people, the people present, and their posterity.

The author interprets that was the intention and meaning of the text; and invites the reader to interpret the text in its own way and for this purpose includes the full text of the constitution of the United States of America in the end note [vii]. The author considers that every citizen should know the content of the constitution that binds the state in which he resides. And it also suggests that colleges and universities (lower and higher division) include classes on the constitution as general graduation requirements. Then let's move on to studying its contents.

Comments to the Text

The people of all the colonies, in unity of thought, drafted the constitution based on implicit and explicit purposes, and on the reasons that gave rise to separation and declaration of independence. The legal basis of the declaration of independence and the preamble to the constitution is the basis of the Constitution. Eight articles specifically broaden and legislate the objectives of that preamble. The author focuses his highlights. On what issues does the constitution need reform?

Article I –

Art. I, Section 1.

House of Representatives: The people elect their members to a period of two years. But what is the real reason that representatives are elected even a period of only two years, while senators are elected to a period of six. In truth, each new representative loses at least one third of their period by learning the protocol system of this chamber before contributing to something positive. Since this chamber is the largest, it should be thought that the election also in alternate groups as for senators.

Art. I, Section 2.

House of Representatives: You have the absolute power to press charges in political trials. The constitution does not clearly specify the procedures of political trials, nor does it criminalize the possible charges that such political trials give rise to, even though it vaguely mentions treason, high crime and misdemeanors. The lack of criminalization of charges leaves open the law to various interpretations that dilute the intent and effective application of the procedures.

We understand as "political judgments" "... a judicial process... to determine the liability of public officials in different facts or situations." The process results in a "judgment (political and arbitrary) ... limited to ordering the dismissal of the accused. But it does not exonerate the accused of possible "civil or criminal liability" and leaves open the possibility of judging [the accused] in subsequent trials "by an ordinary court".[112]

Art. I, Section 3.

Senate House: ... (members elected by the people) will be the only (body) empowered to judge Political Judgments. The scope of the sentence in Political Judgments shall not go beyond the dismissal of office and disqualification from holding and enjoying any honorary, trustworthy or remunerated office, which depends on the United States; but the condemned party will, however, be subject to being accused, prosecuted, judged and punished in accordance with the Law.

This section 3 sets the scope of the statement. And while it states that the convicted party is subject to legal proceedings under the law, the constitution does not mention anything regarding the exoneration of the accused party. The sentence only exonerates the accused of the possibility of being removed from office and does not relieve him of civil or criminal guilt of the act committed. The exoneration of civil and criminal acts can only be sentenced. Nor

---

[112] https://definition.de/juicio-politico

does it mention the civil or criminal responsibilities that the official found not guilty may face. Therefore, the convicted party or the destitute party "shall be subject to being accused, prosecuted, judged and punished in accordance with the law".

Article I, section 3, shows another situation that exposes government, constitution and democracy to political corruption and the deterioration of the separation of powers. Empowering the vice president of the executive branch as president of the Senate, even on certain occasions, and at the same time giving him the power to vote to resolve a tie of votes in the Senate, whatever that situation and or necessity, is an anomaly and openness to possible political corruption, because the executive branch, in this case, presides over two powers at the same time. The possibility of legislating in favor of the executive's interests is imminent. It is preferable to let the president of the Supreme Court take up that position and preside over the Senate with the right to vote a tiebreaker, as well as to preside over political trials in the Senate.

In this same section 3, the constitution empowers the Senate to judge political trials. Neither the constitution nor the amendments to the constitution specify a standard method for the process of political dismissal and in that case the senate is free to create its own rules for the process that may exonerate the accused for party political force.

Article I, section 5 promulgates that "Each Chamber may [or is entitled to] develop its rules of procedure, punish its members for inappropriate behavior, and expel them from its bosom with the consent of two-thirds. This section does not define or specific, much less typifies, inappropriate behavior, and the consequences and punishments of such behavior. The effect of defining such inappropriate behaviors and their corresponding punishments is, and should be, clear with the intention of maintaining ethics and transparency, as well as the separation of powers, avoiding the mixing of interests of powers. The case of Devin Gerald Nunez, a representative of the 22nd district of California and leader of the House Intelligence Committee, who served as a member of the President Trump transition team, did no take place. The investigation of this chamber's ethics committee closed the case without taking any action against Nunez. It was linked to alleged efforts to stop the investigation and to protect President Trump from any possible compromising allegations against the president. The constitution must clarify precisely in detail the limits of the separation of the three powers according to the intention of the republican government.

The role of judges of the supreme court of justice must be for a specific time determined no more than three presidential terms, but a Justice may run for re-election for no more than two additional term of twelve years, but should not participate in another election after their third re-election. The danger of life-making positions is the corruption that Benjamin Franklin anticipated 244 years ago.

Article I, Section 8.

The constitution sanctions in this section 8, the administration of the Military Reserve–provide, organize, arm and discipline the Military Reserve–thus fulfilling the duty of the Common Defense. But keep quiet about the militia. Since the constitution enacts the power of Congress to "Create lower courts than *the* Supreme Court of Justice". These are first instance and are within the federal judicial system of the United States.

The election of the candidates for the position of magistrate of the supreme court is the responsibility of the people. Candidates should not be nominated by any political party, therefore the judiciary is empowered to nominate no more than three candidates to meet the requirements established, including ethics and experience, by the House of Representatives. The election to the position of supreme court magistrate must be on the same date established for the election of the president and vice president. The date on which this amendment takes effect, the president shall be acquitted of the responsibility of nominating candidates for the supreme court and higher districts or courts.

Article II, Section 2.

Currently, the president has the power, by and with the advice and consent of the Senate, to appoint Justices of the Supreme Court of Justice.

This power is another vulnerable point of the constitution and democracy, it is serious and affects the separation of powers from the state because it lends itself to possible corruption of the government. That is, when the presidency (executive power) and the Senate (upper house) of the legislature belong to the same political party, the active president and the Senate approve the nomination of a candidate who favors the interests of that political party—two examples of this were the senate approval processes for Justices of the supreme court of Neil M. Gorsuch. , Brett M. Kavanaugh by Donald Trump. The separation of the powers of the state disappears when one power nominates the representatives of another power. In other words, this process destroys democracy along with the democratic right and duty of the people to elect their representatives. It is the people who, by their popular sovereignty have the absolute right to elect their representatives in the three powers. If the people do not have that right, then the republic is destroyed, and there is neither democracy nor separation of powers. Corruption is established in government, and powers become autocratic, acting under party interests. The constitution deserves an amendment to restore to the people the sovereign power and right to choose their representatives to the different powers.

Article III, Section 1.

Article IV. No comments.

Article V

Amendments. The responsibility for proposing amendments to the constitution is of both Houses of Congress, when they deem it necessary. Individual States in a number equal to or greater than two-thirds are also empowered to convene a Convention to propose Amendments to the Constitution. The question whether the power of central government is above the power of the state has an answer in the hierarchy of authority. We understand that everything that is not sanctioned in the constitution belongs to the power of each state or of the citizens of each state. That is, the power of government is limited to the authority and power that the people bestow upon it in the spirit and letter of the federal constitution.

Amendments to the constitution

Amendments to the US constitution are made in compliance with the constitutional purpose of making a more perfect Union. That is why it should not be weird, extraordinary, or unnecessary to amend the articles of the constitution to adapt it to the socio-political and economic conditions of today. To date, twenty-seven amendments have been enacted, the last revision of which was sanctioned on 7 May 1992, approximately twenty-eight years ago.[113]

Amendment 1. Freedom of worship, expression, press, petition and assembly without government intervention. It was proposed on 25 September 1789. That is to say that any attempt to act or coerce bay any ruler, public or clandestine, to silence, reduce or eliminate such rights, must be considered a high crime against the constitution, and against popular sovereignty.

Amendment 2. The right to bear arms is not a natural right, but is the right then created to legalize the popular defense against the forces of the English monarchy. By decreeing this right, he removed the king's authority to arrest the citizens of the colonies for possessing and carrying weapons. It was a necessary defense argument that also created the militias. In reality, the purpose of having and carrying weapons is controversial, and the purpose is not clarified in these

---

[113] https://es.wikipedia.org/wiki/Anexo:Enmiendas_a_la_Constitución_de_los_ Estados_Unidos

times. It has been said before that the United States has the most powerful armed forces in the world, and also has a military reserve both highly organized, trained and disciplined. While the possible militias of these times, it is neither organized nor trained to defend the people as intended. The author believes that the militias should be organized and trained to fulfil their role.

Fifth Amendment

For a neophyte citizen in the interpretation of the law, this amendment is not entirely clear, so that this same citizen uses the interpretation of scholars in laws. However, the layman understands that the Fifth Amendment extends rights relevant to civil and criminal proceedings. This amendment guarantees the right of a grand jury, self-incrimination protection and receiving fair legal process as part of those proceedings. But the author notes that this amendment makes no mention or reference to political trials, such as a process of elected officials' dismissal of public office—cases that are not criminal or civil. Political trials are explicitly delegated to the legislature with the power to file dismissal charges and recommendation (in the house of representatives) and corresponding trial (in the Senate Chamber). This amendment explicitly states that in criminal cases the right to a grand jury and protection against self-incrimination.

Twelfth Amendment. This amendment replaces Article II, Section 1, clause 2 of the constitution. This section sanctioned a procedure that proved inefficient in its original form in reference to the functioning of the electoral college in the presidential elections. There were two elections in 1796 and the 1800 election that proved certain inefficiencies of that electoral procedure. Now in the 2016 presidential election in which Donald Trump was elected, it is noted that Hilary Clinton won the most votes by a clear percentage and yet the electoral college elected Trump. It may not be an anomaly, but it leaves evidence that democracy does not work and that those who receive the most votes of the people lose the election to the office of president. This case is something that the legislature must study thoroughly with two alternatives, (1) better the electoral college procedure, or (2) eliminate it altogether and establish an effective and secure method to ensure the election of a president deserving of the will of the people.

Twenty-fifth amendment legislates that when the president dies, or resigns from office, the vice president assumes the office of presidency. The constitution and this amendment cover only those two conditions of the president inability to govern the nation. Situations such as difficulties, mental, intellectual, moral and little knowledge to lead the nation in compliance with what the constitution establishes in its single article, its preamble are not included. The constitution should clarify the behavior, and intellectual and moral capacity that is expected of the candidate to, and indeed the, president. The careful qualification of the requirements to the office of president must be clear and constitutionally accurate.

The Government

As far as the government is concerned, the constitution must establish in an amendment the behavior of a president who makes him a monarch, autocrat or dictator. The president has no absolute power over the states, he's not a monarch, he's not a dictator, he's just a president. President D. Trump's actions leave much to be desired, and Mr. Trump's judgment is not fit to govern this great nation; we, the people, are at great risk of irreparably damaging our Republican government, our constitution and our democracy.

Division of powers

The settlers were able to choose any division of powers–of course there are several–however, they adopted the trichotomy of power already known in Europe, thinking that they could avoid any form of absolutism. But, although the intent is morally good, every system always has an intrinsic or innate weakness; a point of failure is a low rate of operation effectiveness: the human factor and its intention. In other words, -when the operator, or operators, in any way ignores (or ignores) the procedures in place for effective system operation and maintenance, the operator or operators, unintentionally or intentionally, alter the objective, behavior and effectiveness of the entire system. That is, a monarchical, autocratic or dictator government can, if left alone, destroy the people's democracy. The founding fathers knew all of the above and expressed it, in fact, they included in the declaration of independence, a precise phrase that says, *"... The Laws of Nature and the God of Nature entitles them* [the people], [and] a decent respect for the *opinions of humanity requires them to declare the causes that drive them to separation* [amend the fault to restore democracy]." This is the control valve that prevents, reduces and cuts the arbitrariness of such despotic governments.

The author finds in the fault tree of the democratic system of the republic that the definition of the legal framework (The Rule of Law) defining the delegation of the three powers is not clear and specific enough to prevent the possible abuse of authority and power of a despotic ruler. And it states that the possible failure is the weaknesses or vulnerabilities of the chosen system, even if the founders have included in the republic respect for the civil liberties of the settlers–now citizens of the United States of America–are the democratic, intrinsic values of a democratic republic that depend on the honesty of elected and unelected officials in government.

The founders thought that dividing the power of central government into Legislative, Judicial and Executive and clarifying the operation of the system in their magna carta would protect or guarantee the existence of the democratic republic. But for the sake of the definition of "democracy and respect for this idea"; perhaps it was the impulse of freedom of choice. Did they leave the operational specifications of the system short?

The author does not think that it was so, on the contrary, observes that they thought about this subject, in fact, they included the remedy of this possibility, in the text of the declaration of independence that says, *"But when a long train of abuses and usurpations, invariably pursuing the same Object evidences a design to reduce them under absolute despotism, it is their right, it is their duty, to discard that government, and to provide new guards for their future security".* This is the political mechanism to safeguard the integrity of the democratic republic which is not yet fully legislated. A restoration procedure is not clearly defined in the constitution, *"the social contract"*. This phrase, however, defines, without a doubt, popular sovereignty, clarifying that no representative of the people, elected or not, with the power and authority granted by the people is not, or may be, above will, of the power of the people–their sovereignty.

In reality, the duty to maintain the integrity of the constitution and its rules of law is the people and the representatives acting on behalf of the people. The phrase with which the founding fathers initiate the constitution reads, *"We, the People of the United States, in order to form a more perfect Union. we establish and sanction this Constitution for the United States of America."* The author understands that the intention expressed in this sentence is a sustained action during the existence of the union; it is not an occasional, isolated, one-moment and one-moment action; the phrase involves a sequence of actions over the time necessary to make, each time, the most perfect union. Thus, the phrase implies the responsibility of all citizens and the government representing the people to continue to seek ways, methods and procedures that improve that union. Where the term *"union"* represents the will and sovereignty of the people, entailing the innate desire to improve their democratic republic; and also considers that everything-standards applicable to states with equality and equal effectiveness-that has to do with the common national interests, such as defense, security, health, diplomatic relations, international exchange and trade (export and import), immigration, and everything compatible with the common interests of all states are the responsibilities of a federal government.

The states and the central government

The principle of popular sovereignty is superlative to national sovereignty, being that the second derives from the first all its authority and powers that are limited to the spirit and letter of the constitution, the social contract.

"Heritage governments have inherent advantages, which will once give them influence and ancestry over the National Government,

and will forever prevent the possibility of federal invasions. That their freedoms, in fact, can be subverted by the federal chief, is repugnant to all rules of political calculation."

So, this being the political relationship between the central government and the states of the Union, there is no idea that the executive component of a government elected by the people can assume, or indeed assume, an autocratic, dictatorial or monarchical position with absolute powers over the states or people. This position is what President Donald Trump has, insinuated, or indeed attempted, or attempts to assume. The darkness of the intention of the text, or deficiency, of the constitution gives possibilities for a misinterpretation of its intention. This is why, in order to form a *more perfect union* and reduce or eliminate the corruption that Benjamin Franklin foresaw, it is necessary to reform the constitution as often as required by the evolution of the people's way of life. These reforms must clearly establish the scope of authority and power that the people confer on the three powers of their government, mainly to the executive branch. These reforms must also fully ensure the separation of the three powers, eliminating any possibility of political interference or influence, for part-party or personal benefits, of power over the other two. No one is above the law.

Government size

In reality, the size of the central government must be clearly defined in terms of the distribution of powers. It is not enough to stipulate that what is not sanctioned in the constitution is the matter and responsibility of the states or the people. The preamble sets out a purpose *in order to form a more perfect union, establish justice, ensure national tranquility, tend to the common defense, promote general welfare and secure the benefits of freedom for us,* the people. These are the terms on which the constitution is founded. The responsibility is to establish, the principles and higher political or legal bases for the exercise of such objectives, in general terms. And the laws of the states must follow these principles and bases covering the details of local situations and circumstances. So, the central government acts as a control over the laws being applied equally in terms of such principles and bases. The distribution of the nation's power is hierarchical following the resolution of problems and circumstances from the bottom up. In this context, the administrative management and control of social, political and economic affairs rests with the states and each state for their environmental characteristics, availability of resources, and idiosyncrasies of their population, in addition to being closer to the source of the problem, they must be responsible for applying the details of governance. So, and in this situation, the central government can be reduced to managing the general guidelines for the application of the constitution commonly applicable to all states. While the particularities of each state are under state responsibility; for example, the health, education, employment and unemployment, environmental control, and others. In short, general rules are handled by central government, while contingent local rules are handled by states that are closest to the sources of situations. Legislative power with the assistance of the executive branch should consider how to expedite governance by balancing the distribution of authority and duties of governments, central and state. Another example, the federal government decrees by stipulating the legal basis and its criminal consequences, that discrimination on the basis of race, religion, sexual tendencies, social status, and the like, in any form, covered or discovered, is intolerable and totally prohibited in the United States. States assume the authority and duty to create their own laws, regulations, and equal application to fulfill those federal purposes. Likewise, the function of resolving environmental impacts are local in nature and states are responsible for acting as first central government-assisted first responders in whatever the state needs. This process should be well established to trigger automatically when a disaster passes, for example, pandemics, hurricanes, earthquakes, etc. In other words, authority and power must be hierarchical, and that hierarchy is what the constitution and its derived laws must clearly sanction.

Civil and political rights[114]

With regard to civil and political rights in relation to the constitution, the author finds that the federal and other state governments do not protect individual freedoms and break the intent and mandate of the constitution. There are repressions, open and covert. One of the murders of recent times was that of George Floyd, captured on the cell camera by eyewitnesses, in broad daylight. Later, during protest demonstrations and public petitions, there was an overlapping crackdown, abuse of authority and power on the part of the executive against the demonstrators. In other words, the federal government (executive power does not guarantee the ability of citizens to participate in the nation's civil and political life equally, without racism or discrimination.

Civil Rights

These are the rights granted within a state acquired by the fact of being born, according to naturalistic concepts, or by the idiosyncrasies of the constitution of each state. It is interesting to note that John Locke proposed *"that natural rights to life, freedom, and property should be converted into civil rights and protected by the sovereign state as an aspect of the social contract (constitutional rights)."* The author agrees with Locke as to the absence of any form of laws, life, freedom granted by Nature and the Creator of nature along with the resources of the environment where man lives, and the property that by man's own efforts he obtains from his environment–this happens without course the presence of groups, societies and or communities. The constitution should clarify the right to Life and Freedom, but remains silent regarding the definition of Property. Constitutional reform must sanction the extension of these inalienable rights of man. Considering the fundamental property necessary to protect and maintain life and economic property as a function of personal enrichment that adds nothing more to the life of the human being,

---

[114] https://es.wikipedia.org/wiki/Derechos_civiles_y_políticos

outside of additional conveniences and pleasures. In this sense water and air being necessary for the support and maintenance of Life should not be owned by private companies, but of the common property of citizens, managed by the government, as a vital article and health. In the hands of the private company whose objective is speculatively to obtain the greatest profit could suppress the supply, make the article more expensive, making man's life impossible.

Let's look at this *"all peoples" "right of self-determination" as a note of evidence. The so-called "collective rights", as opposed to "individual rights", are among the "rights of generation" according to the theory of the three generations of rights.*

Human rights

In addition to the right to life and freedom come other rights necessary to live Life in the best possible way alone and in relation to one or more individuals–without these complementary rights lives is not possible. In other words, all these complementary rights to protect and maintain individual life must also be part of the inalienable right of the right of life.

Political rights

As regards the relationship between individuals there are certain rights that include the expression and participation of individuals in democratic groups and societies and therefore social and public life. In other words, these rights give way to influencing political efforts in participatory democratic societies. In the United States, citizen participation in the event and political management is the best thing in the world, although it is not perfect, it has its flaws. For example, there have been failures of the electoral college process in the selection of presidents. It once happened in 1776 and was instead drastic of that process. In modern times, the electoral college was found to have chosen Donald Trump as president when the opposition candidate won a majority of the popular vote, in the 2016 election. In other words, the electoral college overcame the sovereignty of the popular will. In this case it was a violation of the political right of the people, to the fundamental principles of democracy–the selection of the representatives of the people in the government by the majority of votes.

Natural rights

What are natural rights? Seeing this subject from the point of creation of the universe and the intention of existence, we find that man exists by explicit and implicit human conditions. These physical and mental conditions cannot be revoked, ignored, denied, and in any regular or restricted form. These are innate conditions that no man has written in any rule of law. They exist at the will of Nature and the Creator of nature. They are human conditions that are governed by the laws of existence superlative to laws written by man and which are governed by the universal concepts of good or evil. No positive legal order can contravene or contravene this moral, legal order of existence. Within these rights we find not only the right to life, but the natural right to learn, know, study, and apply knowledge to the extent and extent that the form and live of the individual requires it.

States vs Central Government

It was at the convention of 1787, a year after the end of the war of independence, the founders established a Federal and Democratic Republic. That is, the United States of America, the new nation on the new continent, free and sovereign, was a republic composed of thirteen states and with democratic characteristics. It is just and appropriate to analyze the meaning of this broad title, democratic. A federal republic defines its meaning by its content and nature; in this case it is an organization of a central government that represents and manages the plurality of thirteen local governments, the states, which in turn have their own administrative organizations-their governments. The central government assumes a delegated power by the thirteen states and derived from the powers of those same states. A federal government has a sovereignty that is born of the proper sovereignty of the states, consolidating that sovereignty into a standard criterion applicable to states. Causally, on the cause of effect, these criteria in themselves establish the responsibilities of local governments and central governments according to the origin and proximity of particular and general issues and problems. States have different realities and common realities, i.e. particular and general; therefore, there are issues that are preferable and more efficient to let states handle them and there are issues that it is preferable to let the central government handle. The federal republic then assumes responsibility for managing or managing the needs and problems that affect autonomy in a general way. For example, to maintain the balance of the equal allocation of resources, tax collection is a divided function between local and central government.

Democratic Republic

As for the term Democratic Republic, it is a form of government–very different from a monarchy, an autocracy or a dictatorship–that configures its central (administrative) government structure to receive and manage the power that the people entrust and delegate to their responsibility, based on respect for the legal framework–the social contract.

Origin of political parties

The reason political parties emerge and exist is because, in fact, there are different perspectives of life and the way of life. People stick to another of similar political thoughts and groups are formed based on an ideal thought. In the course of life, too, with experience and as knowledge grows those perspectives and ideals can change and man changes his mental position, clinging to other groups. Freedom of thought and expression is manifested by the advancement of knowledge. And even if some call betrayal those who change groups, it is not-in fact-betrayal but the result of intellectual evolution that changes the old perspectives. This way of thinking is imbued in the preamble to the political constitution of the United States of America hidden in the phrase *"... decent respect for the opinions of humanity requires them to declare the causes that drive them to separation."* The respect that is called for is implicit in the recognition of new opinions–as the prospects of life change with the advancement of knowledge and the growth of experience–that is acquired.

The author acknowledges, on the basis of what he has explained in this book to this point, that the settlers had, at the time, different opinions. Some thought that perhaps it was better to remain under the rule of the English crown, while others, firm in their purpose, longed for total freedom under self-government, structured to their liking. The result of a declaration and subsequently the drafting and implementation of the constitution is an obvious fact of its prospects. After the declaration of independence, and later, after the war, the time came to exercise his authority and manage his own destiny. The political parties of the United States have a common origin. And even though everyone thought of a federal union, it had their differences in how to distribute power. So, the federalist idea of the federalist party was broken up by that controversy. Some thought full control of the government would be in the hands of one central government and another thought states would maintain their political autonomy. And so, came in the Republican Democratic party on one side and on the other the federalist party. By 1816 the federalist party vanished and amid controversial issue of slavery the Republican democratic party departed; some who rejected slavery behind the ideas of Abraham Lincoln, the Wig party (by his name Whig) and others who wanted to maintain slavery formed Andrew Jackson's Democratic party, around the election of John Quincy Adams in 1828. [115] [116] Political thinking is refined or polished with better perspectives and the intellectual position changes course. So philosophical thinking progresses in a natural process that follows the increase in consciousness. Then those who wanted to abolish slavery

---

[115] https://www.aboutespanol.com/origen-de-los-partidos-politicos-en-eeuu-1772313

[116] https://norbertobarreto.blog/2012/05/17/breve-historia-de-los-partidos-politico-en-los-estados-unidos/

marched behind high concepts of *"free territory, free work, freedom of speech, free men";* it was the Republican party.

Hoy en día los republicanos alzan el banderín de *"Haz América grandiosa de nuevo"*, sin aclarar el verdadero significado de dicho concepto. Hay quien dice que *"no sigas lo que dicen, sino observa lo que hacen"*–Rachel Maddox, CNN; así veras la intención de lo que dicen. El autor observa el patrón de acción y hechos del gobierno de Donald Trump esa frase puede implicar una supremacía blanca en el poder y la opresión de clases minoritarias (gente con piel de color).

Purposes of the union

There are only six purposes of the Union stated in the preamble to the constitution, its Unique Article. In the following graph of hexagons, social equality is hexagon 1 in the center above. Human equality is the first objective or purpose of the Union. We have seen, with regard to social equality, that the original intentional one is distorted from the beginning. Long before independence the colonies were embroiled in the slave trade. Colonies like Rhode Island, for

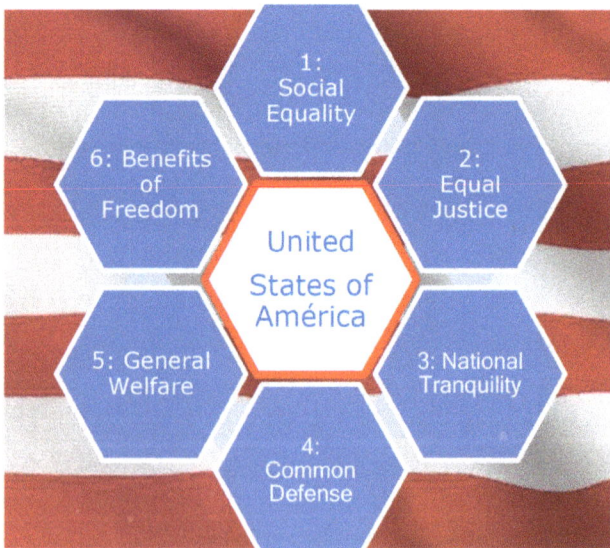

Author's graphic creation

example, settlers captured and sold Native Americans as slaves, in addition to the trafficking and use of slaves by African people. The African slave trade in the New York colony is one of its main trades. There is no equality if there are social differences in the Union, let alone slavery in the United States. It was casually the slavery the cause of the civil war and as a consequence the abolition of slavery in this country. Slavery existed from the beginning of the English colonies in North America. And the bottom line was that even though the declaration of independence says *"we consider these truths to be obvious, that all men (women and men) are created equal,"*, slavery was firmly established when the United States Declaration of Independence was signed. [117] The new republic was divided into slave states and free states on both sides of the Mason-Dixon line. This line separated Maryland (slaver) and Pennsylvania (free).

The differences are obvious; the minority struggles to achieve adequate education and health that allows them to compete with those who hold capital. Most of the middle class down (ninety-nine percent of the population) are below the line between the affluent and poor class. That line of class separation continues to rise, so that the population in poverty increases. The poor class cannot enjoy *the benefits of freedom,* let alone consider enjoying *general welfare or seeking Happiness.* There is no *national tranquility* (social and economic) for them. These differences are part of the mirage of democracy. The cost of living has reached the point where the poor class only sees the benefits from the distance. A minimum wage person cannot afford a ticket to their favorite sport. They can't think of sending their children to college, and it's a miracle that these children get scholarships to a lower-class college. Is this equality? No, it's not. Is this equal opportunity? Obviously, it's not either. The land of opportunity is not for all its citizens, when only a few enjoy the benefits of *freedom.*

Social equality is another part of the Mirage of the Union. There are still deep racial resentment and discrimination, hatred, of certain white members against people of colored skin. The demonstrations

---

[117] https://es.wikipedia.org/wiki/Esclavitud_en_los_Estados_Unidos

in protest of the murder of George Floyd are clear evidence that we, the people indeed, must, demand a general reform of the constitution and the laws that derive from it to make the concept that men are created equally reality not only the initial dream.

The constitution needs reforms to return to the purpose of *to form a more perfect Union, to restore Justice, to ensure tranquility, and to promote general well-being for us, the people, and our posterity.* Perhaps we, the people of the United States, need several years to study the lessons of criminal acts against the constitution and its rules of law that certain government officials have committed. But it is necessary to begin the steps required to restore the course of the Union government, its constitution and its democracy to the original concept of men "... *They are endowed by their Creator with certain inalienable rights, which include Life, Freedom and the Pursuit of Happiness...*"

Democracy should not be effective only on election days, when the people exercise their popular sovereignty and observe and elect their representatives who handle the affairs of the people, supposedly, but a participatory democracy for every day of the existence of this Union and its democracy. It is a fact that when we authorize a representative of one power to elect another representative of another power, democracy ends, for it is not the people who elect their representatives in the different (allegedly) separate powers. The separation of powers ends and corruption is born among the hidden agendas of corrupt politicians and they no longer work for the people, disrespecting the fundamental concept of the constitution it says.

—*"... promote general welfare and ensure for us and our prosperity the benefits of Freedom"*—.

It is a legal anomaly that must be closed as soon as possible. The founders' intention was clear and frank. They saw the possibility that one or many will act on their own to subvert the chaste spirit of the Union. The attempt at subversion has been seen up close, as in the administration of the forty-second president of the United States of America. This president has shown that it is feasible and possible to install a dictatorship—even a monarchy—despotic and autocratic take possession of the government of the people, by the people, and for the people, forgetting or de facto ignoring the constitutional mandate sanctioned.

It must be admitted that rhetorical demagoguery does not represent the reality of commitment; only the subsequent action reveals the true intent behind demagoguery—by that time may be too late—when the damage that fact. After the elections there is eminent danger that representatives will follow party policies that may be incompatible with the will of the people. The republic depends on the ethical integrity of its three powers; and the corruption of executive power only needs a portion of the legislative power to change the history of American democracy in a short time. What happened in the political prosecution of President Trump between December 8, 2019 and February 5, 2020 shows what was said earlier.

The social gaps defined by the level of wealth and power that each one has, marks the socio-economic state. And the political, economic and social dynamics are growing in favor of a few rich. Maybe it shouldn't be, but it's the result of the situation within the mirage floating on the hot, dry sand, the desert, our lives. Natural law points out that the wealth of this nation belongs to the people, but the government—responsible for protecting the people, has mortgaged this great popular heritage at the hands of an *autocratic-capitalism* system. Every system is good if the system works for the benefit of all its components. But the system is harmful if some of its components work for the benefit of a few elements. The poor man's fantasy of economic independence is just that; because the rich and powerful with their hidden agendas turn everything they touch into their own riches. There is no equality-social, political or economic-even if the constitution so says; exists only in the mirage of the great system created. That is, free enterprise and the free market—which a few control—took the government that was created as the people, for the people and by the people; *autocrat—capitalism* I take it for the benefit of those selfish rich; they manipulate capital-money. The absolute power of the English monarchy at the time—the same one that gave rise to the independence of the thirteen colonies—capitalism is the monarchy of today, here we are not talking comparatively about socialism, communism, and capitalism; we are setting up the selfishness of the few who corrupt the good capitalist system. This is the point, past governments culminating in the current one has allowed—or rather fell into the sphere of influence of the great capitals. But capitalism is not the cause of socio-economic differences, but selfish ambition—the boundless accumulation of capital at one end of the economic balance and wealth—allowed by an accomplice and also corrupt government, attacking the power of the people.

The time has come, but not to make another civil war calling for the restoration of the principles of the constitution—actually being a right and duty of popular sovereignty—but to initiate critical changes to the course of our egalitarian democracy in this twentieth century and one. This is the theme of this book; it is the goal of the theme and the essence of its goal. It is the author's view that, pressed by the present situation—economic, social and political—sees a need to reform our way of life in the United States of America. Let's read the following, for example.

General Welfare

The government must establish general welfare in the aspects of health, education, safety, equal opportunities, and individual protection.

Economic aspects

The government must create the economic balance by raising citizens' wages and wages and eliminating the low-middle-middle economic strangle. The government must enforce equal opportunity for all the citizens.

Educational aspects

Release education to an equal, free and hierarchical education in order to create productive individuals from the end of their middle education (secondary schools) to the first university level (first four years). The government should structure the national education on a vocational path. That is, individuals should be equipped to gainfully join the wealth producing force at three levels: end of high school, end of junior college, and end of four years college; and of course at end technical schools, and institutes of technology.

Social Aspects

The federal government must lay the foundations, methods, and procedures to avoid nation-paralyzing situations such as the economy and business and social functions. And must re-train the law enforcing agents and rewrite policies to avoid, reduce, eliminate abuse of force and authority, guaranteeing it does not occur.

Health Aspects

Likewise, the government to establish or reinstate an endemic and or pandemic prevention system that can cried the economic, educational, commercial, etc.

Health Care Crisis

The Pandemic of Coronavirus COVID-19 opened the intimacy of the distribution of powers with state governments and central government. The classic controversy of those who have the power to say what to do regarding the pandemic is clear. The president decided to do nothing at first saying that was a decision of each state. But later said he is the ultimate authority to order the opening of business, schools, services, etc. Meanwhile the western states, California, Oregon, and Washington signed a state pact agreeing to reopen their economies based on certain health conditions, with a system of testing, monitoring, and isolation of the virus.

"If you want to change the model, you can change the model. He is the president of the United States," Said Andrew Cuomo, adding, *"But then change the model and explain it. What does that mean that the federal government is in charge of the opening?"*

We know the central government is responsible of establishing an action plan to deal with disasters, in this case the Covid-19 pandemic, letting the states implement methods to resolve crises according to the actual local situation.

Political Aspects

President Trump thinks he is the ultimate authority, and states should obey his mandates. This is in relation to the process of opening up the economy when Coronavirus Covid-19 is not yet controlled. Governors of California, Oregon, and Washington on the West Coast and New York, Connecticut, Massachusetts, Rhode Island, New Jersey. Pennsylvania, created their own, independent, defense coalitions.

There was a political battle at the beginning of the pandemic. The president said he would likely direct his economic working group to "opening the country" in the days that followed. His actions cleared his intention; his agenda is not to serve the people without benefiting politically and economically taking advantage of pandemic situation. Some state governors on both coasts announced they will drive their decisions by facts, science, and public health professionals, not politics, directing their efforts to ward off the president's actions.

CHAPTER 7

Lessons Learned

What has happened over the years since 1776 happened in the weeks following Memorial Day 2020. Other similar situations of injustice, racial and social economic differences, is what the senate did with the political trial to dismiss president Trump, early in 2020. The Republican Senate supported what this president did against the constitution and the rules of law, and continues supporting what he does. All of these events are evidences of the failure of the government, violating the fundamental principles of the declaration of independence and the Constitution. The Union government walks on the side of the danger of losing its own existence and identity, and we, the people, can only state the lessons we have learned and point the way to restoring America's goal of independence. The current situation (2020) is caused by Donald Trump's inability to govern. However, the president's selfish actions uncovered areas where his government and past governments have failed.

First lesson: Discrimination and Racism

We cannot deny that discrimination and racism exist in the United States. It has been growing for a long time. Racial discrimination is ongoing and not ending. At least that's how they see it and publish at certain news centers. [118],[119]. We read on the headers of a Wikipedia article the following. [120]*After his release during the civil war by Abraham Lincoln, the southern states, resentful of his defeat during the civil war, passed a variety of laws to discriminate against black citizens. This phenomenon occurred during the period of "reconstruction" after the civil war. With the election of Rutherford B. Hayes as the nineteenth president, discrimination spread to the northern states that initially had it more smoothly, to such an extent that at the beginning of the 20th century you could see the severity of discrimination and racism in places like New York, Boston, Detroit, Chicago and Los Angeles. According to a study between 1830 and 1950, 4,000 blacks were lynched in the United States. Which, according to the source, was often a public and popular spectacle with sometimes thousands of witnesses. Where 25% of the accusations were abuse against whites; where the victim was not even required to be recognized by the aggressor and that caused the emigration or ethnic purity of 6,000,000 blacks to the north and west of the country. As states could not eliminate the rights of blacks, which are guaranteed in the constitution, the "segregation" that was legal for many years was used under the idea of... "Separate but equal". The idea was that as long as the opportunities that were awarded were the same for both races, this was legal.* [121]

There are more cases in public records that can be obtained under the right of information we still have. But discrimination is not only with citizens in black skin, but against all citizens who have no white skin. These individuals are considered to be citizens of lower classes, or are inferior, than those of white-skin. Discrimination does not stop on these skin color themes; discrimination against the female sex, for example, the equal pay-as-a-work rule does not apply to women, who receive about 75 percent of what men receive doing the same work. All this happens that despite the constitution considers *"that all men are created equal, that they are endowed by their*

---

[118] https://www.hispantv.com/noticias/ee-uu-/437191/racismo-discriminacion-salarios
[119] https://es.aleteia.org/2017/07/02/eeuu-discriminacion-racial-que-no-acaba/
[120] https://es.wikipedia.org/wiki/Racismo_en_Estados_Unidos
[121] https://es.wikipedia.org/wiki/Racismo_en_Estados_Unidos

Creator with certain inalienable rights, which include life, freedom and the pursuit of Happiness."

We cannot deny that there is discrimination and racism in America. You can't when the abundant evidence confirms it. There is no denying that the Klu Klux Klan still exists in operational form have marched in public streets and places this year 2020. Actually, we don't know how many representatives of the people in government are members of the clan. If the presidents of recent decades are guilty of not doing anything to reduce, eliminate and ensure that discrimination and racism in America will not work. Legislative power is also guilty for failing to pass severe laws aimed at eliminating discrimination and racism that exists open or undercover. In this context there is complicity marked by inaction and silence.

Second lesson: Social inequality

Is there equality in the United States? No, not in the manner mentioned in the constitution. Inequality in the United States that the fundamental concept of equality of men is part of the mirage of democracy that we project to the world. And because of many social, economic and political arbitrariness, we violate the supreme mandate of the constitution of the United States United states that clearly says,

> ... *"We consider that these truths are obvious, that all men are created equal...*

Indeed, large social, economic, and political gaps or differences clearly show that a minority controls the nation's power and wealth. This minority have abducted for them the benefits of freedom achieved in 1776. Ninety-nine percent of the population controls only one percent of national wealth; while one percent of the population controls ninety-nine percent of that wealth. We cannot say that there is economic equality in this great nation.

There are several ways to measure equality in a nation; among these is the coefficient (percentage) of Gini. The author thinks that inequality grows in form and substance over time, and resentment also increases in proportion resisting and fighting against that unfair growth. And this resentement is the time bomb that Bernie Sanders talks about so much. The United States is one of the countries with the highest percentage of inequality.

The distribution of a country's wealth is a misunderstood concept. The author believes that it is not necessary to take away from the rich to give to the poor; it is not about creating a Robin Hood-nation. Distribution is made from the present into the future. And the government prepares the citizens or its people to compete, establishing equal rules and ways for citizens to participate in the competition while normalizing enrichment, all for the sake of equality according to the Single Article of the Constitution—*to form a more perfect Union...* [and so forth].

Third lesson: Corruption in search of power and authority

Corruption, abuse of power and authority is endemic that should not be tolerated. He says it's endemic is generosity; indeed, it should be said that it is a pandemic that occupies the world in all its spheres: social, political, and economic. The three terms, corruption, abuse of power and abuse of authority are man's attitudes that he has dragged from the beginning of time. It is practically man's *modus Vivendi* in modern societies, to the point that societies accept it as a standard behavior.

Corruption

What is corruption in itself? [122] For the author is an attitude of man who breaks the order of behavior that existence expects. Man discusses his behavior between two alternatives in each thought, decision, and action he takes. It is a moral and conscience action

---

[122] https://www.significados.com/corrupcion/

that man assumes in choosing between good and evil, the just and unjust, the right and wrong. And regardless of external influences, internal influences are always the responsibility of man, because man's decision is based on these internal influences. The desirable step of existence is behavior for and for good, just and right.

Benjamin Franklin understood the phenomenon of corruption well and predicted the need to upgrade the Union to a higher state of perfection on the grounds of corruption. Corruption in the political sphere encourages and predisposes the abuse of power and authority, which in most cases is to achieve personal or group-specific benefits. It can be said that the abuse of power and authority are descendants of mother corruption. So, eliminating corruption actually eliminates abuses of power and authority. In truth, reforms to the constitution should focus as major issues on reducing, eliminating and ensuring how not to allow them to occur in the future. As long as the people do not demand and the government does not implement these measures, the Union is at risk of self-extermination, as has happened with other major empires in history. The Ottoman, Persian, Greek or Roman empires.

The author finds on the Internet a definition that partly says, *"Corruption is often related in the popular imagination to the world of politics and illicit enrichment, that is, to money, but not only to that. Corruption applies to many instances. For this reason, there is political corruption, economic corruption, sexual corruption, etc. This is because the two big exchange factors that mobilize corruption are often money, power, and sex."* [123] The author maintains that corruption is born of the human ego when consciousness loses control of the behavior of the ego. That is, corruption is reflected in the action, visible-tangible, of man, but it is the product of his ego. The endemicity of corruption is what the constitution must attack with a reform of the constitution as a matter of urgency.

---

[123] https://www.significados.com/corrupcion/

Abuse of authority

What is abuse of authority? The term authority necessarily implies hierarchical differences in a social, political and economic structure; where a person on a higher rung is in charge or is responsible for other people in lower positions, or rungs, who are their subordinates. Abuse of authority, as a derivative of corruption, is found by the aforementioned areas or structures. But for the matter that concerns us, politics, we focus the issue on the government sector. That is, the use of the authority conferred on a representative of the people for personal benefits or of a group of persons of his choice, be it this attitude applied to the use of resources and or the submission of subordinate persons to perform unlawful acts for and of self-desirability. We have seen Donald Trump's behavior ordered his underlings to alter, destroy, or hide information and/or documents. Important information and/or documents in the investigation pursued by independent or public investigators. As well as abuse of authority, it was an abuse of procedures necessary for the recruitment of close relatives to positions under his charge. Abuse of authority.

Abuse of Authority

What is abuse of authority? The term authority necessarily implies hierarchical differences in a social, political and economic structure; where a person on a higher rung is in charge or is responsible for other people in lower positions, or rungs, who are their subordinates. Abuse of authority, as a derivative of corruption, is found by the aforementioned areas or structures. But for the matter that concerns us, politics, we focus the issue on the government sector. That is, the use of the authority conferred on a representative of the people for personal benefits or of a group of persons of his choice, be it this attitude applied to the use of resources and or the submission of subordinate persons to perform unlawful acts for and of self-desirability. We have seen Donald Trump's behavior ordered his underlings to alter, destroy, or hide information and/or documents. Important information and/or documents in the investigation pursued by independent or public investigators. As well as abuse of authority, it was an abuse of procedures necessary for the recruitment of close relatives to positions under his charge.

Abuse of Power

Power is the freedom and responsibility for decision, action and jurisdiction granted to a person, the proxy, to execute on behalf of another, one or more persons or a people, the grantor, the will, duties and powers, in accordance with the interests of the grantor. The definitions of abuse of power are consistent, perhaps with certain variants, but agree that it is the use of the power conferred in the description of a position, in this case in public management, is the excessive, incorrect, unfair and improper use with respect to the description of the office and in violation of the natural and or positive rights of the citizens they represent, the grantor. There are certain typical actions that stand out among many that have the same purpose or purpose. For example, these.

(1) An authority uses the power it holds and compels a subordinate to do things that are not up to his duties under threat of punishing or depriving him of something. (2) an authority, superior or leader overtakes the exercise of his duties by requiring a subordinate, on the basis of threats such as loss of employment or any other benefit, to perform certain actions or activities that he should not develop. (3) when a person agrees to a position of importance that allows him to make certain decisions and dispose of others, it is common for him to use that influence and power that he gives his position to subdue his subalterns and force them to carry out certain activities with the mission of satisfying his personal interests and have nothing to do with functions for which they were hired. [124] In any case, abuse of power leads to an obvious coercion of an expected outcome, and it is coincidentally that result that shows the intention of coercion. Also, it may be considered abuse of power, the search, selection and application of a person in office for that person to act for the personal benefit of the contracting person, doing jobs not

---

[124] https://www.definicionabc.com/derecho/abuso-de-poder.php

specified in the job description. When a person uses the resources allocated to her or his position, for personal use, she or he abuses her or his power.

The constitution should be reformed with an amendment of national ethics and transparency covering the behavior of officials, elected or assigned, to positions in government and self-governing bodies, including public services. This reform must clearly and without a doubt stipulate its purpose, criminalization of crimes and penalties for certain violations.

Perfection of the Union as stated by the constitution in its Unique Article, corruption cannot never be achieved, even if a revolution is made every two hundred years as anticipated by Benjamin Franklin in 1776. Now let's get back to the constitutional question.

Fourth Lesson: Separation of State Powers

As for the separation of powers, we have already mentioned some ideas above; however, the following should be mentioned. (1) as long as a power has direct interference in structuring or training, including the nomination of interests to the other powers of the state, it will not be complete, nor shall the separation of the three powers be effective. This is the case of the authority and power granted to the president of the republic to elect and nominate candidates for the supreme court of justice and judges of the federal courts, being that the judiciary is an independent, autonomous or separate branch of the and in the structure of the government. It should be remembered that the fundamental principle was that the structure of a government with the separation of its three powers is intended to prevent corruption or the possibility of corruption in the management of the Republican government.

The constitution needs reform to actually make a more perfect Union, to completely separate the three powers from its state. As long as this does not happen political manipulation by the encumbering executive will take advantage of this constitutional anomaly, satisfying his partly interests as seen in the cases of supreme court nominees, Neil Gorsuch, Brett Kavanaugh. In these times when corruption is high and the *modus operandi* is *"I do you a favor and you pay me with another later", the nominating power of federal judges and supreme justices lends itself to corrupt political play.* That is, from a party's point of view, the more federal judges and justices of the supreme court of justice are appointed by presidents of a political party, the more control that party has in the management of justice. Then the surrender of justice is also corrupted.

Fifth Lesson: Electoral College Term

The fundamental principle of a democracy exists in popular sovereignty. And in the author's opinion, understanding the fundamental principles of democracy is essential to seeing the effectiveness of the electoral college. The U.S. State Department gives us guidelines to follow on this issue. [125] This article states that it is the people of the people who maintain sovereign power over their legislature and government. That is, power and civil liability are exercised by citizens directly or through elected representatives. According to the article, democracy is the institutionalization of freedom, in which the rule of the majority governs democratic development, joint with the individual and the rights of the minority. From this point of view, most votes, in a popular election, must, in fact, be a democratic method that elects a candidate to a public office as the president. The system of an electoral college curbs that right to vote popularly and directly to elect its president. The system has already failed on certain occasions, i.e. it does not pass the ineffability test, because its result alters the will of the people. There is one case in the elections of 1776 and another in the 2016 elections, when the electoral college scores a candidate who does not get the majority of the votes from the people. That is, the electoral college obviates the democratic principle of the majority rule. The concept of election through the electoral representation of the people violates the constitution if the electoral college does not abide by the will of the popular majority. Reform of the constitution may not need to be the

---

[125] https://asmarino.com/articles/1442-principles-of-democracy

elimination of the collegiate process, but this process must conform to the democratic majority rule. In any case, the school's procedural process should focus on verifying and authenticating the legitimacy and counting of votes and voting in favor of the majority. Otherwise it's not the people who elects its president without the delegates to the electoral college according to their personal criteria? And this is not democracy.

Sixth lesson: Economic system failures

The author finds no intrinsic anomalies in the concept of free enterprise. It is part of the natural way of living in the human relationship, and falls into the free will of man; that is your right to choose your business and economic relationship with other men. And the decision to form companies in their realm of life is also part of their natural right of life. The author finds no discrepancies with how to exchange goods and services with the other men in the (or) societies around him; it's also the natural way to seek your individual welfare. And from this way of life, the need to produce and create services is born to expedite interpersonal exchange. So, companies and the free market are intrinsic parts of man's way of life. And all this guarantees general welfare and is summed up in the sentence of the second paragraph of the declaration of independence that says, *"that all men are created equal, that they are endowed by their Creator with certain inalienable rights, which include life, freedom and the pursuit of Happiness."*

This is why the government should not intervene, or lay down those rights and freedoms and nor handle the individual and private affairs of citizens.

As for the concept of capitalism, many asserts that capitalism is a social and economic order that operates within the scope of a nation (national sovereignty) by choice and volition of popular sovereignty (the people). In reality, it is not a social system, rather it is a mercantilist system under the concept of the accumulation of wealth or the marketing of what can become products or services. It's not social because it doesn't attend or care for popular welfare if the desire, without limits, of profit. That is, the people allow, and indeed, it causes the government to tolerate the private operation of companies and the free market. Capitalism is born with the usufruct of private property, and private property is part of the right to life of men. So far, the author finds nothing anomalous in the concept of capitalism; rather he argues that capitalism is the instrument that facilitates the free natural trade relationship between men. It is nothing new because it has existed almost since the beginning of humanity in different forms. The analysis of the concept obviously starts with the revision of the basic principles of capitalism. These principles can be summed up in a few concepts sufficient to paint the image of the economic order. We take some of these principles from the footnote reference. [126]

(1) The desire for profit. –What is the "desire for profit? It is the desire of people to accumulate as much capital and resources as they can by spending the least of effort or resources... *includes capitalists who decide to invest their capital and resources in the hope of receiving a great return, and... workers who work for someone else with a desire to make money for themselves.*

(2) Competition and survival of the fittest.–True competition is only among private undertakings that dispute the choice of consumer choice of the goods and services offered by the free market. The factors of this competition are the quality, price, durability, speed of delivery, flexibility of the transaction, among so many others. They say the competition is healthy; but it alone is when such competition is fair.

(3) Supply and demand. -Maybe the supply and demand be a natural function of the business relationship between men. It may be that this couple boosts production to meet demand as long as demand is spontaneous; the problem is

---

[126] https://www.ehowenespanol.com/cuales-son-principios-basicos-del-capitalismo-info_427737/

that the supply is manipulated to the taste and craving of private companies.

The three principles mentioned above represent the foundation of the concept of capitalism. But the author notes certain inconsistencies between those principles of capitalism with the commitment written in the social contract that representatives receive from the people to administer their central government. Since neither the constitution nor its amendments stipulate or legislate the way of life that citizens wish to live; and that the choice of their economic system is part of their private life; and since the constitution is the highest law and nothing and no one can be above the law, he considers that the commitment of the rulers first is with the mandate given to him by the constitution; then, the government does not receive authority or power to intervene, in any way in the economic life of citizens... and the choice of economic system is a private matter outside the constitution and is therefore a right of the states or the people. The author argues that the application of capitalism in the democracy of the American Union has serious drawbacks or incompatibilities with the spirit and letter of the constitution, or its commitments to the sovereignty of the people.

1. Safeguard your rights. -The great commitment of the United States government is to the concept of *"that all men are created equal... endowed by their Creator with certain inalienable rights of men, including Life, Freedom and the pursuit of Happiness."*

2. Maintain and improve the Union. -The constitution orders and establishes a government by the will of the people in *order to form a more perfect Union, establish justice, ensure national tranquility, tend to the common defense, promote general well-being and ensure that the benefits of freedom for us [the people] and for our posterity...".*

3. Protection of popular sovereignty. - Therefore, and in order to fulfil its governance commitments, they are obliged to regulate the formation and operation of the free enterprise

and market to ensure that this economic system does not infringe, lied, squeeze or in any way limit, prevent, reduce or eliminate, natural and positive rights, general well-being, and or prevent citizens from enjoying the benefits of their freedom. The author believes that the desire for profit can move private enterprise to create and implement methods of unfair competition and supply manipulation under selfish tendencies, greed and greed in order to dishonest enrichment. The government cannot and should not allow the formation of major economic empires, such as monopolies, that restrict competition on an equal footing. The government must promote the creation of small businesses and industry with all freedom.

Human capital. –There are several definitions of human capital. The government is responsible for maintaining the union of American states in accordance with the spirit and letter of the constitution representing popular sovereignty–the will of the people. According to the spirit and letter, detailed in the text of the declaration of independence, the government has no authority or power to change the intention and purpose of the will of the people; even if it is an individual private right to choose the way of life and must act in accordance with Article Unique (the preamble) which says *"establish justice, ensure tranquility... promoting general well-being and securing the benefits of freedom for us (the people) ..."* That is why human capital must be treated fairly as an intrinsic part of the general welfare, because it is a direct consequence of the benefits achieved with the freedom from oppression and monarchical exploitation, in 1776. In other words, the government must prevent the exploitation of man by man from continuing, in any form. The author sees that human capital grows out of investing the work of the individual to accumulate knowledge, build skills and establish experience. The human capital is private and with product or service characteristics that is exchanged for something of value like capital-money, usually. This capital has the ability to produce or serve, and create wealth for both the owner of the human capital and for third parties or owners of private companies. In this context, each individual is a free private enterprise that offers their human capital in the form of knowledge, skills and experiences in the free market to private companies. The same forms of protection and support that the government grants to private enterprise must support and protect the small owner of the single-product enterprise, private capital, not only by private entrepreneur in the economy, but because the government has a primary duty to protect each individual's property in the village. But let's read and comment on an article concerning private capital taken from the Internet; For example

First article —*Human capital is the most important within an organization and refers to the productivity of workers based on their training and work experience.*

The author considers, as it is, that human capital is not accumulated productivity of a company's workers. Human capital is also not a working or fixed asset of a company. The article keeps saying.

—In opportunity, the term human capital is used to point out the resources that a company has, its competences that lead to an overall improvement in production, this is given to the old concept that placed human capital as a factor of production and not emphasizing the formation of it... It is a measure to financially assess the professional skills possessed by a certain person. Human capital is only, and uniquely, owned by the individual who offers a private company for an amount agreed in a contract. The owner of such capital reserves the natural right to withdraw it at any time, if it is his wish, because human capital is not a factor of production that is cloistered in the product or services of the contracting company. Human capital is not the resource of a private company that hires it, as the transport service that contracts for its purposes is not owned by the company. In reality, the value of individual human capital is in its ability to contribute to producing products and services, for any private company that hires it. The article keeps saying.

The factor of production of the work is also taken into account in this capital, as these are only the hours that people spend in the production of services and goods. The human capital of a given subject is calculated

according to the current value of all the benefits that that person expects to receive for the work activities that he/she performs until he finally decides to stop working. If you add this with financial capital, it represents a person's total wealth. [127] The definition of this article departs from the intrinsic meaning of human capital. No contracting company values individual human capital for the number of hours worked but for the quality and quantity of products and services that individual human capital produces in those hours. Of course, the contracted company counts in its books, in the labor account, the amount paid per hours worked at the hourly price contracted with the owner of the human capital. It may be that human capital does not appear in current accounts as credit to bank accounts, but appears as disbursements in expense accounts. The private company contracting human capital is not interested in, or not concerned with, the financial benefit or the financial condition of the contractor concerned. No one knows the situation of the owner of human capital, let alone if what he receives for his effort gives him enough to live. But the government responsible for general welfare and the pursuit of happiness must worry that human capital will get the price or fair value according to the cost of living, plus productivity in the means of producing products and services benefiting the contracting enterprise, economically. On the other hand, the owner of human capital is not concerned about calculating the economic benefit at the end of his productive life, he only lives worried that he does not lack work and this attitude is because the wage and salary levels are not fair or high enough to generate significant savings that contribute to his accumulation of individual wealth. The government is responsible for the national tranquility, the general welfare, ensuring that the benefits of freedom are for the citizens, the people.

Let's read another article on this topic of human capital.

Second article. —*Human capital is a measure of the economic value of a person's professional skills. It is also known... human capital to the factor of production of labor,* which are the hours that people spend on the production of goods or *services. A person's human capital*

---

[127] https://conceptodefinicion.de/capital-humano/

is calculated as the current value of all future benefits that person expects to get with his or her work until he stops working. This in addition to financial capital represents a person's total wealth. Being a future amount, human capital is greater the younger a person is, since an older person has already made those profits and consumed or saved them, now forming part of their financial capital. The amount of human capital is not the same over a lifetime and is reduced as the years go by, but can increase through investment. An employee's education, experience, and skills have economic value. [128]

The perspective of this second article is interesting but does not fit with the nature of human capital. First, human capital is not a metric, or instrument, to measure the economic value of human capital, on the one hand and on the other, human capital is not only of professionals but of all levels of work. In addition, human capital is not a factor of production calculated in hours of service but in the productivity it achieves in the hours worked. The contracting undertaking is not so much concerned about working hours but about the units of product or services that human capital produces, because the contracting undertaking deducts the return on investment per unit from the units produced. The person who owns the human capital only has in mind the present value of the income derived from the employment contract; so, the concept of current value in the definition is only an economic mirage not nodding in the financial reality of the owner of human capital. This article argues that the wealth of the individual who owns human capital is a financial capital; this concept is another mirage of capitalism seen as a possible monetary capital that an individual can gain in the years that remains of his productive life. That financial capital referred to is fictitious or unreal because it does not exist; is hypothetical, speculation, an illusion or a deception. In reality, capital is an individual's ability to create products and services, with quality and quantity, in a given time. This ability is based on the individual's knowledge, skills and experience. And the individual invests time and capital-money to achieve and or update their knowledge, skills and experience in the

---

[128] https://economipedia.com/definiciones/capital-financiero.html

right time. The value of knowledge, skills and integrated experiences make a tradable product that guarantees the creation of products and services for a public or private company. This value must be precisely calculated by experts in this matter giving it the meritorious value on the free market. The government is responsible for establishing a scale of human capital values that leaves profit margin (as a return on investment to accumulate human capital). Human capital must be free property of a private and individual company that leases its capital in the form of service. The government has a responsibility to protect these individual free small businesses as part of the pursuit of Happiness and general welfare and national tranquility, legislating the form of fair contracting that benefits each other the small entrepreneur hired and the contractor. Then, we will say that capitalism reached its peak where all companies follow their desire for profit, including small businessmen.

The economic balance sheets. –The responsibility of central and local governments (states) covers the promotion of general welfare; and within this welfare is the economic development of citizens and the people in general without intervening in the operation of the industry and or trade of private enterprise in the free market. But within the general welfare and pursuit of Happiness, the government is responsible for ensuring and defending egalitarian life, promoting equal opportunities and fair competition which gives national peace of mind. The government should not limit either the freedom of action or the productive capacity of private enterprise, including unitary (individual) enterprises, but it must prevent the growth of companies at monopolistic levels or achieve levels of economic influence that eliminate fair competition in the free market.

Small Business Administration (SBA). -We can represent the overall economic well-being in three bands. An upper-class band, a middle-class band and a poverty band. And we can classify these bands hierarchically into sub-bands within each of those three. Then the band above the middle-class band grows at a slow pace, it's a thin amplitude band. There the population increases almost imperceptible or does not grow, but the rich of that band become richer. It's the band that accumulates most of the nation's wealth.

And by the principle of the desire for profit (many uncontrolled, avid and selfish) wealth does not sneak down as many thinks down for the poor and middle classes. The fluctuation of the breadth of these bands implies prosperity and abundance or misery and poverty. The middle-class band reflects the general condition of a country. That is, when this band is broadband it suggests that people move from the poverty band to the middle-class band. The economy in times of depression or recession causes massive economic migration is on the border between the lower middle class and the poverty band. People pass that line according to the swing of the national or state economy. The central government that has to ensure *"general well-being, ensure national peace of mind, establish justice, and secure the benefits of freedom for us (the people)"* must indicate economic guidelines for states and or people to experiment with the rights that were included in the constitution, but that the underrated exercise affects constitutional mandates.

Seventh Lesson: Constitutional Deficiency

The constitution has its flaws, and that is why the founders wisely wrote to manage the nation *"in order to form a more perfect Union,"*); several of these flaws have already been mentioned in previous pages. We add that it is the government's responsibility to perfect the Union through the constitution.

Eighth Lesson: Substitution Process

There is a great flaw, however, that we must mention, because of the danger that the nation is in if the reason, crimes, procedures, and sentences of the political dismissal process are not clarified. In the present situation, crimes, prosecutions, trials, including the criminalization of crimes and their consequences must be clearly established. Thus, the intention of the constitution is not subject to capricious interpretations that benefit those who committed the crime, breaking the concept that no one is above the law.

Ninth Lesson: Political Trials

Article I, Section 2, paragraph 5.). It says, *"The House of Representatives will have the absolute power to bring charges in political trials."* But the constitution does not define or criminalize the crimes to which political trials apply. The lack of clarity opens the door to interpretations of the accusation and the defense that prevent the application of the law fairly. Consequently, it allows any official to commit punishable crimes and hide behind that gloom of the constitution. We know that no one can be accused of what the law does not prescribe; that is why the spirit and letter of the constitution must be clarified.

Section 3, paragraph 6.: Says, *"The Senate will be the sole power to judge Political Judgments."* So, the responsibility to charge, and prosecute political trials with the only consequence of ousting a representative from the public office to which he was elected. But the constitution does not define a standard senate methodology for prosecuting the accused on the charges against him. The failure of this provision allows the political party with the majority in the senate to draft its own rules of judgment, in any case, to follow a process that favors the defendant—this is what happened in Donald Trump's case of political dismissal.

Ethics and transparency in administrative management in government promote national tranquility and promote general well-being. It is necessary for the constitution to list and criminalize crimes of all types and categories for the filing of charges and indictments in the house of representatives; congress needs to clearly define the legislative process to be followed in these cases. Only in this way will the legislature not be able to place defendants above the law, the constitution and popular sovereignty, for party gains.

Requirements to the position of President and Vice President

Section 1 of Article II only places as requirements, citizenship, age and residence of the candidate. These requirements make it possible for people without qualifications, knowledge, skill, or experience to occupy either of these two positions, critical to sovereignty, national security and general well-being, and or maintain common defense. The people put in the president's hands their health, safety, tranquility, peace, and general well-being, in addition to the freedoms of the people. The constitution fails to establish the requirements of posts to president and vice-presidents; encouraging the risk of an autocrat being elected and becoming a dictator. The office of the presidency is not a game of Russian roulette. That's why the choice and choice of candidate must be strict. That is, democracy (the vote) fulfills its duty to elect, but the legislative part fails to establish the minimum requirements for the position of president or vice president. In addition, since the vice president is here to fill the position of president, when necessary, the vice president's credentials must also meet the requirements of the position to be elected by the people. The constitution should sanction that any candidate for public office, including the president and vice president, must present his or her credentials before running for public office. It must also establish that any candidate for any public office, including the president and vice president, must submit his financial statement and tax return for the last ten years. All candidates for public office, including the president and vice president, must present their credentials when subscribing to a public office candidate and the house of representatives must review and approve those credentials according to the requirements of the position for each candidate before starting their campaign and in no other way may be a candidate.

Powers granted to the president

The constitution sanctions in the Article II, section 1 the powers granted to the President of the Republic. But there are legal shadows that President Trump interprets and argues as absolute power and authority to do what he wants to do. This is a constitutional flaw that must be considered and amended as soon as possible.

There are other faults that are obvious and require due attention. (1) Forgiveness: This failure is the power given to the president to forgive criminals guilty before the law by the courts of justice. No one is said to be above the law, but forgiving a culprit implies that the president (or governor) is above the law, the judges, and the courts with the power to overturn a court's decision—a characteristic of monarchs and dictators. It gives the impression that the president and governors still have absolute powers of monarchs, taking a position of judge over judges, and playing with justice—which may well be for ill-intentioned purposes. This ability brings the possibility that justice will be corrupted and used for profit. The action of forgiveness of the rulers is an autocratic action outside of Justice and lends itself to corruption, ignoring the pain and feeling of those affected by the crimes of the individual who is forgiven.

Other high crimes and crimes

One. Actions that can be judged as criminal acts in normal courts must be senior political officials. Embezzlement of funds from the for-profit public purse, which are proven to be high criminal offenses; therefore, they must be criminalized as serious charges of an indictment and trial of political dismissal. Crimes such as sexual abuse, assault and or rape must be criminal charges when repetitive with obvious and proven intent and should also be included as high crimes on the list of charges in a political dismissal trial. We have seen that senior officials in the state's powers committed crimes of the type mentioned in this paragraph in the United States.

Two. The level of moral character of the nation's leaders must be so high, maintaining the ethical and transparent nature of government action to serve as an example to citizens. Otherwise America is a country more of the third world where laws do not count and justice does not exist. We've seen William P. Barr, the U.S. Attorney General, become President D. Trump's personal counsel, and a Secretary of State, Mike Pompeo, becomes President Trump's protective adviser. This is outdoor corruption. Corruption was not born with Trump, it has been growing for some time, but with President Trump it came from the underground in the public, no matter what the people think and say.

The above is part of the great mirage, the virtual reality, in which the people live. From this mirage arises the distrust of the people, or sectors thereof, with regard to the three powers of their sovereign republic and their democracy. Mistrust stems from the action of the government, the moral, ethical and professional quality of the officials representing the people. This is the point of this book, exposing the social, political and economic mirage of the nation. A distant mirage to the dream of the founders of the United States of America. And it is duty and right to restore the nation to the desired course to *form a more perfect Union.*

image borrowed from the Internet

So, we came to end of our discourse, the need for constitutional reforms in the mind of a regular citizen.

Life follows the change sequence of the Existence. We see life between imperceptible changes. All systems, closed or open, also follow these changes. The mind changes with new knowledge and attitudes like the prospects of life do not escape that natural process. The United States Union is a system under the same process, although more complicated because it is under the management and control of human beings. And the political system depends on men's, ethical and transparent, behavior, performing their scope of work.

Existence gives life to every living being at birth—which is not an individual's choice, but the result of conditions and circumstances that existence establishes. And with the right to life every living being, humans for example, have the natural right to take from the universe what they need. Humans need to live and maintain their material life. Existence does not give anyone power or authority to suppress the natural rights of life, to any other man, or the complementary rights for living. No man receives authority, or supremacy over another man, to reduce, prevent, or eliminate human natural rights. Likewise, the choice to form groups, communities, etc., for any purpose, is a natural right of man. But in that choice, man yields some of those natural rights for the benefit, or benefits, derived from other men. This is, the contract, political-social, which is born creating the group, society, or a government of the association. And it is the men in the group who define, by common accord and acceptance, the terms and conditions of the group association. No association has preexisting conditions, excepting those establish by the Existence natural relationship rules. Manmade associations have their unique terms and conditions determining rules of management, self-governance, and group member interactions. And the members of the association reviewed and approved the rules of their relationship. So, the administrations rule derive from the will of the members of the association. And the members that creates the association have the right and authority to change, improve, and or close the association. A government is a system of rules to run the nation (the people's association) on behalf of the people. The nation belong to the people. So, the people write the *carta magna,* the constitution to regulate men interaction, domestic and foreign, for the welfare of the people. The people is the popular sovereignty y the government is the national sovereignty. But the government exist with the consent of the popular sovereignty. The government has no greater authority or power than the authority and power that the members, united, confer on the government. The government is an extension with limited power, not general, derived from the law and power of the members of the group. So, there is no greater authority or power than the power of the people. The power of any agreed government subordinates to the supreme power of the people who formed, shape and approve it.

The above declaration applies the principles of natural law and focuses on the aforementioned popular and national sovereignty. We should also note that the constitution transfers the power of the people with *"political bands that connect them* to another. The other person representing them, as are the people chosen by popular choice for public office in their government. It also states that Nature and the God of Nature gave the people power, therefore, they are inalienable. The government derives their power from the consent of the people; and the declaration says: *"that every time any form of government becomes destructive to these purposes, it is the right of the people to alter or abolish it, and to institute a new government"*. So, the founders realized that the people reserve their absolute duty and right to replace or change a government that does not fulfill the functions conferred by the will of the people. They have the duty and right *"to discard that government, and provide new guards for your future safety, when a long train of abuse and usurpation, invariably pursuing the same Object evidences a design [pattern of behavior] to reduce them under absolute despotism". But we must* follow the aforementioned prudence. The people have the duty and right to change their government or members of their government if they do not fulfill their duties and or oaths. They must respect and subordinate to the power of the people established in their political-social contract-the constitution. This declaration of independence is the intrinsic definition of popular sovereignty discussed above.

The constitution delegates part of the power of the people to representatives *"the absolute power to bring charges in Political Trials", Article 1, section 2".* And senators' duty is to try the accused officer. *"The Senate will be the sole power to judge political trials."* However, neither representatives nor senators have authority or right to alter the course of political judgment, with intent or intentional intent, for advantages or party agendas. Any political trial must be subject to the truth and evidence of the case. That was not the case with the indictment and trial of the 45th president of the United States of America. Is it because people hate D. Trump? No, it is not. It is because no one is above the rule of law. And no one has power to place anybody above the law–not even the president.

As for the behavior, effectiveness and or efficiency of the government, the author exposed evidence of failures that cannot hide. But many politicians try to minimize or suppress evidence with legalistic subterfuge. But the truth is unique and comes to light. We cannot deny there is corruption in the branches of the government. There are many party and personal interests in the political current dragging the government, the constitution and democracy to their destruction. There are powerful capitalists infiltrated in the three branches of government, making them lean towards their benefits. Doe this behavior eliminates equal opportunities? You bet your life they do; and the powerful rich rake these opportunities to their purse and the purse of people's representatives playing the rich game.

image borrowed from the Internet

The government has never been *of the people, by the people, for the people*. That thought was just a dream, or it is the mirage, the author mentioned above. The government became property of capitalists, for capitalists, by capitalists. They break justice; and we apply justice according to the spirit and letter of the law only to the poor, middle class down. There is another rule of law fitting bending, and ruling in favor of the rich, powerful, or famous. And there is still another rule of law for politicians in power. This is not the constitution, the government, the democracy that the founding fathers dreamed of. As Benjamin Franklin once said (244 years ago). Governments become corrupt as its ages; so, we need a revolution every 200 years, to clean up the mess and to bring back the government to the station the founding fathers dreamed.

The Union, the government and democracy are sick, suffering from chronic endemic corruption. And the government lives weaker every day, and the day will come when it can no longer operate and fall over dead, breaking into fifty-two pieces, which are also sick. We, the people, still have time to cure our government, save it form that endemic corruption. The remedy is the so-called *ethics and transparency*, which we must inject into the operational arteries of the three powers. But we, the people, must inoculate our minds because corruption has also infected our entire society. We must reactivate honesty and decency in young people from early stages by education and discipline. But the three powers of the government, the legislative branch, must reform the constitution by adding effective amendments to recover the Union. The people must keep the government in intensive care under the control of the people until the government recovers.

We have the right by our freedom of expression to petition reforms to form a more perfect Union. We have the right to demand our government and the representative we elect to the its offices to establish Justice for all in egalitarian form. But we insist that no one, including any president, is above the law. No politician should shower themselves with immunity, because by so doing they place themselves above the rule of law. We have the right. And when a judge finds a person guilty in our court system, no one should have power to undo the judgement of the court. The act of pardoning a person found guilty is and act that breaks the laws.

Oh, yes, we may demand our government to end, once and for, all forms of racial discrimination, religious discrimination, sexual orientation discrimination, and others. We may demand equal treatment for all, for men and women, for equal pay for equal work, for the government has the responsibility to establish the Justice. We may demand the government ensure national tranquility. But there is no national tranquility when the government steps over, ignoring the separation of power of the equal branches of the government, there is no tranquility. And when the president calls the free press *the enemy of the people* just because they question his actions. We may say; the free press has the right under the first amendment. There is no national tranquility when a president oversteps the constitution responsibilities. He breaks the law when he orders armed federal troops onto a state to reduce and or eliminate people demonstrations covered by freedom of expression. We have the right to protest. And when the president order federal troops to attack the people demanding their rights, just for the president personal whims. We may ask for reforms.

We may demand of our government to tend the common (national) defense. But when the president shrugs his shoulder while facing the worst pandemic ever reaching our nation, we may ask our government for immediate actions. We have the right to worry when more than 6.54 million people reported positive and over 196 thousand die because of the COVID-19. The president never implemented a nationwide safety plan. We have the right to demand constitutional reforms. We may demand protection, aid, and mitigation of our brother in Puerto Rico suffering the effect of hurricanes. They are citizens of the United States of America. We have to demand reforms.

Oh yes, we have the right to demand our government to act and to shore, improve, and promote the general welfare. This general welfare is not socialism; it is a constitutional mandate the founding fathers included in the unique article, the preamble, of the constitution. We have the right to ask for that. And in the general welfare we, the people, are entitled to, and the government is responsible to promote and provide the people with, health, education, peace, morality, and safety. And because the general welfare of the people is the primary reason behind creating the constitution, the people have the right to ask for it. So, when the government let businesses exploit the people's money with high cost of health insurances, medicine, drugs and care, (far over other countries in the world), we may demand change. What is the government doing to promote the general welfare? What is the government doing to establish ethic and transparency in the government, and in businesses?

The people have the right to ask what is the government doing to secure the benefits of the freedom for the people? And so, we question the government performance according to constitutional mandates. We will the legislative branch of government act to form a more perfect Union. We have the right to ask for positive reforms to the constitution.

FINAL NOTES

[i] [https://es.wikipedia.org/wiki/Poblamiento_de_Am wasérich]
The irrefutable evidence that there were inhabitants in the Americas before Europeans arrived in the 14th century and beyond brings the question of where they came from. According to archaeological studies indicate that the first inhabitants of America came from Asia through the Bering Strait settling in the territory we now know as Alaska, Canada and the United States of America. These Asian migrants spread and populated the entire American continent. They founded great civilizations like the Aztecs, Mayans, and Incas, and others throughout the Americas. The point is not the origin of these people, but the fact that they existed for about 20,000 years before the Europeans discovered America. These natives are the true Americans who owned these territories by eminent domain.

[ii] Corruption: (1) [www.siginificados.com/corruption] "Corruption *the action and effect of corrupting, that is, it is the process of deliberately breaking the order of the system, both ethically and functionally, for personal gain. In addition to the corrupt in committing an illegal action, it also pressures or forces others to commit such acts.*" We must understand that the Union of the United States of America is a system of government established for a purpose specified in the declaration, in the preamble and in the text of the constitution of this Union. Any act of elected representatives or not to any public office in the United States government that breaks the order of the republic and democracy is an act of corruption perpetrated against the Union, the constitution and the will of the people. It is a betrayal of the oath taken when the public office is in place. *"Corruptions often related in the popular imagination to the world of politics and illicit enrichment, that is, to money, but not just to that. Corruption applies to many instances. For this reason, there is political corruption, economic corruption, sexual corruption, etc. This is because the three big exchange factors mobilizing corruption are often money, power, and sex."* The people choose their representatives by popular vote, expecting to have individuals with high moral and ethical level, responsible, swearing to defend and protect the constitution. We do not expect to appoint corrupt persons to positions in the government. Therefore, money, power, and sex factors must be criteria required in the qualifications of candidates for any government public office. *"In each country, the law clearly criminalizes forms of corruption and establishes specific penalties*

for each one by degree. Even so, there may be other forms of corruption that are not contemplated in it, but which are considered forms of corruption according to the ethical system of a given worldview." The constitution does not specify the corruption mentioned by Benjamin Franklin, so it is outside the behavior of the people's representatives in the government. The inclusion of this crime concept in the articulation of the constitution, mainly in Article I and II, is a legal necessity to perfect the Union. Some of the typical acts universally known are the following, *(1) Bribery, (2) Illegal use of public resources , (3) Illicit or Hidden Enrichment, (4) Abuse of Power, (5) Abuse of authority, (6) Trafficking of drugs, humans, and other Influences, (7) Collusion, (8) Conspiracy to Commit Crimes of Corruption, (9) Obstruction of Justice, (10) Nepotism, (11) Illegal use of confidential or false information, (12) Tax evasion, (13) Use of government property and resources for personal gain, and (14) participation in or association with Organized crime.*

iii Abuse of authority [www.significados/abuse-of-power] Abuse of power (or authority) is a corrupt act by a representative, elected or not, to a public office in government. that betrays the trust and will of the people. This crime or high crime must be included in the articulation of the constitution. The source of information cited here in this endnote says, *"Abuse of power is to take advantage of the authority you have to extort another person or entity in order to fulfill personal interests.. Abuse is an act of trust violation and power is generally associated with authority, even though it is not exclusive. Power is an advantage that is held above another person. For example: the power of a friend's closeness or the power of couple complicity are non-authoritarian powers."* A person elected to a pubic service office, or a person assigned by the people or by an elected representative to a public service position commits abuse of power when he or she violates the oath of service.

iv [https://www.significados.com/crimen-organizado]. *"Organized crime, also called mafia, cartel, is that organization composed of a group of people with certain hierarchies, roles and functions, whose main objective is to obtain material or economic benefits through the commission of crimes. There is talk of a crime "organized" by the fact that it is precisely a society or association created specifically for the purpose of carrying out, in a concerted and directed way, actions of a criminal type to achieve economic, political or social power. Organized crime is usually made up of individuals linked to or close to groups of power, which is why their heads manage to avoid falling into the hands of justice."*

v Great philosophers and thinkers of the centuriesXV, XVI y XVII. Rene Descartes (1596-1650)
https://www.biografiasyvidas.com/biografia/d/descartes.htm
Galileo Galilei (1564-1642)
https://www.biografiasyvidas.com/monografia/galileo/
Immanuel Kant (1724-1804)
https://www.biografiasyvidas.com/biografia/k/kant.htm

Benedict (Barruch) Spinoza (1632-1677)
https://www.biografiasyvidas.com/biografia/s/spinoza.htm
Gottfried Wilhelm Leibniz (1646-1716)
https://www.biografiasyvidas.com/biografia/l/leibniz.htm
Thomas Hobbes (1588-1679)
https://www.biografiasyvidas.com/biografia/h/hobbes.htm
Francis Bacon (1561-1626).
https://www.biografiasyvidas.com/biografia/b/bacon_filosofo.htm

vi Text of the political constitution of the United States of America.

THE CONSTITUTION OF THE UNITED STATES.

We, the People of the United States, in order to form a more perfect Union, establish Justice, ensure inner tranquility, provide for the common defense, promote general well-being and ensure for us and our prosperity the benefits of Freedom, establish and sanction this Constitution for the United States of America.

ARTICLE I

SECTION 1.

The House of Representatives shall consist of members elected every two years by the people of the various States, and voters shall possess in each State the conditions required for voters in the largest branch of the State legislature.

SECTION 2.

The House of Representatives shall consist of members elected every two years by the people of the various States, and voters shall possess in each State the conditions required for voters in the largest branch of the State legislature.

No person who has not turned 25 years of age and has not been a united state citizen for seven years, and who is not a resident of the State in which he is appointed, at the time of the election, shall be a Representative.

[Representatives and direct taxes shall be apportioned between the various States that are part of this Union, in accordance with their respective numbers, which shall be determined by adding to the total number of free persons, including those required to provide services for a certain period of years and excluding Non-Taxable Indians, three-fifths of all remaining persons] [1] The listing itself must be carried out within three years of the first session of the United States Congress and thereafter every ten years, in the manner established by law. The number of Representatives shall not exceed one for every thirty thousand inhabitants provided that each State has at least one Representative; and until such an enumeration is made, the State of New Hampshire shall have the right to choose three; Massachussets, eight; Rhode Island and the Providence Plantations, one; Connecticut, five; New York, six;

265

New Jersey, four; Pennsylvania, eight; Delaware, one; Maryland six; Virginia, ten; North Carolina, five; South Carolina, five; and Georgia, three.

Where vacancies occur in the representation of any State, the Executive Authority of the State shall issue a decree convening election in order to fill them.

The House of Representatives shall elect its president and other officials and shall have the absolute power to bring charges in Political Trials.

[Representatives and direct taxes shall be apportioned between the various States that are part of this Union, in accordance with their respective numbers, which shall be determined by adding to the total number of free persons, including those required to provide services for a certain period of years and excluding Non-Taxable Indians, three-fifths of all remaining persons] [1] The listing itself must be carried out within three years of the first session of the United States Congress and thereafter every ten years, in the manner established by law. The number of Representatives shall not exceed one for every thirty thousand inhabitants provided that each State has at least one Representative; and until such an enumeration is made, the State of New Hampshire shall have the right to choose three; Massachussets, eight; Rhode Island and the Providence Plantations, one; Connecticut, five; New York, six; New Jersey, four; Pennsylvania, eight; Delaware, one; Maryland six; Virginia, ten; North Carolina, five; South Carolina, five; and Georgia, three.

Where vacancies occur in the representation of any State, the Executive Authority of the State shall issue a decree convening election in order to fill them.

The House of Representatives shall elect its president and other officials and shall have the absolute power to bring charges in Political Trials.

SECTION 3.

The United States Senate will consist of two Senators for each state [elected for six years by the U.S. legislature] [2] and each Senator will have one vote.

As soon as they have met under the initial election, they will be divided into three groups as equal as possible. The seats of the senators of the first group will be vacant at the end of the second year; the second group, at the expiration of the fourth year and those of the third group, at the end of the sixth year, so that it is feasible to choose a third party every two years; [and if vacancies occur, by resignation or other cause, during the recess of the legislature of a State, the Executive of the State may make provisional appointments until the next session of the legislature, which shall proceed to fill such vacancies.] [3]

No person who has not turned thirty years of age and has been a U.S. citizen for nine years and who, at the time of the election, is not a resident of the state by which he was elected will not be a Senator.

The vice president of the United States will be president of the Senate, but will not have a vote except in the case of equally divided senators.

The Senate will elect its other officials, as well as a pro tempore president, in the absence of the vice president or when he is serving the presidency of the United States.

The Senate will be the sole power to judge political trials. When you meet with this item, your members must take an oath or promise. When the President of the United States is tried, he shall preside over the President of the Supreme Court: and no person shall be convicted if the vote of two thirds of the members present does not take place.

The scope of the sentence in Political Judgments shall not go beyond the dismissal of office and disqualification from holding and enjoying any honorary, trustworthy or remunerated office, which depends on the United States; but the condemned party will, however, be subject to being accused, prosecuted, judged and punished in accordance with the Law.

SECTION 4.

The venues, dates and manner of holding elections for Senators and Representatives shall be prescribed in each State by the respective legislature; but Congress may formulate or alter such rules, at any time, through a law, except as regards the senators' choices.

Congress will meet at least once a year, [and this meeting will be the first Monday of December] [4] unless otherwise set by law.

SECTION 5.

Each House shall rate the elections, reports on counting and the legal capacity of its own members, and a majority of each shall constitute the quorum necessary to session; but a smaller number may suspend overnight sessions and will be authorized to require absent members to attend, in the manner and under sanctions determined by each House.

Each Chamber may draw up its rules of procedure, punish its members for inappropriate behavior and expel them from its bosom with the consent of two-thirds.

Each House shall keep a Diary of its sessions and publish it from time to time, with the exception of those parties which it believes require reservation, and the affirmative and negative votes of its members with respect to any question shall be recorded in the Journal, at the request of one fifth of those present.

During the session of Congress, neither House may suspend them for more than three days or agree to be held in a different place from the one in which the two Houses meet without the consent of the other.

SECTION 6.

Senators and Representatives will receive for their services remuneration that will be fixed by law and paid by the United States Treasury. In all cases, with the exception of treason, serious crime and disturbance of public order, they shall enjoy the privilege of not being arrested for the time they attend the sessions of their respective Chambers, as well as by going to or returning from them, and may not be subject to any inquisition for discussion or debate in one of the Houses elsewhere.

No Senator or Representative shall be appointed, during the time for which he or she has been elected, to hold any civilian office that depends on the United States, which has been created or whose remuneration has been increased during that time, and no person holding a public office in the United States may be part of the Chambers while it remains in office.

SECTION 7.

Any bill for revenue must originate in the House of Representatives; but the Senate may propose reforms or agree on them in the same way as other projects.

Any bill approved by the House and Senate will be submitted to the President of the United States before it becomes law; if he approves it, he will sign it; otherwise it will be returned, together with its objections, to the House in which it originated, which will settle the objections into its Journal and proceed to reconsider it. If, after such a review, the two-thirds of that House agrees to approve the draft, it shall, accompanied by the objections, be forwarded to the other House, by which it will also be reconsidered, and if it were adopted by two-thirds of that House, it will become law. But in all these cases, the vote of both Houses will be nominal and the names of the people voting for or against the project will be based in the Journal of each of the Houses. If any bill was not returned by the president within ten days (except on Sundays) after being introduced to him, it will become law, in the same way as if he had signed it, unless the suspension of congressional sessions prevented its return, in which case it will not become law.

Any order, resolution or vote for which the concurrence of the Senate and the House of Representatives (except for the suspension of the sessions) is necessary, shall be submitted to the President of the United States; and will have no effect before it is approved by him, or in the event that he rejects it, if it is re-approved by two-thirds of the Senate and the House of Representatives, in accordance with the rules and limitations prescribed in the case of a bill.

SECTION 8.

Congress shall have the power to: establish and collect taxes, tariffs, duties and contributions; to pay off debts and provide for the common defense and general well-being of the United States; but all taxes, tariffs, duties will be uniform across the United States.

Borrowing from U.S. credit.

Regulate trade with foreign nations, between different states and with indigenous tribes.

Establish a uniform naturalization regulation and uniform bankruptcy laws across the United States.

Issue money and regulate its value as well as its relationship with foreign currency. Fix weight patterns and measurements.

Provide what is necessary for the punishment of those who falsify the securities and the current currency of the United States.

Set up post offices and postal routes

Promote the progress of Science and Useful Arts, assuring authors and inventors, for a limited time, the exclusive right to their respective writings and discoveries.

Create lower courts than the Supreme Court of Justice.

Define and punish piracy and other serious crimes committed on the high seas; violations against the Law of Nations.

Declare war, award March cards and retaliation, and dictate rules regarding catches at sea and land.

Recruiting and sustaining armies, but no appropriation of funds with that fate will be for more than two years.

Enable and maintain an armada.

To dictate rules for the government and regulation of naval and ground forces.

Arrange when the Military Reserve must be called in order to enforce union laws, quell insurrections and reject invasions.

Provide what is necessary to organize, assemble and discipline the Military Reserve, and to regulate the part of the Military Reserve used in U.S. service; reserving to the corresponding States the appointment of the officers, and the power to train the Military Reserve in accordance with the discipline prescribed by the Congress.

Legislate exclusively on everything relating to the District (which may not be larger than ten square miles) that, as a result of the transfer of the States in which it is located, becomes the seat of the United States government; and apply such authority to all places acquired with the consent of the State Legislature in which the District is located, for the construction of forts, warehouses, arsenals, shipyards and other necessary buildings.

Issue all laws that are necessary and appropriate to implement the above powers and all other powers conferred on the government of the United States or any of its departments or officials.

SECTION 9.

Immigration or importation of persons that any of the now-existing States deems appropriate to admit may not be prohibited by Congress, before the year of one thousand eight hundred and eight, but may impose on such importation a contribution or fee not exceeding ten dollars per person.

The privilege of habeas corpus shall not be suspended, except where public safety requires it in cases of rebellion or invasion.

No prohibition decrees or ex post facto laws will be passed. [No direct or captaincy tax shall be established, other than proportionate to the census or enumeration previously ordered to be practiced.] [5]

No tax or duty shall be established on articles exported from any State.

The ports of one State shall not take precedence over those of any other under any commercial or tax regulations; nor shall vessels heading to or from a State be obliged to enter, issue their documents or cover rights in another State.

No amount of money may be withdrawn from the Treasury if it is not as a result of Statutory Allocations, and from time to time, an orderly statement and balance of public money income and expenses shall be published. The United States shall not grant any noble title: and no person holding a paid or honorary position dependent on the United States will accept any gift, emolument, office, or title, whatever kind, of any monarch, prince, or foreign state, without the consent of Congress. Section 10.

SECTION 10.

No State may enter into any Treaty, Alliance or Confederation; award March and Retaliation cards; issue currency, legalize a method other than gold and silver coins as a means of repaying debts; pass proscription decrees, ex post facto laws, or laws that impair obligations arising from contracts, or grant any noble degree.

No State may, without the consent of Congress, impose tariffs or duties on imports and exports, except as is absolutely necessary for compliance with its inspection laws, and the net proceeds of all duties and tariffs imposed by States on imports and exports, shall be for use by the United States Treasury; and all such laws will be subject to congressional review and control.

Without such consent from Congress, no State may establish rights of tonnage, maintain troops or warships in peacetime, enter into any agreement or pact with another State or with a foreign power, or enter war, unless invaded or in such imminent danger that it does not admit delay.

ARTICLE II

SECTION 1.

Executive power will be conferred on a president of the United States of America. He will carry out his commission for a period of four years and, together with the Vice-President appointed for the same term, shall be elected as follows:

Each State shall appoint, as its legislature provides, a number of voters equal to the total number of Senators and Representatives to which the State is entitled to in Congress, but no Senator, representative, or person in an honorary or remunerated position dependent on the United States may be designated as a voter.

[Voters shall meet in their respective States and elect by secret ballot between two persons, one of whom shall at least not be a resident of the same State as them. And they will form a list of all the people they voted for and the number of votes for each; who will sign and certify, and refer sealed to U.S. Government Headquarters, addressed to the President of the Senate. The President of the Senate will open all certificates in the presence of the Senate and the House of Representatives, and the votes will then be counted. The person who obtains the highest number of votes shall be the President, provided that that number represents the majority of all voters appointed: and if there is more than one who has that majority and has equal number of votes, then the House of Representatives, by secret ballot, shall elect one of them immediately for President; and if no person has a majority then the House will choose the President in the same way from the five names with the highest number of votes on the list. But to elect the president the vote will be taken by States, having the representation of each State one vote; for this purpose, the quorum shall consist of one or more members of two-thirds of the States, and a majority of all States will be required for the election to be made. In all cases, and once the president is elected, the person with the highest number of voters will be the Vice-President. But if there are two or more of the same number of votes left, the Senate will choose from among them the vice president, by secret ballot.] [6]

Congress may set the date of appointment of the Electors, as well as the day on which they must cast their votes, which must be the same throughout the United States.

No person who is not a citizen by birth or who has been a citizen of the United States at the time of the adoption of this Constitution shall be eligible for the office of president; nor will any person who has not turned thirty-five years of age and who has not resided in the United States be eligible for that office.

[In the event that the President is separated from office, death, resignation, or inability to perform the Powers and Duties of that Position, the Powers and Duties of that Office shall pass to the Vice-President, and Congress may provide by law for the case of separation, death, resignation or incapacity, of both the President and the Vice President, and declare that an official will serve as president until the cause of incapacity disappears or a president is elected.] [z]

The President shall receive remuneration for his services, on the specified dates, which may not be increased or diminished during the period for which he has been appointed and may not receive any other emoluments from the United States or any of the States during that time.

Before he begins his office, he will give the following oath or promise: "I solemnly swear (or promise) that I will fairly serve as President of the United States and that I will sustain, protect, and defend the Constitution of the United States, to the fullest of my powers."

SECTION 2.

The President will be commander-in-chief of the United States Army and Navy and the Military Reserve of the various States, when called to active service in the United States; May seek the written opinion of the chief official of each of the administrative departments in relation to any matter relating to the duties of their respective charges, and shall be entitled to suspend the execution of sentences and grant pardons for crimes against the United States, except in the cases of Political Trials.

He shall have the power, by and with the advice and consent of the Senate, to conclude treaties, provided that two-thirds of the Senators present consent; and with the advice and consent of the Senate, it shall appoint Ambassadors, other public ministers and Consuls, Supreme Court Justice Judges and all other officials of the United States whose appointment does not provide this document in any other form and who have been established by law: but Congress may, by law, confer the appointment of the lower officers it deems appropriate, to the President, only to the Courts of court or to the Heads of Departmental.

The president shall have the right to fill all vacancies that occur during the Senate recess, extending provisional appointments, which will end at the end of the next session.

SECTION 3.

Periodically, it shall provide Congress with State of the Union reports, recommending for consideration by Congress, any measures it deems necessary and appropriate; on occasions of an extraordinary nature, it may convene both Houses or any of them, and in the event that they disagree as to the date on which they are to go into recess, it may suspend its sessions, on the date it deems appropriate; will receive Ambassadors and other public ministers; will ensure that laws are enforced on time and extend the offices of all U.S. officials.

SECTION 4.

The president, vice president, and all civil servants in the United States will be separated from their charges by being charged and convicted in Political Judgment, Treason, Bribery, or Other Serious Crimes and Misdemeanors.

ARTICLE III

SECTION 1.

The united states judiciary shall be deposited in a Supreme Court and in the lower courts that Congress establishes and establishes thereafter. The judges of both the Supreme Court and the Lower Courts will continue in their duties as long as they observe good conduct and will receive on certain dates a remuneration for their services that will not be diminished during the time of their commission.

SECTION 2.

The Judiciary shall understand in all disputes, both law and equity, arising as a result of this Constitution, the laws of the United States and treaties concluded or concluded under the authority of the United States; - in all disputes relating to Ambassadors, other public ministers and Consuls; - in all disputes of maritime jurisdiction and Admiralty; -in disputes in which the United States is a party; -in disputes between two or more States; - [between one State and the citizens of another], between citizens of different States, -between citizens of the same State who claim land under concessions from different States, [and between a State or citizens thereof and States, foreign citizens or subjects.] [8]

In all cases involving Ambassadors, other public ministers and Consuls, as well as those to which a State is a party, the Supreme Court shall have jurisdiction in a single instance. In all other cases mentioned above, the Supreme Court will be aware on appeal, both law and facts, with exceptions and in accordance with the regulations made by Congress.

All offences will be tried by jury except in Political Trial cases; and such a trial will take place in the State in which the crime has been committed; but where it has not been committed within the limits of any State, the trial will be held in the place or places that Congress has provided by law.

SECTION 3.

Betrayal against the United States will consist only of declaring war against them or joining its enemies, giving them help and protection. No person shall be convicted of treason if it is not based on the statement of two witnesses who have witnessed the same openly perpetrated act or a confession in public session before a Court.

Congress shall be empowered to set the penalty for treason; but no conviction for treason can deprive the right to transmit property by inheritance, nor will it result in the confiscation of his property, beyond in the life of the convicted person.

ARTICLE IV

SECTION 1.
Full faith and credit in each State shall be given to the Public Acts, Records and Judicial Procedures of all other States. And Congress may prescribe, through general laws, how such Acts, Records and Procedures will be proven and the effect of them.

SECTION 2.
Citizens of each State shall be entitled to all the privileges and immunities of the citizens of the other States.

A person accused in any State of treason, felony or other crime, who flees justice and is found in another State, shall be handed over, at the request of the Executive Authority of the State from which he has escaped, in order to be brought to the State which has jurisdiction over the crime.

[No person obliged to serve or work in a State, under the laws of the State, who escapes another State, shall be released, as a result of any law or regulation of that State, from such services or work, but shall be delivered upon claim by the interested party to whom such service or work is due.] [2]

SECTION 3.
Congress may admit new States to this Union, but no new State may be formed or built within the boundaries of another State, nor a State may be constituted by the union of two or more States or parts of States, without the consent of the legislatures of the States concerned, as well as congress.

Congress shall have the power to provide and formulate all necessary regulations and rules with respect to the Territory and other goods belonging to the United States, and no part of this Constitution shall be construed in a manner that prejudices the rights claimed by the United States or any individual State.

SECTION 4.
The United States will guarantee every State of this Union a form of republican government, and will protect each state against invasions; and at the request of the Legislature, or the Executive (if it is not possible to bring the legislature together) against internal unrest.

ARTICLE V

Whenever the two-thirds of both Houses deem it necessary, Congress shall propose amendments to this Constitution, or, at the request of the legislatures of the two thirds of the various States, convene a Convention in order to propose Amendments, which, in any event, shall have the same validity as if they were part of this Constitution, for all purposes, once they have been ratified by the legislatures of three-quarters of States separately or through conventions meeting in three-quarters thereof, according to Congress has proposed one or the other mode for ratification; and provided that no Amendment that is made before the year of one thousand eight hundred and eight, modifies in any way the first and fourth clauses of the Ninth Section of The First Article; and that no State shall be deprived, without its consent, of equal voting in the Senate.

ARTICLE VI

All debts incurred and commitments made prior to the adoption of this Constitution will be as valid against the United States under this Constitution as under the Confederacy.

This Constitution, and the Laws of the United States issued pursuant to it; and all Treaties concluded or concluded under the authority of the United States shall be the Supreme Law of the country; and the Judges of each State shall therefore be obliged to observe them, without regard to anything to the contrary in the Constitution or the laws of any State.

The aforementioned Senators and Representatives, members of the various state legislatures and all executive and judicial officials, both in the United States and of the various States, shall be bound by oath or promise to uphold this Constitution; but a Religious Test will never be required as a condition of any public office or mandate that depends on the United States.

ARTICLE VII

Ratification by the Conventions of nine States will suffice for this Constitution to enter into force with regard to ratifying States.

Given in Convention, by the unanimous consent of the States present, on the seventeenth day of September of the year of Our Lord of one thousand seven hundred and eighty-seven, and twelfth of the Independence of the United States of America. As witnesses to this, we sign our names below,